A Beginner's Guide to
Writing Minecraft® Plugins
in JavaScript

Peachpit Press

Walter Higgins

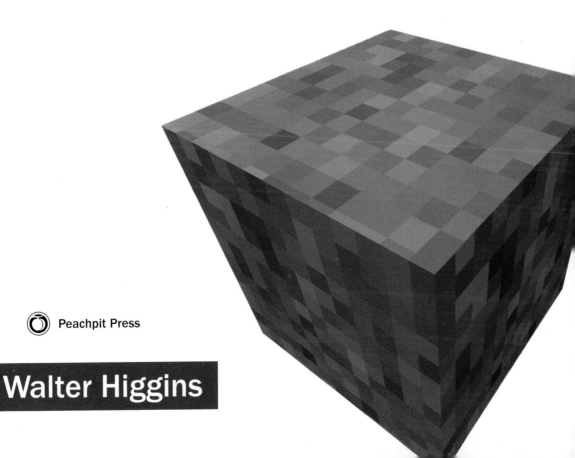

A Beginner's Guide to Writing Minecraft® Plugins in JavaScript
Walter Higgins

Peachpit Press

www.peachpit.com
To report errors, please send a note to errata@peachpit.com

Peachpit Press is a division of Pearson Education.

Copyright 2015 by Walter Higgins

Editor: Kim Wimpsett
Production editor: Rebecca Chapman-Winter
Compositor: Danielle Foster
Indexer: Valerie Haynes Perry
Cover design: Mimi Heft
Interior design: Mimi Heft

ISBN-13: 978-0-133-93014-6
ISBN-10: 0-133-93014-9

9 8 7 6 5 4 3 2 1

Printed and bound in the United States of America

For my family.

Acknowledgments

I'd like to thank—in no particular order—the many contributors to ScriptCraft (the software used in this book); the teachers and volunteers who have used and improved ScriptCraft; my editors, Cliff Colby and Kim Wimpsett; and the production editor and proofreader for their diligence and enormous help in writing this book. This book took a big chunk of time to write, and I must thank my wife Ursula and kids, Kate and Sean, for their patience, love, and support. I'd also like to thank my dad, Paul Higgins, for instilling in me a love of books.

This book would not be possible without the work of the hundreds of open source programmers who developed or contributed to the open source Bukkit and CanaryMod projects. These projects are the lifeblood of Minecraft and the Minecraft modding community. Thanks to Jason Jones (`@darkdiplomat`) for heroic work maintaining CanaryMod, Michael Madden for creating great ScriptCraft resources for CoderDojo, Athijegannathan Sundararajan for patiently answering all my questions about Nashorn, Chris Cacciatore for his fun Script-Craft contributions, and Jon Ippolito for his forum contributions.

About the Author

Walter Higgins has more than 20 years' experience in software development working at Microsoft, Apple, EMC, and IBM. When not programming, he enjoys tinkering with new technology, reading, and running. He lives in Cork, Ireland.

Contents

Preface

Who Is This Book For?

This book is for anyone who is curious about programming and creating Minecraft plugins. It teaches how to create Minecraft server plugins and assumes the reader has no previous programming experience. Specifically, this book is for beginning programmers age 10 and older.

Why I Wrote This Book

I've been playing Minecraft since 2010 and have been playing multiplayer Minecraft with my two kids on a shared server at home since 2011. I developed software as a hobby in my teens and have been developing software professionally for more than 20 years. I took my kids to local CoderDojo sessions where they learned to use Scratch and create simple web pages using HTML and JavaScript. I thought "Wouldn't it be cool if kids could learn to program using Minecraft?" When I first looked into developing Minecraft plugins, I was bewildered by the number of options available.

All of the options available required you to write code in Java. Java is the programming language that Minecraft is written in. It is a fine general-purpose language and is especially suited to developing large, complex business applications. However, it is not ideal as a first language to learn. Learning Java can take some time, and you need to write a lot of Java code to get things done. Even for a seasoned Java developer, the options available for modding Minecraft were bewildering. That's why I came up with the idea of making modding easier by letting plugin developers use JavaScript instead.

In late 2012 I launched ScriptCraft—a way of writing Minecraft plugins using JavaScript, which is a much simpler language than Java.

I wrote this book to make learning to program fun and easy. I believe that learning even a little about software—how it's made and how it works—is good. Developing Minecraft plugins is a great way to learn programming and create something fun for yourself and your friends. Maybe you want to create your own Minecraft mini-game or you can't find a plugin that does exactly what you want. This book will teach you how to create your own plugins and mini-games. Playing Minecraft is fun. Creating Minecraft plugins is a whole different level of fun.

Walter Higgins, April 2014

Introduction

This book shows you how to create your own Minecraft server plugins using JavaScript. There's often confusion about the words *mod* and *plugin*. For the purpose of this book, they mean the same thing. Mojang—the makers of Minecraft—prefers to use the term *plugin API* rather than *modding API* when referring to its forthcoming official API, which will make extending Minecraft easier.

Before I begin, I will explain some of the words I'll use throughout this book.

- **Plugin**: A modification you add to Minecraft that changes the game in some way. The plugin is usually in the form of one or more files.

- **Mod**: Mod is short for "modification." In this book, *mod* and *plugin* are used interchangeably (they mean the same thing).

- **Modding**: The practice of writing modifications or plugins for Minecraft. Modding requires some programming knowledge, which you will learn in this book.

- **API**: API is short for "application programming interface," which is an official way to write Minecraft plugins using a guide. Players and regular users of software don't need to care about APIs, but they are essential for programmers because they make it easier to develop plugins. An API is like a list of recipes; you probably crafted your first pick-axe by referring to an online guide—how much more difficult would it be to have tried creating one without knowing where all the materials should go in the crafting grid? Similarly, programmers need APIs to provide help and guidance in building plugins. The API you will use in this book is the CanaryMod API.

- **Multiplayer**: The mode of playing Minecraft with other players all connected to the same server.

- **Server**: A computer that is running the Minecraft server software. In this book I will show you how to set up and run your own Minecraft server.

Why JavaScript?

In this book I will teach you how to program using the JavaScript programming language. JavaScript is just one of many programming languages. When I set out with the goal of making Minecraft plugin development easier, I chose JavaScript for a few reasons.

- JavaScript is an easy language to learn.

- I like JavaScript. I enjoy writing code in JavaScript and hope you will too.

- JavaScript is expressive. You can do more with less. A little bit of JavaScript code can do quite a lot compared to other programming languages such as Java. The shorter your programs are, the easier they are to understand.

- JavaScript is bundled with Java. The latest versions of Java include JavaScript. This means you won't need to install any additional software to use ScriptCraft.

- Anything you can do using Java, you can do using JavaScript. In this book you'll learn about the CanaryMod API—a set of guidelines for creating Minecraft plugins. The CanaryMod API is Java-based, but you can use JavaScript too!

- JavaScript isn't a toy. JavaScript is a proper programming language used professionally by thousands of programmers around the world. Although originally used only for adding simple extensions to web pages, it's now used for developing all kinds of software and has become one of the most popular programming languages.

- JavaScript is cross-platform. This means JavaScript is available on Macintosh, Windows, and Linux.

The JavaScript programming language is a simple language to get started with, but it can be quite flexible in how you do things. In JavaScript there's usually more than one way to do it. This book is not intended as a comprehensive tour of all of JavaScript's features. Its aim is to focus on the fun parts of JavaScript and to help those who are curious about programming get a taste for what programming in JavaScript is like.

About the Upcoming Minecraft API

When I created ScriptCraft in 2012, there was no one true way to write Minecraft plugins because there was no official API provided by Mojang. At the time of writing (September 2014), Mojang has announced an upcoming official way to write Minecraft plugins using the Plugin API. The Plugin API will provide a standard way for plugin developers to extend the Minecraft game. There is still no official release date for the Plugin API, but I'll be watching closely and will make any necessary changes to ScriptCraft when the API is released.

Online Bonus Appendixes

We have provided some additional bonus material in the form of five appendixes, which you can find online at `www.peachpit.com`. They cover the variables provided by ScriptCraft, working with plug-ins, and more. Visit peachpit.com/register, log in or create an account, and register the book's ISBN to download companion files.

Part I

Building a Modding Workbench

WELCOME TO THE EXCITING WORLD of Minecraft plugin development. In this first part of the book, I'll introduce you to the tools you'll need to start programming. In Minecraft, you need to first create a *workbench* (also sometimes called a *crafting table*) before you can craft more sophisticated tools. So too in real life you'll need to first gather some resources and set up a work area where you can create sophisticated Minecraft plugins. This part of the book describes the resources you'll need, how to get them, and how to set up your "modding workbench." All of the resources you'll need are freely available online. The ingredients you'll need to construct your modding workbench are as follows:

- **CanaryMod:** A freely available open source Minecraft server

- **ScriptCraft:** A plugin for CanaryMod

- **A text editor:** gedit, TextWrangler, or any other text editor suitable for programming

The following chapters will show you how to install and set up each of these.

Chapter 1

Running Your Own Minecraft Server

I BEGAN PLAYING MINECRAFT in 2010 in single-player mode. It was a fun and relaxing way to pass the time. Later I installed the Minecraft server software on one of the computers on our kitchen table. My youngest son, Sean, had just finished his homework, so I asked him if he wanted to join the home server. Seeing each other in the game was quite a novelty. Soon my eldest daughter, Kate, joined in, and we began some serious building together (**FIGURE 1.1**). Building in Minecraft is much more fun with others.

FIGURE 1.1 Multiplayer Minecraft

When you play Minecraft in multiplayer mode, chatting, building, and min-
ing with other players, you do so on a Minecraft *server*. The Minecraft server is
just a computer program (like the Minecraft client, Microsoft Word, or Internet
Explorer) that provides a shared virtual place for Minecraft players to connect,
build, and chat. You don't need to buy any special type of computer to run a
Minecraft server. You can run one on your laptop computer—assuming it's not
too old. Minecraft server software won't run on an iPad, Android tablet, or phone.
It runs only on Windows, Macintosh, and Linux computers.

Client-Server Networking

Minecraft multiplayer is "client-server," which means that one or more "client"
computers (computers running the Minecraft game) can connect to a central
"server" (a computer that is responsible for storing all of the Minecraft world information so that players can play together in the same world). **FIGURE 1.2** shows a
simple client-server network with just one client (player) connected to a server.

The client must be connected to the server over some kind of network. The line
between the client and the server in Figure 1.2 represents the network. A server
with just one client computer isn't much fun, though. Servers really become fun
when many players are connected to the same server, as in **FIGURE 1.3**.

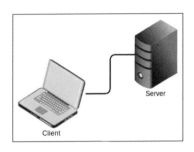

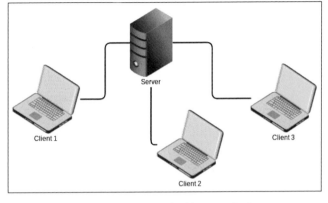

FIGURE 1.2 A simple client-server network

FIGURE 1.3 A client-server network with many clients

In Figure 1.3, the server must chat with all of the connected clients. For example, if it starts raining in the game, the server must send a message to each client that it's begun raining. In Minecraft multiplayer, the server is responsible for many things. The server decides what the weather will be like in the in-game world, what time of day it is, and so on. This is so that the time of day and weather *will be the same for all connected players.*

You'll notice that in Figure 1.3, the server is shown as a separate computer. This is just for illustration. While often server software *does* run on a separate computers, you won't need a separate computer to run Minecraft server or to follow the tutorials in this book. In fact, for learning how to create Minecraft plugins and to get the best from this book, I recommend running a Minecraft server on the same computer you play Minecraft on. This means your computer will act as both a client and a server (see **FIGURE 1.4**). This is by far the most convenient and cost-effective way to run a server and learn how to create Minecraft server plugins.

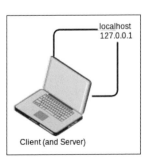

FIGURE 1.4 A computer that is both a client and a server

When you play Minecraft in multiplayer mode, before you can connect to a server, you have to enter the server details into the game. The server details are a hostname or an IP address; either one of these provides a way for the Minecraft client (the game) to connect to a computer running the Minecraft server. The hostname or IP address are how computers uniquely identify one another on the Internet, much like how you identify each other by name and/or address. When you run a Minecraft server on your own computer, you will use a special hostname called localhost or IP address 127.0.0.1. I'll talk more about these in the following sections.

Anyone can run a server. In the following sections, I'll show you how to set up and run your own Minecraft server.

Why Run Your Own Server?

Why should you run your own server? Running your own server means you have total control over the Minecraft world you want to create and share with your friends. You can decide what type of server and world you and your friends will play in, what server plugins to install, what rules will govern the server and world, and who can and cannot join the server. As a server *operator*, you will have access to commands that normal players don't. You can control the weather using Minecraft commands, start and stop thunderstorms, or even change the time of day. You can also install popular Minecraft server mods like Hunger Games and MobArena. The real power of running your own server comes when you add ScriptCraft, which makes it easier to create your own Minecraft server plugins. If you have an idea for a new Minecraft mod or would like to do something that current mods don't support, you can create your own mod and test it on your own server.

Running your own server is essential for plugin development. Minecraft server plugin developers run their own servers because they need to be able to test their creations before releasing them into the wild for others to use. Serious modders would not consider releasing a plugin that they hadn't first tested on their own servers.

Which Minecraft Server Software Should I Use?

There are a couple of different flavors of Minecraft server. Mojang provides its own server software that can be downloaded from the Minecraft.net website. This was the first server software released for Minecraft. This is often referred to as the "vanilla" Minecraft server. At the time of writing, it doesn't provide any way to add plugins, although this will probably change once Mojang releases the official Plugin API. The Minecraft server provided by Mojang is fine if you want to run a server with no modifications. The problems with running such a server is that there's no reliable way to protect against *griefing*.

TERM Griefing

Griefing is when a player in a multiplayer video game deliberately irritates and harasses other players within the game, using aspects of the game in unintended ways. A griefer enjoys annoying other users by destroying other players' work or cursing and harassing players and server administrators.

The standard (vanilla) Minecraft server has only limited ways to protect against griefing. Because of this, other more popular Minecraft server software arose that allowed administrators to strictly control who could join the server and to enforce penalties and bans on players who misbehaved. CanaryMod, which you'll use in this book, let administrators add any number of antigriefing plugins to make the server as safe, secure, and player-friendly as possible.

CanaryMod

In this book, you'll use CanaryMod as your Minecraft server software. You'll look at the CanaryMod API in more detail later. For now, all you need to know is that CanaryMod is the name of the server software, and it has an API that makes it easy to modify the game.

I highly recommend browsing the CanaryMod website at *www.canarymod.net/*. It provides a wealth of information for both administrators (the people who run CanaryMod servers) and developers (the people who create plugins for CanaryMod).

Installing CanaryMod

The first step in constructing your modding workbench is to install CanaryMod. Unlike many games, Minecraft is in ongoing development. This means new versions of Minecraft are released often. When you purchase and download the

TERM **Bug**

Bugs in software are errors or mistakes in the software code that can cause problems. Nobody quite knows for sure why errors in software are called bugs, but one story goes that a problem with an early mechanical computer in the 1940s was caused by a moth that somehow found its way inside. The term bug had been used to describe errors long before computers came along, so when the engineers captured the moth, they kept it with a note that said "First actual case of bug being found."

Minecraft client, you automatically get new versions of the game when they are released. This is great for players because you get the latest and greatest version for free, which often includes bug fixes and new features. If you've played Minecraft multiplayer before on one of the popular public servers, you'll know that there's a downside to Mojang's commitment to improving Minecraft: Server software upgrades do not happen as often as client software upgrades. This can lead to client software and server software that are *incompatible*. When the client and server versions are incompatible, they cannot communicate (see FIGURE 1.5).

Usually, a compatible version of the Minecraft server software is released shortly after the Minecraft client is upgraded. One thing to keep in mind is that CanaryMod is an open source and voluntary project—this means that the people who develop CanaryMod don't get paid to do so. They do it for fun. Upgrading server software takes a lot of work, and the software needs to be tested (by volunteers) before it can be released. That's why sometimes it may take a while for a new version of the Minecraft server software to be released that is compatible with the latest and greatest client. Be patient and remember that the developers who work on CanaryMod do it for fun and don't get paid, so posting questions on the Canary-Mod forums, asking when the new version will be ready, won't speed things up.

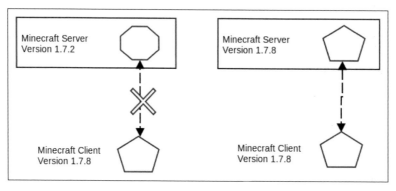

FIGURE 1.5 Compatibility between client and server

At the time of writing, 1.8 is the most current version of Minecraft, and the CanaryMod development team are working to support version 1.8, but the most stable version of CanaryMod (at the time of writing) is version 1.7.10. The example code in this book is tested against CanaryMod version 1.7.10, so I strongly recommend downloading and installing that particular version. There's a way you can safely and temporarily *downgrade* your Minecraft client software so that it will be compatible with your server software.

Since version 1.6, the Minecraft Launcher (the software you run on your computer to start the Minecraft client and to upgrade to new versions when they become available) lets you choose which version of the client software to run. By default the Launcher is configured to always download and run the latest version, but you can easily change this using the new profiles feature. The following are step-by-step instructions for changing your Launcher profile to use a different version of Minecraft client:

1. Launch Minecraft.

2. Click the New Profile button on the bottom left of the Launcher screen (see **FIGURE 1.6**).

3. Fill in the Profile Name field. For example, you should call it something like Version 1.7.10. I find it helpful to include the version name in a new profile so I can see at a glance which client version the profile will use.

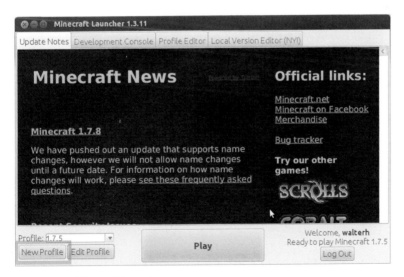

FIGURE 1.6 Minecraft Launcher

4. Choose the appropriate version from the Use Version drop-down list (see **FIGURE 1.7**).

5. Click the Save Profile button.

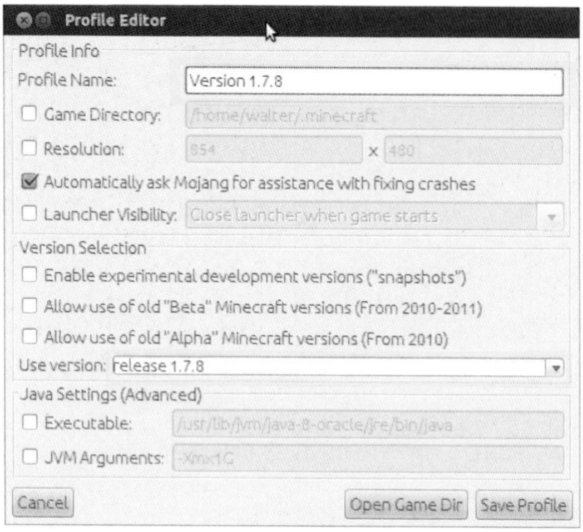

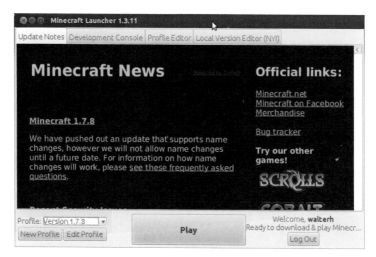

FIGURE 1.7 Minecraft Profile Editor

The newly created profile should now be automatically selected in the Profile drop-down list on the main Launcher page. Click the Play button to begin playing using the chosen version of Minecraft client software (see **FIGURE 1.8**).

FIGURE 1.8 Profile selection

By using the Profile Editor to downgrade your Minecraft client software, you can ensure that your client and server are compatible and that you can play multiplayer Minecraft even when the server software is not as up-to-date as the current latest version of Minecraft client. This means you can always use the most stable recommended build of CanaryMod.

Depending on which browser software you use (Chrome, Safari, Internet Explorer, or Firefox), the instructions for downloading will differ. Please read the instructions for the browser you use.

Download Instructions

Follow these steps to download CanaryMod:

1. Create a new folder on your computer called mcserver.

2. Visit *http://scriptcraftjs.org/download/latest/*. Right-click the `canarymod.jar` link and choose "Save link as."

3. Save the JAR file in the folder created in step 1.

Once downloaded, the next step is to install CanaryMod on your computer. The instructions are slightly different for each operating system, so skip directly to the instructions for your operating system.

Installing CanaryMod on Windows

Follow these steps to install CanaryMod on Windows:

1. Open Notepad (you can find it by clicking the Start or Windows button in the bottom left of the screen and then typing **Notepad** in the search box).

2. Type the following into Notepad:

```
java -Xmx1024M -jar canarymod.jar -o true
PAUSE
```

3. Save the document as **run.bat** in the **mcserver** folder you created earlier. It's important that you change the Save As Type option from Text Documents to All Files. Otherwise, Notepad will try to save the document as **run.bat.txt**, and it will not be executable.

TERM JAR File

 The CanaryMod software is downloadable as a JAR file. Programs that are created using the Java programming language are often distributed as JAR files and will have a name that ends with **.jar**. JAR is short for **J**ava **AR**chive file. It's an archive of all the code and resources needed by Java to run the software. CanaryMod is distributed as a JAR file. So too are all of the plugins for CanaryMod.

4. Double-click the **run.bat** file you saved in the previous step, and CanaryMod should start running. If you see the error message "Java is not recognized as an internal or external command, operable program or batch file," then you need to reinstall Java. Java is the programming language Minecraft is written in. It's also the programming language the CanaryMod Minecraft server is written in. You can download Java by visiting *www.java.com* and following the instructions. If after installing Java you still get the same error, then follow the instructions at *www.java.com/en/download/help/path.xml*.

5. Assuming the server has started (you didn't see any errors), you can shut down the server by issuing the **stop** command at the server console (type **stop** and then hit Enter).

Installing CanaryMod on Mac OS

Follow these steps to install CanaryMod on Mac OS:

1. The first thing you'll need to do is install Java. Since OS X 10.7, Java no longer comes bundled with OS X, so you will need to install Java from Apple's Java Install page at *http://support.apple.com/kb/DL1421*.

2. Open TextEdit. (You can find it by typing **TextEdit** in the Spotlight field in the top right of the screen. Click the magnifying glass icon to bring up Spotlight.)

   Under the Format menu, choose Make Plain Text and then type the following:

```
#!/bin/bash
cd "$( dirname "$0" )"
java -Xmx1024M -jar canarymod.jar -o true
Save the file in your mcserver folder as
start_server.command.
```

3. You will need to be able to run this newly created file, so follow these steps:

   a. Open the Terminal application. (To find it, click the magnifying glass icon and type **Terminal** in the Spotlight field.)

   b. Type **chmod a+x** (don't hit Enter yet).

   c. Find the file you just created in the Finder and drag and drop it into the Terminal window.

   d. The name of the file you just dropped into the Terminal window will be appended to the **chmod a+x** command, so you can now hit Enter.

4. Start the server by double-clicking the **start_server.command** file.

5. To stop the server, issue the **stop** command in the Terminal window (type **stop** and then hit Enter).

Installing CanaryMod on Linux (Ubuntu)

Follow these steps to install CanaryMod on Linux:

1. Open Text Editor by clicking the Dash Home button in the top-left corner of the screen; then type **Edit** to see a list of editors (you can choose Text Editor or another editor of your choice).

2. Type the following into the editor:

```
#!/bin/sh
BINDIR=$(dirname "$(readlink -fn "$0")")
cd "$BINDIR"
java -Xmx1024M -jar canarymod.jar -o true
```

3. Save the file as **canarymod.sh** in the **mcserver** folder you created earlier.

4. You will need to make this new file executable. In Nautilus (Linux's File browser) right-click the file and select Properties. In the Properties dialog, click the Permissions tab and ensure that the Execute checkbox is ticked. (You can also make the file executable by issuing the Unix command **chmodx canarymod.sh`** from the folder where you saved the file.)

5. Launch the Terminal application and type **~/mcserver/canarymod.sh** (assuming you created a folder called **mcserver** in your home folder).

6. Once the CanaryMod server console has launched, you can stop it by issuing the **stop** command (type **stop** and then hit Enter).

Agreeing to the End User License Agreement

As of version 1.7.10 of the Minecraft server, you are required to agree to Mojang's end-user license agreement before running the Minecraft server for the first time. The first time you run CanaryMod, the server will stop immediately and issue the following error message: "You need to agree to the EULA in order to run the server."

To agree to the EULA, open the `eula.txt` file in the `mcserver` folder and change it so it reads as follows:

```
eula=true
```

Save the `eula.txt` file and the start CanaryMod again. This time it should run without error.

Configuring Your Server

Once you've installed CanaryMod, the next step is configuration. This is where you decide what kind of Minecraft server you want to run. Will it have monsters? Will it be Survival mode or Creative mode? Will it be player versus player, and so on? While configuration is something you'll probably do only once, you can later change the server configuration at any time you like. The server configuration isn't set in stone; just bear in mind you will need to restart your server if you change the configuration.

The server.cfg File

When you first launch CanaryMod, a couple of configuration files and folders will be created in the `mcserver/config` folder. When configuring your server, the most important file is `server.cfg`. This is a plain-text file (meaning it can be edited using any text editor) containing all of the configuration for your server. The first few lines of my own `server.cfg` look like this:

```
#Minecraft server properties
#Sun Apr 20 11:11:20 IST 2014
op-permission-level=4
allow-nether=false
allow-flight=false
announce-player-achievements=true
server-port=25565
```

The first two lines—the lines that begin with a # character (also known as the *hash symbol*)—are comments, so they are ignored by the server. The configuration begins properly on line 3. The settings for the server are specified using *name-value* pairs, which is programmer-speak for how settings are written. For example, `allow-flight=false` is a name-value pair where the name is `allow-flight` and the value is `false`. In property files, the name and value are separated by the = (equal) symbol. Let's look at just some of the properties you might want to change.

WORLD TYPE

Later in the book I'll show you how to use JavaScript to create roads and sky-scrapers. If you plan to eventually put your newfound programming prowess to use building large-scale places for others to visit, you'll probably want to edit the `mcserver/config/worlds/default/default_NORMAL.cfg` file and change the `world-type` property from **DEFAULT** (Minecraft's standard setting where worlds are made of varied landscapes of hills, valleys, and oceans) to **FLAT**. In a **FLAT** world, there are no hills and no valleys, just flat terrain for as far as you can see. While this might be considered boring, it does have the advantage of being easier to build on. If you plan to build roads, houses, and other large-scale con-structions, a **FLAT** world might be the best place to start. It's not essential that `world-type` is set to **FLAT**; you can always leave this setting at **DEFAULT** and just flatten the area you want to build on first. (If you later decide to change the level type, the setting applies only when creating new worlds. Existing worlds will not be modified.)

If you decide to create a new world and want to use a level type other than **DEFAULT**, you have two options.

- Change both the `world-name` and `world-type` properties to create a new world while keeping the old world. (The old world will not be wiped out— it will still be on your computer stored in the **worlds** folder.) This is the best option if you want to keep your existing world data. You need to change the `world-name` setting to something other than the default value. Call your new world something memorable like **flat-world**.
- If you don't care about keeping the existing world, delete the **worlds** folder from the **mcserver** folder and change the `world-type` property. The next time the server starts, a new world and a new **worlds** folder will be created.

MONSTERS

The next setting you'll probably want to change is the `spawn-monsters` setting in the world's config file located in the `mcserver/config/worlds/` folder. This determines whether monsters will be spawned. By default it's set to **true**, which means monsters will appear at night. I recommend changing this setting from **true** to **false** because the last thing you need while learning to program is to be attacked by giant spiders. You can change this setting any time you like. The setting won't take effect until you restart the server. I'll talk about starting and stopping the server shortly.

GAME MODE

For the same reason I suggest making your server a monster-free zone, I also suggest changing your server's **gamemode** property from 0 (Survival) to 1 (Creative). In Survival mode, you will need to constantly seek food and be careful not to fall. In Creative mode, you can give your full attention to learning to program.

The ops.cfg File

The **ops.cfg** file is a configuration file listing all of the *operators* for the server. Operators are players who have special privileges on the server. Operators (also sometimes called *administrators* or *admins*) are responsible for keeping the server running and ensuring that players play nice and don't grief. If players don't play nice, operators have to power to ban or kick players off the server using special commands available only to them.

There may already be an **ops.cfg** file present in your **mcserver/config** folder. If there isn't, then one will be created automatically when you run the **op** command from the server console. You will need to be an operator to issue JavaScript commands in the game, so one of the first things you should do once you've installed the Minecraft server is make yourself an operator by issuing the **op username** command, replacing **username** with your own Minecraft username. For example, I would issue the command **op walterh** because **walterh** is my Minecraft username. ScriptCraft—the plugin you'll install later—allows only operators to issue JavaScript commands.

You're done with all of the server configuration you'll need for now. If you want to delve deeper into server configuration, a good place to start is by reading the *http://minecraft.gamepedia.com/Server.properties* page.

Permissions

CanaryMod provides a default set of groups: visitors, players, mods, and admins. Players who join a CanaryMod server are assigned to the **visitors** group by default. The **visitors** group can't place or break blocks by default, so you'll need to run the following command once:

```
groupmod permission add visitors canary.world.build
```

You can find out more about CanaryMod permissions by visiting the following links:

- *http://canarymod.net/books/canarymod-admin-guide/permissions-and-groups*
- *http://canarymod.net/books/canarymod-admin-guide/list-permissions*

Basic Server Administration Commands

CanaryMod's usefulness as a Minecraft server comes from its ability to be extended and made more interesting by adding plugins. In this book you'll use just one plugin—ScriptCraft—which lets operators extend the game using JavaScript. There are just a few things you'll need to know about server administration to get the most from this book.

Starting and Stopping Your Server

To start your Minecraft server, double-click the startup script you created earlier in this chapter. This launches the Minecraft server in a Terminal window. The Terminal window will look something like **FIGURE 1.9**.

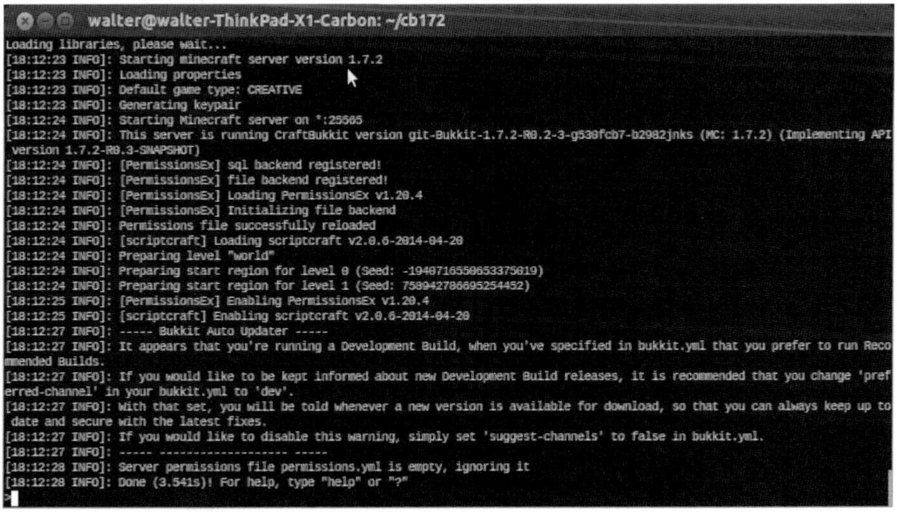

FIGURE 1.9 The Minecraft server console window

Don't worry if your Terminal window doesn't look exactly like this or has slightly different content. The important thing is that after starting up, your server should display a server console prompt—the right arrow (>) symbol—in the bottom left of the screen along with a blinking cursor. This is called the *server console*, and you can issue administration commands here even if you aren't an operator. Try it: issue the `help` command to see the full list of commands you can use as the server console user.

In the server console window, you don't need to put a forward slash (/) in front of commands the way you do in the Minecraft client. So, you simply type the command name without the leading /. Remember: `help` instead of /`help`, `toggledownfall` instead of /`toggledownfall`, and so on.

Another thing to note about the server console is that when you enter commands there, you do so as a special player called CONSOLE. In Minecraft the /`me` command is used to send a message to other players in the form of *yourname action*. For example, if I issue the command /`me sneezes` in the Minecraft client, all other players on the server will see `walterh sneezes`. However, if you issue the same command in the server console, you will see * @ `sneezes` instead of your own name. CONSOLE is not visible to other players and does not inhabit the Minecraft world. Normally only the person who starts the server can issue commands as CONSOLE.

To stop the server, you should issue the `stop` command at the server console. If you plan to administer a Minecraft server for others to play, the `stop` command will come in handy whenever you want to shut down the server for maintenance or troubleshooting.

Connecting to Your Server

To check that your server is running and accepting connections, follow these steps:

1. Launch the Minecraft game as you would normally.

2. Once Minecraft has launched and you have logged in, click the Multiplayer button.

3. If this is the first time you're connecting to your own server, click the Add Server button. If it's not the first time you've connected to your own server, skip to step 8.

4. Fill in the Server Name field. You can call the server any name you like. The default name, Minecraft Server, will do if you can't think of something imaginative right now.

5. In the Server Address field, you should type **localhost**. As mentioned earlier, localhost is a special server address meaning "the same computer." You could also use 127.0.0.1, which is the IP address of localhost (servers usually have a name and/or address, and it's usually possible to connect to them using either name or address). Use either localhost or 127.0.0.1 but not both; either one will do fine.

6. Once you've entered the server address, click the Done button.

7. The new server you just added should appear in the list of servers. If it's not visible, use the scroll bar to scroll down. If you have already added other servers, it may not appear at the top of the list. Because you've added this server using the Add Server button rather than the Direct Connect button, it should appear in the list of multiplayer servers every time you launch Minecraft.

8. Select the server and click the Join Server button.

If you get an error when trying to connect, ensure that your server is first running (see the earlier section on starting your server). If your server is not running, you will see an error "Failed to connect to the server. java.net.ConnectException: Connection refused." If you see this error, click the Back to Title Screen button; then start your server and try again.

Once you've logged into your server, take a look around. It's important that you have operator (administrator) privileges on your own server. You can check that you have the right privileges by issuing the **/time set 4000** command. If you can run this command without error, then you're all set up. If you see a warning message "You do not have permission to perform this command," then you'll need to make yourself an operator at the server console window. Switch to the server console window (Alt+Tab on Windows, Cmd+Tab on OS X) and type **op username**, replacing **username** with your own username; then switch back to the Minecraft game and try issuing the **/time set 4000** command from the in-game prompt. Once you've verified you have operator permissions, kick back and relax. Or, if you have a spare computer on your home network, invite a friend or family member to join you on your server. If this is the first time you've played Minecraft multiplayer with friends or family, you'll have great fun.

Achievement Unlocked!

By now you should have your very own
Minecraft server installed and running.
Congratulations, you're well on your way
to becoming a Minecraft modder!

Other Server Options

Other Minecraft server options are available, but installing and running your own
server is the only sensible option if you want to start modding.

Commercial Minecraft Hosting

Once you've mastered server administration and modding, you might eventually decide to use one of the many commercial Minecraft hosting plans available online. These Minecraft hosting providers usually charge a monthly fee, so
they are not free. For your money, they provide you with a Minecraft server you
and your friends can connect to and play. They usually offer managed install
of plugins through a web-based administration portal (a web page where you
can choose which plugins your server should use). Commercial Minecraft hosting isn't cheap, and it's not as flexible as running your own server. You certainly
don't need to sign up to commercial Minecraft hosting to get the most from this
book. You can find a list of Minecraft hosting providers by searching for *Minecraft
hosting* online.

Minecraft Realms

Mojang has rolled out its own Minecraft hosting solution—Minecraft Realms—
throughout the world. Minecraft Realms does not currently support plugins of
any kind, although that may change in the future.

Chapter 2

Setting Up ScriptCraft

IN THE PREVIOUS CHAPTER you downloaded and installed CanaryMod, a customizable Minecraft server. In this chapter, you'll install ScriptCraft—a server plugin that lets you write your own plugins using the JavaScript programming language.

What Is ScriptCraft?

ScriptCraft is a plugin for Minecraft that lets you create plugins using JavaScript instead of Java. It is a server plugin, which means it is installed on a server (CanaryMod) but once installed can be used by all players connected to that server. I created ScriptCraft for several reasons:

- To make it easier for myself to create Minecraft mods

- To make it easier for my kids (and others) to create Minecraft mods

- To make it easier to teach programming to kids using JavaScript and Minecraft as tools

Most Minecraft plugins are written in a language called Java. Java was invented in the 1990s as a simpler way to program. Before Java, programmers used languages such as C and C++, which were difficult to learn and use. C and C++ were difficult because if you wrote a program that wanted to grab some space in the computer's memory, you had to remember to free up that space when you no longer needed it. Otherwise, the computer would quickly run out of memory, and the program would crash. Java solved this problem by having automatic *garbage collection* (yes, that's what programmers actually call it), which automatically frees up memory when it is no longer needed. Java has many other advantages too. It has a large library of functions to do common tasks so you don't have to write those functions yourself. Java is *cross-platform*, which mean it runs on Windows, Linux, and Mac OS. Minecraft is written in Java and so too are Minecraft servers.

Java is a fine language and is widely used. However, it can be a little difficult to learn, especially if you are completely new to programming. Java can be verbose, meaning you need to write a lot of Java code to do even simple things. Java code can't be executed right away either. You need to first *compile* it. Compiling is the process of converting Java source code into a form the computer can understand.

JavaScript came along shortly after Java. It was invented in the mid-1990s just when the Internet was becoming really popular. Although their names sound alike, they are very different languages. JavaScript is simpler than Java in many ways. In recent years, it has become popular as a language not just for web programming but for all kinds of uses.

Installing ScriptCraft

To download and install ScriptCraft, follow these steps:

1. Visit *http://scriptcraftjs.org/download/latest/*.

2. Right-click the `scriptcraft.jar` file and select Save Link As from the pop-up menu.

3. Save the file to the `mcserver/plugins` folder. If there is no `plugins` folder, it's probably because you haven't yet launched CanaryMod. The first time CanaryMod is launched, it creates a couple of configuration files and a `plugins` folder, so make sure you've launched CanaryMod at least once before attempting to download ScriptCraft.

If there is already a `scriptcraft.jar` file in your `plugins` folder (if this isn't the first time you've installed ScriptCraft), make sure to remove it first before saving the new file.

If CanaryMod is running, stop it by issuing the `stop` command in the server console.

Launch CanaryMod by double-clicking the launch script you created in Chapter 1. When CanaryMod starts up, you should see an "Enabling scriptcraft" message appear in the server console. The first time it's loaded, the ScriptCraft plugin will unzip a lot of files into a new `mcserver/scriptcraft` folder. Your server console output might look something like **FIGURE 2.1**.

```
Enabling scriptcraft v3.0.0-2014-10-14
Directory /home/walter/mcserver/plugins/scriptcraft does not exist.
Initializing /home/walter/mcserver/scriptcraft directory with contents from plugin archive.
Unzipping /home/walter/mcserver/scriptcraft/lib/command.js (NE)
Unzipping /home/walter/mcserver/scriptcraft/lib/console.js (NE)
Unzipping /home/walter/mcserver/scriptcraft/lib/events.js (NE)
```

FIGURE 2.1 Unzipping files

There will be many more entries because many files are bundled with ScriptCraft.

The `mcserver/plugins` subfolder is important. It's where all Minecraft server plugins should be stored. This is true not just for `ScriptCraft.jar` but for all server plugins. If you save a Server plugin JAR file to any other location except the plugins folder, then it will not be loaded when CanaryMod starts. CanaryMod looks only in the `plugins` folder for plugins to load at startup.

Verifying ScriptCraft Is Installed

You can verify that ScriptCraft has been successfully installed by issuing the following command at the server console:

```
js 2 + 3
```

Make sure to type this text exactly as you see it and then hit the Enter key. The response you get from the server console should of course be 5.

Achievement Unlocked!

Congratulations! You've just installed ScriptCraft and executed your first line of JavaScript code.

ScriptCraft adds just two new server commands to the Minecraft server: **js** and **jsp**. I'll talk about **jsp** later in the book. The **js** command is short for "JavaScript," and it lets you execute JavaScript code right away. You'll learn more about this in the next chapter.

Chapter 3

Exploring JavaScript in Minecraft

ONCE YOU'VE INSTALLED SCRIPTCRAFT, you can use the **js** command to evaluate JavaScript code. The **js** command will try to evaluate any of the text that follows it as JavaScript. You must enter a space between the **js** and the JavaScript you want to evaluate. The **js** command will evaluate the JavaScript and print out the result of the expression. So if you type **js 2 + 7**, the **js** command will take **2 + 7**, will try to evaluate it, and, if it can, will print the result. Let's practice with a few simple JavaScript expressions.

Basic Math Operations

The expressions you've used so far are simple addition operations. JavaScript has a number of mathematical operations. I want you to type each of the following expressions into the server console as you read them. It will be good practice for you. As a general rule, you should try executing the code yourself. The best way to learn programming is to try stuff out rather than just reading. Try executing each of the following mathematical operations.

Addition uses the + operator.

```
js 2 + 2
```

Division uses the / symbol (there's no ÷ key on your keyboard, so / is used instead).

```
js 2 / 3
```

To subtract numbers, you use this:

```
js 2 - 3
```

Multiplication uses the * symbol (this is called the asterisk symbol; it's usually typed by pressing Shift+8).

```
js 2 * 3
```

Comparing Numbers

JavaScript can also be used to compare numbers, so you can ask "Is 3 greater than 5?" like this:

```
js 3 > 5
```

The answer to the previous is **false** (3 is not greater than 5). You can ask "Is 3 less than 5?" like this:

```
js 3 < 5
```

The answer of course is **true**. You can also ask "Is 3 equal to 5?" like this:

```
js 3 == 5
```

Notice that I use *two* = symbols, not just a single one, and that's very important. The result of the previous expression should of course be **false**. I'll talk about what a single = symbol means shortly. The **true** and **false** values are really important because they are used in computer programming to make the computer behave differently in different circumstances. For instance, in the Minecraft game, there is a section of code that asks "Does the player have any health points left?" and if the answer to that question is **true**, then the player can continue playing.

Variables

Variables provide a way to give names to numbers and other types of data so that they can be easily remembered, retrieved, and worked with.

Creating Variables

You can't type just anything after the **js** command and expect an answer. You have to use expressions that JavaScript understands. For example, if I type the following:

```
js hearts
```

then the server responds with the error message **javax.script. ScriptException: ReferenceError: "hearts" is not defined**, which is JavaScript's way of saying "I don't understand what you mean by **hearts**."

Right now JavaScript does not know what you mean by **hearts**. If you want to tell the computer what **hearts** is, you do so like this:

```
js hearts = 8;
```

This basically says that **hearts** is equal to 8. A couple of things are worth noting about the previous expression. First, **hearts** is now a variable. A variable is just something JavaScript uses to store things in. Variables are used in all programming languages to store information. When you want the computer to remember something and to keep track of it, you use a variable. You can think of a variable as a named storage location. It's like a storage chest in Minecraft (see **FIGURE 3.1**). You can put stuff in a variable and come back to it later, and it will still be there.

FIGURE 3.1 Variables are like chests. You can store stuff in them.

Now when you type **js hearts**, JavaScript understands what **hearts** is, remembers its value, and prints it out. Try it:

```
js hearts
```

It should print out **8**. Second, what I've done in the **js hearts = 8** expression is made an *assignment*. That is, I've *assigned* the value 8 to the variable **hearts** using a *single* = sign. I can reassign a different value to the variable **hearts** like this:

```
js hearts = 9
```

That's why variables are called *variables*—they can vary (or change). Now when you issue the following command, the result is **9**:

```
js hearts
```

Just as you can do math with numbers in JavaScript, you can also do math with variables. Try this command:

```
js hearts + 1
```

The previous statement should print out **10** as the result. That's because the computer now knows that **hearts** is equal to 9 and that 9 + 1 is 10. Try each of the following commands yourself:

- `js hearts + 5`
- `js hearts - 2`
- `js hearts * 2`
- `js hearts / 3`

After executing all of these commands, issue the following command:

```
js hearts
```

You'll notice that the value of the **hearts** variable is unchanged. It's still **9**. If you want to change the value of **hearts** by some amount, you need to reassign it the new value. You can do so like this:

```
js hearts = hearts + 1
```

What you've done here is combine a math operation and an assignment in a single statement. Now issue the command `js hearts`, and you'll see that hearts is now **10**.

String Variables

Let's create another variable called `healthmessage` and assign it a value, like so:

```
js healthMessage = 'You have ' + hearts + ' health remaining'
```

What you've done here is created a new variable and assigned it a value. The value is the text "You have" plus the value of the **hearts** variable plus the text "health remaining". Everything between `' '` (single quote symbols) or `" "` (double quote symbols) in JavaScript is treated as text. The result of this expression is as follows:

```
You have 10 health remaining
```

JavaScript creates a new variable called `healthMessage` and then joins together the three values `'You have '` (which is text), `hearts` (which is a number), and `' health remaining'` (more text) and constructs a new value `'You have 10 health remaining'` and assigns it to the `healthMessage` variable.

In JavaScript, a piece of text is also called a *string*. In Minecraft a string is the material spiders sometimes drop when slain. *String* is also the word programmers use when talking about text. Here are some examples of strings (text) in JavaScript:

- `js "Hello"`
- `js 'Goodbye'`
- `js "Minecraft 1.7.9"`
- `js "123"`

That last one might surprise you. JavaScript treats anything between quotes as a string even if it's a number! In our first string example, `js healthMessage = 'You have ' + hearts + ' health remaining'`, I used the + operator to add strings together. The + operator can be used to add numbers or strings. When used to add strings, the + operator behaves differently. Adding strings in JavaScript is also called *concatenation*. You concatenate two or more strings together to form bigger, longer strings. This is a technique you will use quite often in programming Minecraft plugins when you want to display information to players.

The letters, numbers, and other symbols that form a string are known as *characters*. A *character* is any single letter, number, or symbol. a, B, 9, -, ., /, and : are all examples of characters.

Escaping Quotes

In JavaScript you can enclose a string in either single quotes (' ') or double quotes (" "), but what if your string needs to include these characters? In JavaScript there are a couple of ways to do this.

If your string contains only single quotes, you can enclose the string in double quotes.

```js
"I'm a String!"
```

If your string contains only double quotes, you can enclose the string in single quotes.

```js
'He said "No"'
```

You can escape each single or double quote character by putting a backslash character \ in front of it.

```js
'He said "I\'m a String!".'
"He said \"No\""
```

Naming Variables

You can create as many variables as you like in JavaScript. You'll notice that both the **hearts** and **healthmessage** variables use one-word names. I could not call the **healthMessage** variable **health message** because variable names cannot have space characters. There are a few other rules about what JavaScript will accept as a valid variable name. It doesn't like variable names that begin with numbers, so **2player** is not a valid variable name, but **player2** is.

JavaScript programmers, as a habit, generally use lowercase letters for variable names, and if the variable name is made of two words joined together (as in **healthMessage**), then the first letter of the second word is usually uppercase. This style of variable naming is called *camelCase* and is considered "good practice" among JavaScript programmers. This means that using this naming convention makes it easier for programmers to read and understand each other's (and their own) code.

You can read more about camelCase on Wikipedia (*http://en.wikipedia.org/wiki/CamelCase*).

Making Mistakes

Feel free to experiment at this point. Create your own variables using your own numbers, strings, and operators. If you make a mistake, you'll see a long-winded error message in your console window. These error messages are called *stack traces*, and they're the computer's way of telling you something went wrong. Stack traces can be useful for Java programmers but not so useful for JavaScript. Remember, the Minecraft server software is written in Java, not JavaScript. You can think of ScriptCraft (the plugin you use when you type the **js** command in the server console) as a translator. It translates the JavaScript code you type into Java code so that the server can understand it. If the JavaScript code doesn't make sense, then the translation won't work.

Don't worry about making mistakes. Making mistakes is an essential part of learning something new. Computers are finicky about code and will point-blank refuse to execute code that isn't correct. We humans are good at conversation because we allow for errors and can make pretty good guesses at what someone else means even when there's background noise. Computers, on the other hand, are pretty dumb and aren't able to guess at what you really meant if your code isn't correct. The good news is every time you make a mistake, you learn something new. Each of the following statements will cause an error:

```
js help
ReferenceError: "help" is not defined
```

This is JavaScript's way of saying "I don't know what **help** is".

```
js 'steve
EvaluatorException: unterminated String literal
```

This means JavaScript encountered a string **'steve** that didn't have a closing quote symbol. Strings must begin and end with either a single quote (') or a double quote ("). What's more, you can't mix them; you can't start a string with a single quote and end it with a double quote. The strings **'this is good'** and **"so is this"** are both valid, but the strings **'this is bad"** and **"another bad one'** are not.

```
js :-)
EvaluatorException: syntax error
```

JavaScript will respond with a *syntax error* if it simply doesn't understand your code. It's clear from this example JavaScript doesn't know what a smiley is.

TERM Exception

An exception is something the computer did not expect—that's what makes it "exceptional." In JavaScript, *throwing an exception* is JavaScript's way of saying something unexpected happened. An exception will often include a stack trace, which is a breadcrumb trail of where the program was when the exception occurred.

As you learn to program, you will encounter errors. One misplaced comma, quote, or period and the computer will complain by *throwing an exception*. Just remember to be patient. Computers aren't as smart as us, so we have to be extra careful when typing code.

The var Keyword

I said earlier that you can create a new variable by typing a name and assigning it a value. In the earlier example, shown here:

```
js hearts = 8
```

two things happen with this statement.

- A new variable called **hearts** is *declared*. To declare a variable is to create a variable.

- The variable is also *assigned* a new value (8). *Assigning* a value to a variable means storing the value in the variable.

So in the previous statement, you both declare a new variable and assign a value to it. It's considered good practice to declare variables using the **var** keyword. **var** as you can probably guess is short for "variable." So, a better way to declare the variable is like this:

```
js var hearts = 8
```

You should always declare variables using the **var** keyword. If variables aren't declared using the **var** keyword, they become what are called *global* variables, that is, variables that can be seen everywhere in the program. Global variables can lead to confusion because different parts of your program can access and change the variable, which can lead to unexpected results. Global variables often end up becoming a source of bugs in the program. Using the **var** keyword to create a new variable is another good habit you should adopt when writing JavaScript code.

Another thing to note is that you don't always have to both declare and assign a variable in the same statement. You can create a variable just by issuing this command:

```
js var hungerBar
```

Notice that `hungerBar` doesn't yet have a value. You haven't assigned it one; you've just created the variable. Right now the `hungerBar` variable has a special value called **undefined**, which is another keyword in JavaScript—it means there's nothing there. You can test this using the following code:

```js
hungerBar == undefined
```

The result of this expression will be **true** . Note that I used two equal symbols, which means I'm comparing. I want to see whether `hungerBar` is equal to the special value **undefined**. Now that I know `hungerBar` is undefined, I can assign it a value:

```js
hungerBar = 10
```

Note that I didn't need to use the **var** keyword here because the `hungerBar` variable has *already* been declared. All I'm doing is assigning the variable a new value. You should use the **var** keyword only when declaring a variable.

The `null` Keyword

The `null` keyword in JavaScript is a special object that is used by programmers to mean there is no value. When you declare a new variable, you can explicitly assign it a **null** value to make it clearer that the variable is empty.

```js
var hungerBar = null
```

This is the conventional way to declare a variable and assign it a nonvalue.

Declaring Multiple Variables

You can use the **var** keyword to declare just one variable, or you can use it to declare any number of variables in a single statement. For example, to declare the two variables `gameMode` and `allowFlight`, you could use two separate statements like this:

```js
var gameMode = 1
```

```js
var allowFlight = true
```

Or you could declare both in a single statement like this:

```js
var gameMode = 1, allowFlight = true
```

It has become commonplace to declare many variables using a single statement.

Adding and Subtracting

You're going to play with the **hungerBar** variable while exploring some more JavaScript math operations. In Minecraft your *hunger bar* is the bar along the bottom of the screen next to your health bar that tells you how hungry you are. The hunger bar drains as you become exhausted and is replenished when you eat. This is done using addition and subtraction. In JavaScript there's more than one way to do addition with variables. You can *increment* (increment means add 1) using the following operation:

```js
js hungerBar = hungerBar + 1
```

This increases the **hungerBar** variable by 1. The result (assuming **hunger-Bar**'s previous value was 10) will be 11. In most programming languages, this kind of operation is so common that the language designers provide shorthand ways to do it, like so:

```js
js hungerBar += 1
```

That does the same thing using fewer characters. This statement can be made shorter again and can be written as follows:

```js
js ++hungerBar
```

The **++** (two **+** signs next to each other) is a convention used in many programming languages—including JavaScript—to increment values. Similarly, the same rules apply for subtracting values from a variable. All three of the following statements do the same thing—they each subtract 1:

```js
js hungerBar = hungerBar - 1
```

```js
js hungerBar -= 1
```

```js
js --hungerBar
```

Which statement you use is a matter of personal taste and style. While **--hungerBar** is easier to type, I personally prefer **hungerBar = hungerBar - 1** because I think it reads better.

Data Types

Variables are used to store values. Those values can be numbers, text, or one of the many other data types available in JavaScript. You can ask what "type of" data a variable has using the **typeof** operator. For example, to find out what type of data the **hungerBar** variable holds, use this:

```js
js typeof hungerBar
```

The result is **number**. The **typeof** operator doesn't tell you what the value is, only its type. These are the different data types in JavaScript:

- Number
- String
- Boolean
- Object
- Undefined
- Function

To get some practice using the **typeof** operator, try each of the following examples in your server console window:

```js
js typeof false
```

```js
js typeof true
```

```js
js typeof 5
```

```js
js typeof 9.99
```

```js
js typeof 'Hello'
```

```js
js typeof "Goodbye"
```

```js
js typeof "5"
```

```js
js typeof console
```

```js
js typeof Herobrine
```

```js
js typeof parseInt
```

The values **true** and **false** are both *boolean* values. A boolean type can only ever have the value **true** or **false**. Boolean values are really important in programming because, as you'll learn later, they are the values the computer uses when making decisions. When deciding what to do, the computer uses only these two values—there's no gray area or "maybe" when it comes to boolean logic.

The result of the expression **typeof "5"** might surprise you. Even though 5 is a number, because it is inside quote characters, JavaScript thinks of it as a string. Everything inside quote characters is considered a string—even if there is a number inside the quotes.

The **console** variable is one of the built-in variables in ScriptCraft, and its type is object. I'll talk about objects later. The **typeof Herobrine** returns **undefined** because there is no variable or value called **Herobrine** in the system. You can safely use the **typeof** operator to test for the existence of variables in the system. If the variable doesn't exist, then **typeof** will return **false**. If you were to try to access the undefined **Herobrine** variable, you'd get a **ReferenceError** exception. Try it to see for yourself:

```
js Herobrine
```

The type of a variable is important because it determines what you can do with it and how it behaves. Finally, the **typeof parseInt** expression returns **function**. You'll dive into functions next.

Functions

Functions in JavaScript are powerful because they are containers for code that can be called any number of times. You can write your own functions or use any of the *built-in* functions provided by the language. A built-in function is simply a function that comes bundled with JavaScript. Let's look at one of the built-in functions—the **parseInt()** function.

Using Functions

The **parseInt()** function is a useful function that will take any piece of text and try to extract (or *parse*) a number from it. Say you have some text **'4 hours until sunset'**. If you pass this text to the **parseInt()** function, it will try to figure out what number is in the text. Let's try it.

```
js parseInt('4 hours until sunset')
```

The result should be 4. What you did here was *pass* the `'4 hours until sunset'` text to the `parseInt()` function, which processed the text and returned a value: 4.

You are effectively saying `"here's some text; give me the number (and only the number) from it"`. You pass the text to the `parseInt()` function by putting it between the round brackets—the `(` and `)` symbols. Any values between the `(` and `)` symbols are passed into the function and are called *parameters*. Functions typically process (or do something) with the parameters and return a value. The great thing about functions is they can be called over and over again with different parameters. Try the following examples yourself:

```
js parseInt('5 hearts left');
js parseInt('This is not a number');
js parseInt('3 blind mice');
```

Writing Your Own Functions

One of the really cool things about programming is that you're not limited to using only the built-in functions provided by the language. You can create your own functions. In this book you're going to create a lot of functions to do cool things you wouldn't normally be able to do in Minecraft. For now let's create a simple new function that adds two numbers together. You will need to type the following code on a single line in Minecraft. The code is presented here with line breaks for readability only.

```
js function add(firstNumber, secondNumber) {
    return firstNumber + secondNumber;
}
```

When you enter this command, nothing happens. That's because what you've just done is declared a new function called **add**. The function won't do anything until you call it. Let's do that.

```
js add( 1, 2 )
```

The result is 3. Try calling it with different values to test that the function works.

```
js add( 5, 6 )
js add( 9, 1 )
```

Now let's look at the earlier function declaration in more detail. A function is a way to package up code so that it can be reused over and over. When you create a

TERM **Reuse**

Reuse is important in programming. While programming, you'll often find that a problem you're working on is similar to a problem you already solved some time ago. In that case, it's always good to be able to use code you've already written to solve new problems. There are two ways to do this: You can copy and paste the code you've already written, but a better way is to change the code you wrote earlier so that it works in both the earlier program and the new program you're currently working on. There are a couple of ways to write reusable code—packaging up code in functions is just one of them. You'll explore more ways to create reusable code throughout this book.

new function, you must say what parameters the function will expect. You do that by putting names between the round brackets—the (and) symbols. A function can take one or more parameters. If it takes more than one parameter, then each parameter must be separated with a comma (,). So, the first part of the function declaration `function add( firstNumber, secondNumber )` gives the function a name (**add**) and says what the function should expect. The next step in defining the function is to say what the function should do. Everything between the opening and closing curly brackets—the { and } symbols—is code that will be executed whenever the function is called. **FIGURE 3.2** illustrates the different parts of the function definition statement.

When you create a new function of your own, you should give the function a meaningful and memorable name. You can name the function parameters however you like. They don't have to be called **firstNumber** and **secondNumber**, but you should give your parameters names that are memorable so you don't forget what the parameters are for.

In the previous example function, there's one statement, `return firstNumber + secondNumber`, which will be executed every time this function is called. The **return** keyword is another special word in JavaScript. It's used in functions to return something to the caller. In this case, you return the sum of the two numbers passed in. The **return** keyword should only ever be used inside functions.

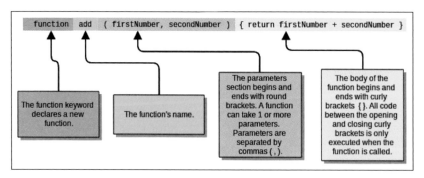

FIGURE 3.2 Function outline

Achievement Unlocked!

You've created and invoked your first function. Functions are an important part of JavaScript, and you'll create many more functions in the course of this book.

We've only scratched the surface of functions in JavaScript. You'll explore them more in later chapters.

Summary

In this chapter, you learned about how to execute JavaScript at the server console prompt. You explored math operations, variables, and strings and the kinds of errors you'll encounter when learning JavaScript. I also touched on functions—how to call them and how to create them. In the next chapter, you'll learn about programming editors—the last piece of the puzzle in constructing your modding workbench.

Chapter 4

Choosing and Using a Text Editor

UP TO NOW you've been executing JavaScript at the server console window using the **js** command. This is a perfectly good way to try JavaScript. It's nice to have a command-line interpreter when trying things out and exploring a new language. However, once you want to start doing some real work with JavaScript, you'll want to be able to save your work and run it, without issuing many **js** commands at the server console window each time your server starts.

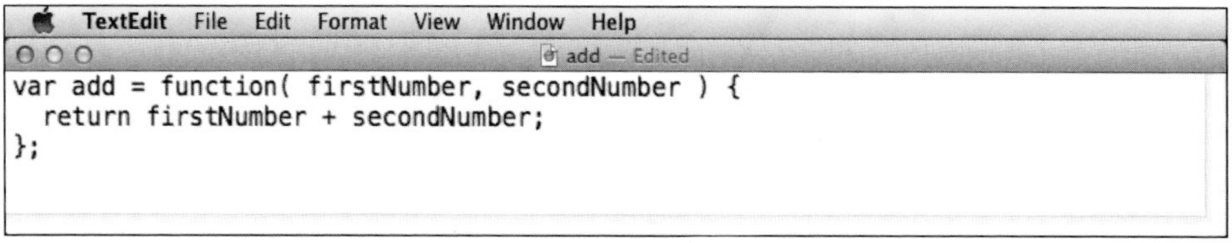

```
  TextEdit   File   Edit   Format   View   Window   Help
○ ○ ○                          add — Edited
var add = function( firstNumber, secondNumber ) {
  return firstNumber + secondNumber;
};
```

FIGURE 4.1 JavaScript code in an editor with no syntax highlighting

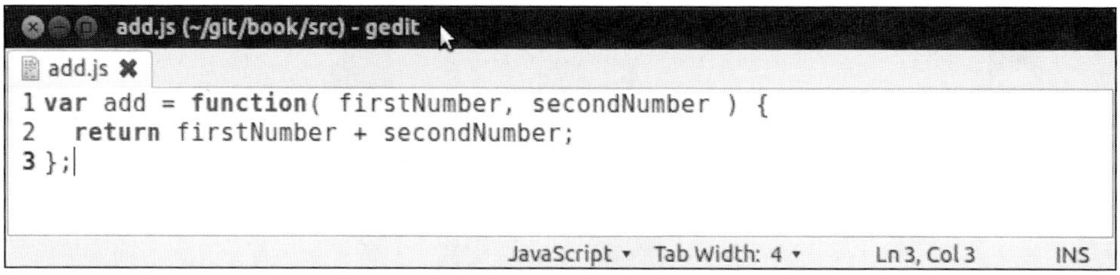

```
add.js (~/git/book/src) - gedit
add.js ✖
1 var add = function( firstNumber, secondNumber ) {
2   return firstNumber + secondNumber;
3 };|
                      JavaScript ▾  Tab Width: 4 ▾   Ln 3, Col 3   INS
```

FIGURE 4.2 JavaScript code in an editor with syntax highlighting turned on

ScriptCraft lets you load JavaScript files you've saved and either can run them automatically when the server starts up or can run your code *on-demand*. If you plan on saving your work, you'll need to write your code using a text editor. Any text editor could do, but I strongly recommend using a text editor dedicated to programming. A programming text editor will have a few extra bells and whistles to make writing code easier than it would be in a plain old text editor like Notepad. Most programming editors have what's called *syntax highlighting*, which colors different parts of your code to make it easier to read. Compare FIGURE 4.1 from a regular text editor to FIGURE 4.2 from a programming editor.

I think you'll agree that the syntax highlighting in Figure 4.2 makes the code more pleasant to read.

Choosing an Editor

There are many programming editors to choose from. Which editor you choose is ultimately up to you. I've been using Emacs—an open source editor—for many years, but I don't recommend it to beginning programmers because, while powerful, it takes some time to learn. Programmers get very attached to their programming editors after time. You should start with an editor that's easy to use and learn. In this chapter, I'll talk about gedit, but you can use any of the following programming editors to get started programming:

- Notepad++ is a free editor for Windows you can download at *http://notepad-plus-plus.org/*.

- TextWrangler from BareBones Software is a free editor for Mac OS X you can download at *http://www.barebones.com/products/textwrangler/*.

- Sublime Text is a cross-platform editor that you can evaluate for free for as long as you like. You can download Sublime at *http://www.sublimetext.com/*.

Let's get started installing gedit. You can skip this section if you've already installed and use a programming editor on your computer. Mac OS users can skip the following section and go straight to "Installing TextWrangler on Mac OS."

gedit

The editor I use for screenshots in this book is called gedit. I chose gedit for use in this book because:

- It is cross-platform, meaning it runs on Windows and Linux. gedit also runs on older versions of Mac OS (up to version 10.5), but I recommend using TextWrangler for Mac OS.

- It is lightweight and easy to use. It installs quickly, doesn't take up much disk space, and doesn't have a whole lot of features you'll need to learn. It has just enough features to get started in programming.

- It has a Disk Explorer Pane, which shows the folders with which you'll be working. This can be really handy when you want to quickly browse the folders for files to edit.

- It is free to use. It won't cost you to download, and it won't nag you to upgrade to a paid version.

You don't have to use gedit. Any programming editor will do. All programming editors have similar features; they let you create new files, edit, and save files.

You can download gedit at *https://wiki.gnome.org/Apps/Gedit/*. Follow the download instructions for your platform.

Installing gedit on Linux

If you use Linux, then gedit is probably already installed on your computer (click the Dash Home button in the top left of your Linux screen and type **gedit** to find it). If it's not already installed, you can install it by opening the Ubuntu Software Center application and searching for *gedit* or by issuing the following command in a Terminal window:

```
sudo apt-get install gedit
```

Once gedit is installed, you can launch it by typing **gedit** into the Dash Home search window (click the Dash Home button).

Installing gedit on Windows

Follow these steps to install gedit on Windows:

1. Open your browser and go to *https://wiki.gnome.rog/Apps/Gedit*.
2. Go to the Download section of the page and click the Windows Binaries link.
3. Click the link for the latest version (at the time of writing this is 2.30).
4. Click the **gedit-setup.exe** link (it might be called a slightly different name).
5. Once it's downloaded, open the **gedit-setup.exe** file to begin the install.
6. Follow all of the install wizard steps. You can use the default values.

Once installed, gedit should appear in your Start menu. If it doesn't appear in your Start menu, you can search for it by typing **gedit** in the Start menu's Search field.

The File Browser

Most modern programming editors provide a file browsing view where you can see—at a glance—all of your folders and files. The disk browser is super useful when you want to quickly navigate around your JavaScript folders and files. To enable the file browsing view in gedit, choose View > Side Panel to open the Side Panel view. In the bottom of the Side Panel view there is a File Browser tab that you should click to switch to the File Browser. From the File Browser (Disk Browser in TextWrangler on Mac OS), you can quickly open files, view folder contents, and create new files and subfolders (see **FIGURE 4.3**). Once you enable the Side Panel view, it will be displayed the next time you launch gedit.

FIGURE 4.3 gedit's File Browser

The gedit File Browser on Microsoft Windows

The first time you launch gedit for Windows, you will need to change one of the default settings so that all files and folders appear in the File Browser window. By default only folders are shown in the Windows File Browser. This isn't very useful because you'll want to work with folders and JavaScript files. To ensure you can see all types of files, do the following: In the File Browser window, right-click anywhere (click the right mouse button) and make sure that the Show Binary option is selected under the Filter menu. This will ensure all file types are visible (see **FIGURE 4.4**).

gedit Preferences

The next step is to set some preferences for how the editor should behave. You do this by choosing Edit > Preferences to open the Preferences dialog (see **FIGURE 4.5**). Let's look at each of the preferences sections in turn.

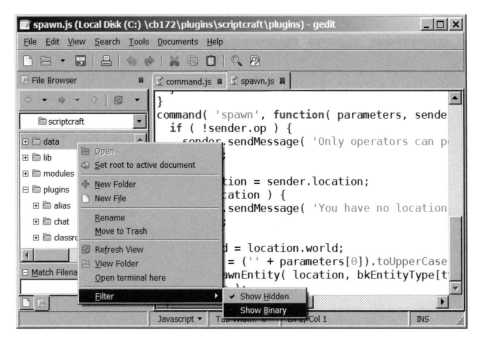

FIGURE 4.4 Ensuring all file types are visible in gedit for Windows

FIGURE 4.5 View preferences

View Preferences

It's useful to have gedit display line numbers alongside your code. The line numbers appear in the left margin of the window and are not part of your actual code.

gedit will display a faint margin along the right side of the window in column 80. This margin is just a guide to indicate that perhaps your line of code is too long. It's only a guide, though, and can be safely ignored. It's generally considered good practice to keep lines of code shorter than 80 characters long to help readability, but there will always be exceptions to this rule.

The Enable Text Wrapping setting should be turned off for programming. It's useful if you're writing a letter, essay, or other nonprogramming text, but it can be confusing if turned on while programming.

Highlight Current Line makes it easier to see where you currently are in the code. When looking at a large JavaScript file, it can be difficult to see the cursor (the blinking block that appears next to letters as you type).

Highlight Matching Brackets is a super useful programming feature. As you move the cursor around your JavaScript source, when the cursor is next to any of the following characters, it will match the opening or closing character.

- Round brackets: ( )
- Curly brackets: { }
- Square brackets: [ ]

This can really help when writing or editing code. In **FIGURE 4.6**, you can see the cursor on line 1 next to the { character with both the opening and closing curly brackets highlighted in gray.

```
add.js ✖
1 var add = function( firstNumber, secondNumber ) {
2   return firstNumber + secondNumber;
3 };
```

FIGURE 4.6 Bracket matching

Editor Preferences

FIGURE 4.7 shows the settings available on the Editor tab.

I recommend using either two or four spaces for tabs to make your code more readable. This is largely a matter of style and personal taste. When starting out, you should probably use four spaces.

Automatic indentation is a handy feature that saves you having to press Tab and the spacebar when you start writing a new line of code.

gedit can create a backup of your files before you save them. This is usually a good idea.

Fonts & Colors

FIGURE 4.8 shows the settings available on the Fonts & Colors tab.

You can change the font and color scheme to suit your own tastes. Some people prefer dark text on a light background, and some prefer light text on a dark background. Pick the color scheme you like. You can always change it later.

Plugins

FIGURE 4.9 shows the settings available on the Plugins tab.

gedit comes with a couple of editing plugins. You should make sure that the File Browser Panel plugin is selected.

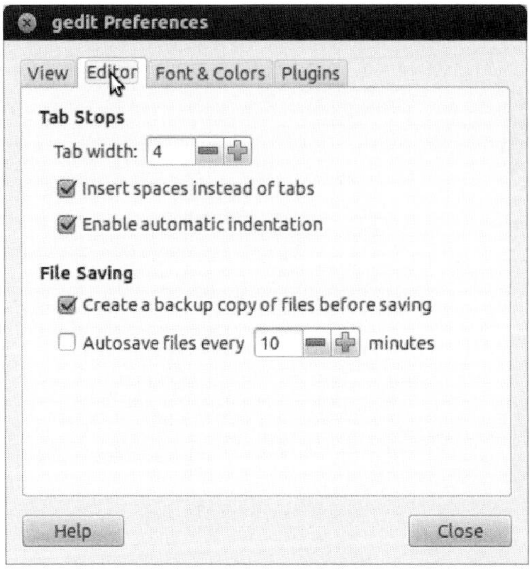

FIGURE 4.7 Editor preferences

FIGURE 4.8 Fonts & Colors preferences

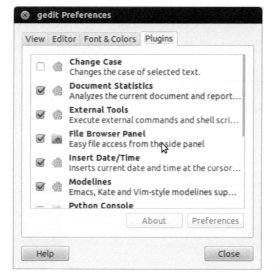

FIGURE 4.9 Plugins preferences

Installing TextWrangler on Mac OS

Follow these steps to install TextWrangler on Mac OS:

1. Open the App Store application and search for *TextWrangler* in the search box in the top right.

2. Click the Free/Install App button to begin installing.

Once installed, you can launch TextWrangler by typing `textw` in the Spotlight search field in the top right of the screen and clicking the TextWrangler result.

Whenever you launch TextWrangler, you should open a Disk Browser window by choosing File > New > Disk Browser. The Disk Browser in TextWrangler lets you quickly navigate around different files in the ScriptCraft folder and subfolders (see **FIGURE 4.10**).

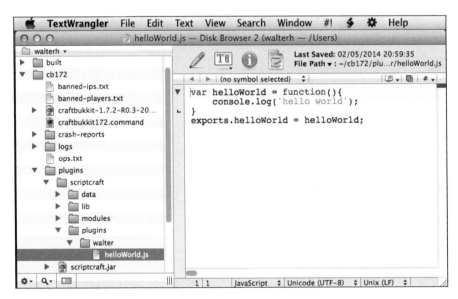

FIGURE 4.10 TextWrangler's Disk Browser

First Steps with Your Editor

To get used to working with a programming editor, you're going to create a new folder and file in the ScriptCraft plugins folder and save the new file.

Create a New Folder

In the File Browser pane (the Disk Browser in TextWrangler on Mac OS), locate and select the **mcserver** folder. Then navigate to the **scriptcraft/plugins** subfolder. Once that folder is selected, right-click the folder and choose New Folder from the menu (see **FIGURE 4.11**). Call your new folder **learning** for now. You can call it something else as long as it's memorable—you'll come back to this folder later.

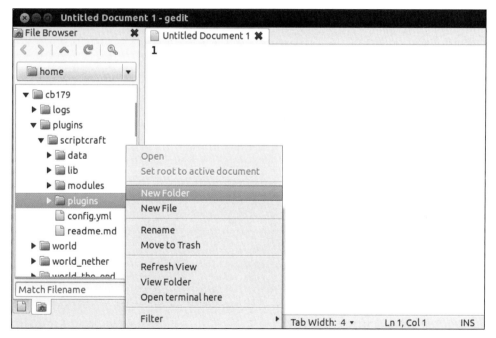

FIGURE 4.11 Creating a new folder

Your new folder will now appear in the File/Disk Browser pane.

Create a New JavaScript File

The next step is to create a new JavaScript file in the subfolder you just created. The file won't do much just yet, but you'll work some more on it soon. Right-click the folder you just created and choose New File from the menu (see **FIGURE 4.12**). Call the new file `helloWorld.js`.

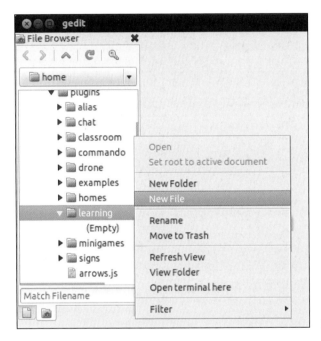

FIGURE 4.12 Creating a new file

The file has just been created but hasn't been opened. If using TextWrangler, click the file to open it. If using gedit, double-click the file to open it. The file contents now appear in the editing pane on the right. The file is, as you'd expect, empty. Type in the following code exactly as you see it:

```
// TO DO : Add some code later
```

The previous code is just a *comment* you've added to remind yourself that you must add some proper code later. This comment isn't understandable to the computer, so you can write whatever you like on a line beginning with `//`. The computer will not try to interpret and execute it. Comments like this can be useful for programmers because they make understanding code easier. Writing code is like any kind of writing—you should try to make your code readable by yourself and others, so if you look at your code later, you can figure out what you did.

Most programming languages provide a way to add comments. In JavaScript there are different ways you can add comments. You can add a single-line comment like the one shown previously by inserting two forward slashes (`//`), and then any text after is a comment and will be ignored by the computer until the next line. I'll talk more about comments later in this book.

Saving Your Work

Save the file by choosing Save from the File menu or by pressing Ctrl+S (Cmd+S on Mac OS). The file is now saved. You can verify this by closing the file and opening it once more. To close the file, choose File > Close or click the close icon next to the filename at the top of the editor pane.

Reopen the file by double-clicking it in the File/Disk Browser pane. The text you entered previously should still be present. Saving your work is really important because code you edit will not take effect unless you first save it. You'd be surprised how often even experienced programmers forget this simple rule and are left wondering why their code isn't working as expected.

When using ScriptCraft, the folder where you save your work is important. You can't just save your files anywhere and hope they'll be executed by ScriptCraft. For now you've saved the newly created `helloWorld.js` file in the `mcserver/scriptcraft/plugins/learning` subfolder. Just as the Minecraft server looks for JAR files in its plugins subfolder to load Java-based plugins, ScriptCraft too looks for JS files in its own `scriptcraft/plugins` folder to load JavaScript-based plugins.

Summary

You've installed a programming editor and have taken your first steps creating and editing a new JavaScript file. In the next part of the book, you'll dive into creating working JavaScript plugins for Minecraft.

This is where the fun begins.

Part II

Basic Modding

IN THE PREVIOUS PART, you assembled all of the pieces needed to construct your modding workbench. Now you're ready to begin developing Minecraft plugins. In this part of the book, you'll learn about how to create plugins, and you'll also learn more about JavaScript. In each chapter in this part, you'll develop a working plugin and learn about JavaScript along the way.

Chapter 5

Your First Minecraft Plugin

IN THIS CHAPTER you'll dive in and create your first Minecraft plugin. A *plugin* is a small program that is loaded and executed by a larger program. The larger program you'll be using is, of course, your Minecraft server. This first plugin will be short—just a couple of lines of code—so you won't have to type too much, but you should read through this first chapter and try to understand the code and the notes. You'll build on the knowledge learned here when creating more sophisticated plugins in later chapters.

Hello World

Launch your editor and open the `helloWorld.js` file you created in Chapter 4. Once opened, you can remove the comment entered previously and type the following text:

```
console.log('Hello World');
```

You haven't used the `console.log()` function before. It's a built-in function that will print out a message in the server console window. You can also use the `console.log()` function in interactive mode at the server console window. Issue `js console.log( 8 + 3 )`, and you'll see it prints the following result:

```
[scriptcraft] 11
```

Whenever you use the `console.log()` function, the output will start with `[scriptcraft]` because `console.log()` writes to the server's log file, which is used by the core server and all plugins. The server software inserts the plugin name at the front of the message to make it easy for server administrators to tell which plugin is responsible for messages in the log file. I'll use `console.log()` in upcoming examples. This function is also really useful for debugging code: adding logging statements in your code so you know it's being executed.

You may be wondering what the semicolon (`;`) is doing at the end of the line. The semicolon is used to end each statement in JavaScript. If you think of a statement as a sentence, then the semicolon is to statements what the period (`.`) is to sentences. In JavaScript, the semicolon isn't strictly needed, but you should use it anyway.

Another thing you might notice is there is no `js` command in the `helloWorld.js` file. The `js` prefix (text that is placed in front of other text) is needed only when executing JavaScript at the server console or in-game prompt. It should never be used inside JavaScript files.

After you've changed the `helloWorld.js` file, make sure to save it (choose Save from the File menu).

If your server isn't already started, then start it by running the script you created earlier. If the server is already started, restart your server by issuing the `stop` command in the server console window and then start the server. After starting or restarting your server, you should see the text "Hello World" appear in your server console window. In fact, you will see it every time the server starts.

Achievement Unlocked!

Believe it or not, you've just written your
first Minecraft plugin!

Well, that was easy, wasn't it? This
might be a trivially simple plugin, but it demonstrates essentially what a plugin
is—some code that is "embedded" in a larger program and is loaded every time
the host program loads. The plugin code never runs on its own; it can be run only
as part of some bigger "host" program (Minecraft server). You've just added new
code to the Minecraft server!

Making Your Function Reusable

So far, the plugin you've written works fine; it is loaded and executed when the
Minecraft server starts. Sometimes that's all you might want or need, but what
if you want to be able to execute the code later? Let's start by putting the code
inside a function (see **LISTING 5.1**).

Now restart the server.

What just happened? The message no longer displays at startup! That's
because you've put the code inside a function, but you haven't called the function
yet! Declaring a new function and invoking the function are two different things.
Just because you declare a function does not mean the function is automatically

LISTING 5.1 helloWorld() Function Declaration

```
function helloWorld( ) {
  console.log('Hello World');
};
```

LISTING 5.2 helloWorld() Function Declaration and Execution

```
function helloWorld( ) {
  console.log('Hello World');
};
helloWorld();
```

invoked when the file is loaded. Let's change the code once more, this time adding a call to the function you just created (see LISTING 5.2).

Now restart the server again. Once again, the message will appear every time the server starts up. The `helloWorld()` function you wrote will be loaded and executed by the Minecraft server every time it starts.

So, you've wrapped the original code in a function of your own, and you call that function. So far so good. Sometimes you'll want to write functions to use at the in-game or server console prompt. Try running the `helloWorld()` function at the in-game or server console prompt.

```
js helloWorld()
```

This command fails with the error `ReferenceError: helloWorld is not defined`. That's odd, no? The function obviously exists and works because it successfully executed when the server started. How can it now claim the function isn't there? That's because functions that are loaded from the `plugins/scriptcraft/plugins` directory aren't automatically made available for use by others. The `helloWorld.js` file loads, and all code in the file is evaluated and executed at startup. However, once it's loaded and executed, the code is basically invisible to others and can't be run again. You can make your code visible to others using a special variable called `exports`. The `exports` variable (as its name implies) "exports" code for use by others. It's how you provide code for use outside of the plugin itself. Let's revisit the `helloWorld.js` file one more time (see LISTING 5.3).

Restart the server again. Now the message appears in the server console. Let's look at the last statement in the code.

```
exports.helloWorld = helloWorld;
```

LISTING 5.3 Making helloWorld() Public

```
function helloWorld( ) {
  console.log('Hello World');
};
helloWorld();
exports.helloWorld = helloWorld;
```

What you are doing here is *exporting* the `helloWorld()` function for use outside of the plugin.

The `exports` variable isn't part of the JavaScript core language. It's provided by ScriptCraft, which uses a module system called *CommonJS*. CommonJS is a set of rules that say how modules (and other things not provided by JavaScript itself) should work. The CommonJS rules for modules are easy to understand and adopt, and so have become very popular lately, especially with the rising popularity of Node.js, which is a JavaScript environment used by professional programmers.

Private and Public Variables

When you create a new variable in a JavaScript file, it is *private*, which means no other parts of the system can see it. Only code within the file itself can see variables declared in a file. That's why, earlier, you couldn't execute the `helloWorld()` function even though it was defined and used within the file. Having variables be private by default is a good thing. If every variable you created was visible everywhere in the system, it would lead to confusion. Imagine you created a file called `MySuperDooperPlugin.js` and another called `MyExplodingZombiesPlugin.js` and in both these files you have a variable called `livesRemaining`. If the `livesRemaining` variable wasn't private, then both `MySuperDooperPlugin` and `MyExplodingZombiesPlugin` would end up using the same variable, which may not be what was intended at all.

Making variables private by default means that two or more plugins don't have to worry about stepping on each other's toes when updating or reading variables. In short, private variables are good.

There are times when you want to make a variable public so it can be used by other parts of the system. To do this, you attach the variable to the special **exports** variable as you did earlier. As a general rule, you should not make all of your variables public unless you really think they'll be needed elsewhere. I'll talk more about public and private variables later.

A Short Note About Objects

The **exports** variable is a special type of variable—it is an *object*. An object in JavaScript is something that can hold or contain other variables and functions. So, you can create a new variable that belongs to the **exports** object much like you'd normally create a new variable, shown here:

```
exports.favoriteGame = 'Minecraft';
```

The difference is that because you're attaching a new variable **favoriteGame** to an existing object **exports**, you don't need to use the **var** keyword. Variables that belong to objects are also called *properties*. For example, every player in Minecraft is essentially (from the game's point of view) an object with certain properties. Each player has a health level, experience points, the ability to fly (or not), and so on. In fact, everything in Minecraft is an object: players, blocks, tools, animals, biomes, worlds, recipes, and even the server itself. Everything is an object because Minecraft is written in Java, and Java is an object-oriented programming language. All of these objects in turn have properties. Each world has a **time** property, which dictates what time it is in the game. Primed TNT blocks have a **yield** property, which says how wide the TNT explosion would be.

Players have dozens of properties. For example, to give yourself full health, issue the following command at the in-game prompt:

```
js self.health = 20
```

To make yourself invisible, issue this command:

```
js self.invisible = true
```

To make yourself visible once more, issue the command `js self.invisible = false`. The `self` variable is one of the built-in variables provided by ScriptCraft. When used at the command prompt, it refers to the player or console sender who issues the `/js` command. The `self` variable should not be used anywhere except at the in-game or server console prompt. Everything in Minecraft is an object, and every object has properties. Knowing how to use these objects and properties is the key to creating cool plugins for Minecraft. I'll talk more about objects in later chapters where you'll learn how to explore the CanaryMod API documentation.

> **TERM Property**
>
> A property is an attribute of an object; for example, in real life, we all have properties: eye color, date of birth, name, and so on. Objects in JavaScript also have properties and so too do in-game objects. The server object has motd (message of the day) and port properties. Each player has food level, experience, and name properties. You can think of properties as variables that belong to or are attached to other variables.

Summary

In this chapter, you wrote your first plugin and used the special `exports` variable to export your code so it can be reused elsewhere at the in-game or server console prompt.

Chapter 6

Rolling Dice

TRADITIONAL BOARD GAMES such as Ludo, Monopoly, and Snake & Ladders all have an element of chance. Success is sometimes based solely on luck and the roll of the dice. In this chapter, you'll create a JavaScript module that mimics a six-sided die (the standard die that comes with most board games). You'll reuse this module in later chapters to give random greetings to players who join the game.

In this chapter, I'll walk you through creating your first *reusable* JavaScript module.

Randomness

When you throw a six-sided die, there's no way of knowing what the throw will be; it can be any number between 1 and 6, but it's impossible to know ahead of time. The number thrown is said to be *random*. Computers can also provide random numbers. In the JavaScript programming language, there's a special method of getting a random number: `Math.random()`. In this chapter, you'll use the `Math.random()` method to get a random number.

Think of a Number Between 0 and 1

Before writing the module, let's do some command-prompt exploration. At the in-game prompt, type the following and hit Enter:

```
/js Math.random()
```

You should see something like this returned:

```
0.7184312066528946
```

TIP

You can quickly perform the previous command at the in-game prompt by pressing the slash (/) key and then pressing the Up Arrow key.

The number you see will be different, but it will be a number between 0 and 1. Try it again: Type the same command at the in-game prompt and hit Enter. This time you'll see a different number than the previous number, but it too will be between 0 and 1. You can do this as many times as you like, and the number will be different each time.

The numbers that `Math.random()` returns are called *floating-point numbers*. You might not think there are any numbers between 0 and 1, but there are in fact many, many numbers. The actual range of numbers is 0.0000000000000000 to 0.9999999999999999. That's 9 quadrillion, 999 trillion, 999 billion, 999 million, 999 thousand, and 999 possible numbers. JavaScript uses this range of numbers when picking a random number.

A Special Six-Sided Die

A regular six-sided die has numbers from 1 through 6 printed or etched on each of the six sides. That's because humans typically count from 1. The number 1 is usually the starting point when you want to count up to something. JavaScript (like many programming languages) is different. In JavaScript, counting begins at the number 0. So if you want to count 10 numbers, where normally you'd count like this:

1, 2, 3, 4, 5, 6, 7, 8, 9, 10

...in JavaScript the count would look like this:

0, 1, 2, 3, 4, 5, 6, 7, 8, 9

This can be confusing for beginning and experienced programmers alike and takes some getting used to. I'll explain why counting from 0 is important in the following chapters. Your virtual six-sided die will have the numbers 0, 1, 2, 3, 4, 5 rather than the usual 1, 2, 3, 4, 5, 6.

Playing with Numbers

You have a problem to solve. `Math.random()` will give you a number between 0.0 and 0.9999999999999999, which isn't useful for most everyday uses. Here you're interested only in six possible numbers, so you need to do some math to get the result you need. We'll explore some basic math you can do in JavaScript and some operations you can perform on floating-point numbers, but first let's think about what you want to be able to do once your first plugin is complete.

Ideally you'd like to be able to issue the following command at the in-game prompt and have a useful number returned:

```
/js dice.roll()
```

That is, calling `dice.roll()` should return a random number between 0 and 5 behaving much like a real-world die. If you try to run the previous command now, it will fail because you haven't yet created this function. That's what we're going to do now.

Launch your editor and in the file/disk browser, select the `scriptcraft/modules` folder.

> **IMPORTANT**
>
> You must select the `scriptcraft/modules` folder, not the `scriptcraft/plugins` folder.

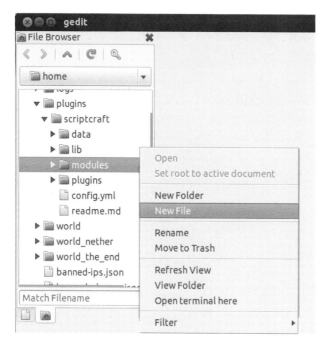

FIGURE 6.1 Creating a new file in the `modules` folder

Right-click and choose New File from the menu (**FIGURE 6.1**). Call your new file `dice.js` and then double-click it to open it (a single click will do for TextWrangler); then type the code shown in **LISTING 6.1** into the newly created file.

I'll talk about this code later. For now, type the code as you see it in the listing. Once you've typed the code, save your work (select the File menu and choose Save).

LISTING 6.1 Rolling Dice

```
function roll(){
  var result = Math.random();
  result = result * 6;
  result = Math.floor(result);
  return result;
};
exports.roll = roll;
```

Once you've saved your work, go back to Minecraft and at the in-game command prompt (remember, you can bring up the prompt by pressing the / key on your computer's keyboard) type the following:

```
/js refresh()
```

The `refresh()` function is a ScriptCraft function that reloads all of the JavaScript code.

The `refresh()` function is important; you should execute it every time you change your JavaScript code because changes to your code won't be activated in the game until you do so.

Once you've executed the `refresh()` function, you're ready to try your new function. Try issuing the following command:

> **TIP**
>
> While working on a Minecraft plugin, if the plugin isn't working as you expect, make sure you've run the `refresh()` function first.

```
/js dice.roll()
```

You should see an error message like this: `ReferenceError: "dice" is not defined`. OK, let's try calling `roll()` on its own.

```
/js roll()
```

You'll see another error message: `ReferenceError: "roll" is not defined`. Why doesn't this work?

ScriptCraft Folders

If you remember, the new file you just created—**dice.js**—was saved in the **scriptcraft/modules** folder, not the **scriptcraft/plugins** folder. Script-Craft has two subfolders you'll work in throughout this book.

The scriptcraft/plugins Folder

The **scriptcraft/plugins** folder is special for a couple of reasons.

- All JavaScript files in the **scriptcraft/plugins** folder are automatically loaded and executed when the server starts.

- All variables "exported" from files within the **scriptcraft/plugins** folder become what are called *global* variables. That means they are public for all the rest of the system to see.

The scriptcraft/modules Folder

There are other folders in **scriptcraft**. The **scriptcraft/modules** folder is much like the **plugins** folder. It's a folder where you can create new JavaScript files. It's similar to **scriptcraft/plugins** except

- JavaScript files inside the **scriptcraft/modules** folder are *not* automatically loaded or executed when the server starts.

- Variables exported from files in the **scriptcraft/modules** folder are not automatically available everywhere—they are not "global" variables.

You've written some useful code, but how do you get to use it?

Modules

A module in ScriptCraft is simply a JavaScript file. Throughout this book I will use the words *module* and *file* interchangeably because in ScriptCraft they mean the same thing. ScriptCraft uses a module system called CommonJS, which is also used by NodeJS—an increasingly popular JavaScript programming environment. Modules provide yet another way to make your code *reusable*. You've already used functions to package up statements that you want to call over and over. Well, modules provide a way to package up functions. So far, you've written only one function in your file, but in later chapters you'll create modules that have many functions.

Modular systems are good when programming. They're good because modules can be combined to form larger systems. Modules usually perform a set of related functions to serve a single purpose. So, for example, in **FIGURE 6.2** the Lunar Lander module was only used to land on the moon. That was its only purpose. Similarly, when writing JavaScript modules, it's considered good practice to have each module serve a single purpose. You'll learn more about modules throughout this book. If you're interested in exploring the CommonJS modules specification, check out the CommonJS website at *http://www.commonjs.org/specs/modules/1.0/* for more information.

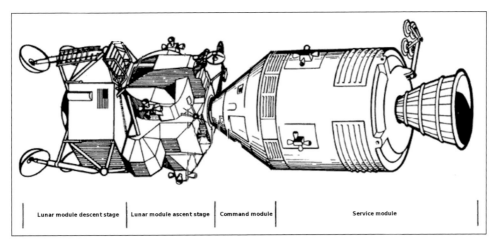

| Lunar module descent stage | Lunar module ascent stage | Command module | Service module |

FIGURE 6.2 Apollo Spacecraft Modules. Image Courtesy of NASA.

Using Modules

Getting back to the earlier problem, how do you use the new `dice.js` module you just created? Remember earlier you learned about the special `exports` variable that is used to expose private variables for use by others? Well, you may be wondering how you get at variables exposed in this way. Fortunately, there's a special function called `require()` that lets you do just that. The `require()` function is the counterpart to the `exports` variable. In the `dice.js` file, you use `exports` to say "Here's some of my code you can use," and you use `require()` to say "Hey, I'd like to use the code in the `dice` module."

So to use the code you just wrote inside the `dice.js` module, you first need to `require()` it. You do so using a statement like this:

```
/js var dice = require('dice')
```

The previous statement loads your newly created `dice.js` module into the computer's memory. The `require()` function is how ScriptCraft loads JavaScript modules. You'll notice I didn't need to include the `.js` suffix (the last part of the filename). This is because the `require()` function is smart enough to know that it should look only for `.js` files anyway. It's also smart enough to know it should look in the `modules` folder, so you didn't need to write `require('/modules/dice.js')`.

After you load your module using the **require()** function, you should almost always assign it to a variable. In this case, the variable has the same name as the module, but it doesn't have to be the same. I could have written **var steve = require('dice')**, and it would work just as well.

Calling Module Functions

You'll notice that the previous statement doesn't appear to have called **roll()** yet. Loading a module will execute any code in the module, but remember, the module just defines a function. *Defining a function and calling a function are not the same thing.* To call the **roll()** function on the module you just loaded, issue the following command:

```
/js dice.roll()
```

A random number between 0 and 5 should be displayed. Try running the previous command a couple of times. Each time you should see a different number returned. Remember, you can run the previous command quickly by typing / and then pressing the Up Arrow key.

Troubleshooting

If you don't see a number or if the **/js var dice = require('dice')** command didn't work (you saw an error), take a look at the server console window to see what kind of error occurred. More than likely there was a typing error when entering the code. Double-check the code to make sure it's exactly the same as the code in Listing 6.1.

Modules as Objects

You may be wondering why you call the **roll()** function the way you do: **dice.roll()**. When you **require** a module, what you get back is an **Object**. An object, remember, is a special type of variable that can hold more than one value in what are called *properties*. So, **require('dice')** actually returns an object—the **exports** object that you used inside the module itself to make public the **roll()** function. When you call a function that's attached to an object, you have to call it by putting the object name in front, then a period, and then the function name. So, you say **console.log()** because **console** is an object, and **log()** is a function attached to the object. Similarly, you say **dice.roll()** because **dice** is an object and **roll()** is the function attached to it. This can take a little getting used to but becomes second nature over time.

Achievement Unlocked!

Major kudos! You've created your first JavaScript module, loaded it, and used it! You've taken your second giant step to creating reusable code.

Digging Deeper

Let's look at the code you've just added to Minecraft (see **LISTING 6.2**).

A JavaScript module is a file with one or more related functions. In Listing 6.2 you see a single function called **roll()**. You let others use functions by exporting them. You'll dive deeper into the **exports** object and modules in later chapters. For now let's look at the function body itself (lines 2 through 5).

LISTING 6.2 Rolling Dice

```
function roll(){
  var result = Math.random();
  result = result * 6;
  result = Math.floor(result);
  return result;
};
exports.roll = roll;
```

1. The first statement of the function, `var result = Math.random();`, declares a new variable called `result` and assigns a random number to it. Remember, `Math.random()` will return a random number between 0 and 1.

2. The next statement, `result = result * 6`, takes the number and multiplies it by 6. The `*` symbol is used in JavaScript to multiply numbers.

3. Next, you convert the number to a integer by passing it to the `Math.floor()` function and storing the result. `Math.floor()` is used to round down a number. `Math.floor()` will chop off the fraction from any number, so, for example, 3.5 becomes 3.0, 4.9 becomes 4.0 , 1.1 becomes 1.0, and so on. The `Math` object is a built-in object and comes with many functions for performing math operations.

4. Finally, the last statement in the function uses the special `return` statement to return a value from the function. The function stops executing when it hits the `return` statement and either returns an expression if one is provided or returns no value (undefined) if no expression is given. In this example, you want the `roll()` function to return the `result` variable.

As in the previous plugin, the last line of the file makes the `roll()` function available for use outside of this file by *exporting* it. Note that you don't *invoke* the function in this last line (to *invoke* a function means to call it or to run it); you just attach it to the special `exports` variable whose sole purpose is to reveal what your file can do. `exports.roll = roll` effectively says this file has a **public** function called `roll` (`exports.roll`), which is actually the same as the **private** function of the same name (the function declaration that begins on line 1 of the file).

Don't worry if this seems confusing at first. You'll use the `exports` variable throughout this book, and its purpose should become clearer with repetition.

Rounding Numbers

All numbers in JavaScript are floating-point numbers; they have an integer part (before the dot) and a fractional part (after the dot). The number "two and a half" is represented in JavaScript as follows:

```
2.5
```

This number is a floating-point number. The integer part is 2. In JavaScript if you want to "round up" or "round down" a number to its nearest integer, you use one of the `Math` functions.

- **Math.floor(n)**: Takes a number and chops off the fractional part. It rounds down the number. For example, 2.5 becomes 2.0.

- **Math.ceil(n)**: Rounds up a number to the nearest integer. For example, 2.5 becomes 3.0, 2.1 becomes 3.0, and so on.

- **Math.round(n)**: Rounds up or rounds down a number to the nearest integer. It will round up any fraction part greater than .5, so, for example, 2.5 is rounded up to 3.0, but 2.4 is rounded down to 2.0.

Math

The built-in `Math` object has many other useful properties and functions. Here are just some:

- **Math.PI**: The number value for ϖ, the ratio of the circumference of a circle to its diameter, is roughly 3.1415926535897932. This value is used, for example, when constructing spheres, cylinders, and arcs in ScriptCraft.

- **Math.abs(n)**: The absolute value of a number is its value as a positive number. `Math.abs()` is used to convert negative numbers (numbers less than 0) to positive numbers, so, for example, `Math.abs(-3)` returns 3.

- **Math.max(n,m,...)**: This will take any number of numbers and return the largest number. For example, `Math.max( 3, 9, 2, 5)` returns 9.

- **Math.min(n,m)**: This will take any number of numbers and return the smallest number. For example, `Math.min( 3, 9, 2, 5)` returns 2.

- **Math.sqrt(n)**: This will return the square root of a number. For example, `Math.sqrt(9)` returns 3, `Math.sqrt(4)` returns 2, `Math.sqrt(16)` returns 4, and so on.

I encourage you to try each of the previous properties and functions at the in-game prompt. Remember that in interactive mode you must prefix each JavaScript statement with `/js`.

For more information about the `Math` object, visit *http://www.ecma-international.org/ecma-262/5.1/#sec-15.8.*

The return Statement

The `return` statement is used inside functions to do the following:

- Stop execution of the function
- Return a value to the caller of the function

The `return` statement can be used only inside a function. It's possible to have functions that don't have a `return` statement at all in which case the function stops executing when it runs the last statement in the function. Functions don't *have* to return a value; in fact, many of the functions you'll write later won't.

Summary

In this chapter you created your first truly reusable module. You learned about modules, random numbers, and the `Math` object. In the next chapter, you'll enhance this module further, and in the chapter after you'll use the module to create custom greetings for players joining the server.

Chapter 7

Multisided Die

IN THIS CHAPTER, you'll build on the code written in the previous chapter to let you roll a die of any number of sides. Sometimes you want a random number that doesn't fit in the range 1 to 6. Ideally, you'd like your virtual dice module to return a random number for any range you give it. You're going to take your six-sided die from the previous chapter and enhance it so it can change shape to any number of sides like the multisided die used in some tabletop and role-playing games (see **FIGURE 7.1**).

FIGURE 7.1 Multisided dice

Flexible Functions

If you wanted to expand on what you've already done to support dice of four, six, and eight sides, you might write new functions for each type of dice.

```
function rollSixSided(){
  ...
}
function rollFourSided(){
  ...
}
function rollEightSided(){
  ...
}
exports.rollSixSided = rollSixSided;
exports.rollFourSided = rollFourSided;
exports.rollEightSided = rollEightSided;
...
```

That would be time-consuming, repetitive, and laborious, and the whole point of programming is to make the computer do the work! The problem with this approach—apart from being time-consuming to type—is that every time you want to support a new type of dice (say 10-, 12-, and 20-sided dice), you have to write a new function. If you then wanted to simulate the roll of a 24-sided dice, you'd have to write *yet another* function. Fortunately, there's a better way.

What if, when you call the **roll()** function, you could tell the function how many sides the die has and the **roll()** function behaved accordingly? What if you could say "Hey, throw a six-sided die" or "Hey, throw a 20-sided die" and `roll()` would do the right thing (return a random number between 0 and 5 for the first call and return a random number between 0 and 19 for the second call)? This is where *parameters* come in.

You've already been using parameters in earlier code examples. In an earlier chapter you used the `console.log()` function and passed it a parameter. Try issuing the following statements at the server console window:

```js
js console.log('Hello world');
```

You should see the message "Hello world" appear in your server window. "Hello world" is the instruction (or *parameter* to use the formal term) you gave to the `console.log()` function when you ran it. Try again with the following command:

```js
js console.log( 5 + 9 );
```

You should see "14" appear in your server window. The expression **5 + 9** is the parameter you gave to the `console.log()` function, which just printed the resulting value. An important point is that the `console.log()` function did not do the math; that was done just before the function was called, so the parameter that `console.log()` received was 14. The `console.log()` function is commonly used for *logging*. Logging is the practice of printing output to screen, usually for the purpose of debugging or better understanding your code's behavior.

Just as `console.log()` and many other functions can take parameters, you can write your own functions so that they take parameters when they are called. Let's take a look at a slightly modified version of the code from the previous chapter. You don't have to type **LISTING 7.1**; I just want to highlight some changes.

The previous code is similar to code from the previous chapter except I declare a new variable called **sides**, and the number 6 is assigned to it. On the following line, the math used is **result = result * sides** instead of **result = result * 6** as in the previous chapter. So, all I've done is create a new variable called **sides** to store the number of sides. This function behaves the same as the function from the previous chapter. But what if you could somehow change the value of the **sides** variable before each call to `roll()`? Let's change the code once more (see **LISTING 7.2**).

> **TERM Parameter**
>
> *Parameters* provide a way to give information to functions. You can pass values to a function, and the function will treat them like variables. There's another word often used in programming that can mean the same thing: arguments. You pass arguments to functions, and the function receives them as parameters. The distinction isn't important. You can use the word *arguments* or *parameters* when talking about passing values to functions.

LISTING 7.1 Rolling Dice: Sides as a Variable

```
function roll( ) {
  var result = Math.random();
  var sides = 6;
  result = result * sides;
  result = Math.floor(result);
  return result;
};
exports.roll = roll;
```

LISTING 7.2 Rolling Dice: Sides as a Parameter

```
function roll( sides ) {
  var result = Math.random();
  result = result * sides;
  result = Math.floor(result);
  return result;
};
exports.roll = roll;
```

Can you spot the difference? I removed the **var sides = 6;** statement and put a new name **sides** between the function's parentheses. The **sides** variable is no longer a private variable and is instead a parameter. Because it's a parameter, you can say what it should be each time you call the **roll()** function. **FIGURE 7.2** illustrates the changes the function has just undergone.

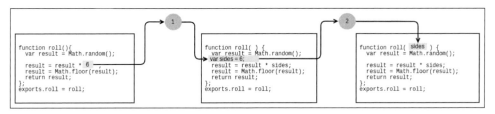

FIGURE 7.2 Using parameters

The first change was to make the number 6 used in the computation a variable. The next change was to make the variable a parameter. Parameters are like variables. In the first version of this program (on the left side), the number 6 is *hard-coded*, which is when you have a specific number or text or other data in your function that at the time seemed like it might never need to change (this would be true if you assumed you'd only ever need a number between 0 and 5). It's usually a good idea to instead turn these values into parameters so you don't have to change your code every time the data changes. Once you've edited your `dice.js` file to match the version on the right, save it and then type `/js refresh()` at the in-game prompt. Then try each of the following commands in turn:

```
/js var dice = require('dice');
/js dice.roll(6);
/js dice.roll(20);
```

Try calling `dice.roll(20)` a couple of times to confirm that it does in fact choose random numbers between 0 and 19.

The updated `roll()` function now takes a parameter that says how many sides the die should have. The type of parameter this function takes is of type **Number**. Functions can take parameters of any type, such as numbers, strings (text), booleans (**true** or **false**), and even other functions! You'll see an example in the next chapter of a function that takes another function as a parameter. Remember, functions are just values like anything else in JavaScript, so they too can be assigned to variables (as you've already seen) or passed as parameters (as you'll soon see).

Default Parameter Values

What happens if you call **dice.roll()** *without* passing a parameter? You can see for yourself by issuing this command at the in-game prompt:

```
/js dice.roll()
```

You should see **NaN** as the result. **NaN** is short for "not a number" in JavaScript, and it means the computed value was not a number. Do you know why? Your function always expects a number (how many sides the dice has), and if you don't give it one, the math won't work as expected. Wouldn't it be nice if when no number is passed to **dice.roll()**, it just assumes that you want the roll of a six-sided die? Six-sided dice are, after all, the most common type of dice. Let's make another minor change to the **roll** function; see **LISTING 7.3**.

LISTING 7.3   Rolling Dice: Default Parameters

```
function roll( sides ) {
  if ( typeof sides === 'undefined' ) {
    sides = 6;
  }
  var result = Math.random();
  result = result * sides;
  result = Math.floor(result);
  return result;
};
exports.roll = roll;
```

What I've done here is add three new lines of code near the top of the **roll()** function. The rest of the function remains unchanged.

```
if ( typeof sides === 'undefined' ) {
  sides = 6;
}
```

The **if** statement is how decisions are made in JavaScript. It's used to test something (a condition), and if the test is true, then the code inside the **{** and **}** (called the *if block*) is executed. In English, you'd write the previous code like this:

```
if there is no 'sides' parameter then
    let sides be equal to 6
```

We'll look at the **if** statement in more detail in later chapters. All you need to know for now is that it can be useful for controlling how your programs behave under different conditions. The code inside the parentheses, **typeof sides === 'undefined'**, returns the type of the **sides** parameter. If no parameter was supplied, then it will be of type **undefined**, in which case you set the **sides** parameter to a default value of 6. Once you've edited and saved your **dice.js** file, make sure to issue the **/js refresh()** command at the in-game prompt and then issue the following statements:

```
/js var dice = require('dice');
/js dice.roll(20);
/js dice.roll();
/js dice.roll(4);
/js dice.roll();
```

You should see a random number output for each of the previous calls. The **roll()** function is now robust enough to handle parameters and use a sensible default value of 6 if no parameters are given when it's called.

Assigning to the exports Variable

Let's say you want to create a new module that provides farm animals. You could write it like this:

```
var cow = 'Cow';
var sheep = 'Sheep';
var pig = 'Pig';
exports.cow = cow;
exports.sheep = sheep;
exports.pig = pig;
```

But since the first three parameters aren't really used except to assign to `exports`, you could simply write this, which saves you some typing:

```
exports.cow = 'Cow';
exports.sheep = 'Sheep';
exports.pig = 'Pig';
```

Sometimes this isn't suitable. If the **cow** variable is used inside the module, then it makes sense to declare it and assign to the **exports** variable. If not, then it's simpler to just assign the value directly to the **exports** variable rather than creating an extra variable that won't be used for any other purpose.

More on Comments

Before you move on to the next chapter, I want to talk more about comments. In the first JavaScript file you created, you started with a single line.

```
// TO DO : Add some code later
```

This is called a *comment*. Comments are notes you write in your code to help you remember things. Source code can be difficult to understand even when you yourself have written it. In the heat of tackling a tricky problem or coding up a cool new plugin, you might end up writing some clever code, but you'll often find that when you come back to it a couple of days or weeks later, you no longer understand what you've written. This is where comments come in. It's a good habit to write comments alongside your code, especially if your code is tricky.

Comments aren't read by the computer, so you can write whatever you like in a comment. Comments should be helpful and provide signposts to yourself and others about what the code does. You can comment as much or as little as you like. When working with others on the same source code, it's considered good practice to comment your code. How much you comment your code is a matter of personal taste. Commenting can be really useful for *documenting* your code. For example, the ScriptCraft API reference documentation available at *http://scriptcraftjs.org/api* is created automatically from comments in the ScriptCraft source code.

Single-Line Comments

You can make any line into a comment by starting it with two forward slashes (//):

```
// this is a JavaScript comment
console.log('this is not a comment');
```

If you were to run the previous code, you'd get the following output:

```
this is not a comment
```

The first line is ignored and is readable only by programmers.

End-of-Line Comments

You can also add comments to the end of lines like this:

```
console.log('The rain in Spain'); // falls mainly in the plain
```

If you run the previous code, you see the following:

```
The rain in Spain
```

Everything before the // is regular code; everything after the // is a comment.

Multiline Comments

Sometimes you will want to write a lot of comments in your code. You might have a section of code that requires some explaining. You can do so using multiple // comments like this:

```
// -------------------------
// Drone Plugin
// The Drone is a convenience class for building.
// It can be used for ...
// 1. Building
// 2. Copying and Pasting
```

If your comments span more than one line (as shown previously), you can use opening and closing comments that must begin with /* and end with */, like this:

```
/* --------------------------
   Drone Plugin
   The Drone is a convenience class for building.
   It can be used for...
   1. Building
   2. Copying and Pasting
*/
```

Most programming editors will display comments in a different color so that they stand out from the rest of the code. Comments can be really helpful in reading and understanding source code.

Commenting Out Code

You can also use comments to *turn off* the execution of code. This can be useful if you want to temporarily change your code or if you have sections of code that you no longer need but do not want to remove just yet.

```
console.log('Pig says: Oink');
// console.log('Cow says: Moo');
console.log('Sheep says: Baa');
```

The output from the previous code would be as follows:

```
Pig says: Oink
Sheep says: Baa
```

The second statement is ignored because it has a // in front of it. Remember, everything after // on a line is treated as a comment.

Comments in This Book

Most of the source listings in this book will not include comments because the code is explained throughout. If you look at the ScriptCraft source code, you will see that the code is commented.

Commenting dice.js

Open `dice.js` in your editor and add a comment section at the top of the file. The comment section should briefly describe what the module does. You can use either `//` comments or `/* */` comments. The comment text can be as short or as long as you like. **LISTING 7.4** shows an example.

Make sure to save the file after you've changed it, run `/js refresh()` at the in-game prompt and then run the following commands to ensure your code still works.

```
/js var dice = require('dice');
/js dice.roll();
/js dice.roll(20);
```

LISTING 7.4 Commenting Code

```
/*
this module provides a roll() function which returns a
random number.
the range of numbers is set using the sides parameter.
if no sides parameter is provided, the default is 6.
Usage:
   var dice = require('dice');
   var randomNumber1 = dice.roll();
   var randomNumber2 = dice.roll();
*/
exports.roll = function( sides ) {
  if ( typeof sides === 'undefined' ) {
    sides = 6;
  }
  var result = Math.random();
  result = result * sides;
  result = Math.floor(result);
  return result;
};
```

Achievement Unlocked!

Congratulations! You've taken another step toward becoming a responsible plugin developer. Your code is robust and well commented. Commenting code is really important if you want to share your work with others.

Summary

You've seen that functions can both return and take a value as a parameter. Parameters can be really useful when you want to provide information to a function. It's usually a good idea to have default values if your function is called without parameters. You've also learned about comments and how they can be used to add useful notes for yourself and others to help understand your code.

Chapter 8

Greeting Players

IN THIS CHAPTER, you'll change the Minecraft game for all players. The best plugins enhance the Minecraft experience and at the same time feel like they are an intrinsic part of the game. In this plugin, each player will be greeted with a new random message each time they join the server. This will be the first plugin that uses *event-driven programming*, which is a way to listen and react to happenings or events in the game. Along the way, you'll learn about *arrays*, a special type in JavaScript for storing lists of items.

Event-Driven Programming

In the early days of programming there was no such thing as event-driven programming. Programs were started and ran to completion; then they exited. If your program needed to ask the user a question, it did so using a command prompt and did not resume until the user had typed a response and hit Enter. With the advent of graphical user interfaces in the 1980s and 1990s, programs and user interaction became more sophisticated. Programs had to be written differently to accommodate new ways users could interact with their computers using menus, buttons, windows, and so on. When you click a link or a button on a web page or other application, that click is an *event*. In Minecraft, when you fire an arrow, break a block, open a door, join the server, or do pretty much anything, that's an *event*. Event-driven programming lets programmers write functions that listen and react to such events.

In the first part of this chapter, you're going to write a module with a single function that will return a random greeting each time it's called. This new module will depend on the module you created in Chapter 7 to return a random number for you. Create a new file in the **scriptcraft/modules** folder and call it **greeting.js**. Then type in the code shown in LISTING 8.1 and save your file.

LISTING 8.1 Random Greetings

```
var dice = require('dice');
var greetings = [ 'Hello ', 'Hola ', 'Bonjour ',
                  'Konnichiwa ' ];
var len = greetings.length;
function random(){
  var index = dice.roll(len);
  var greeting = greetings[ index ];
  return greeting;
}
exports.random = random;
```

You're already getting the benefit of modules and reuse in that you can reuse the **dice** module you created earlier. The first statement in your new module *requires* the use of the **dice** module from the previous chapter. If your module depends on other modules, it's usually a good idea to load those modules at the top of your code. It's another of those good habits you should adopt as a JavaScript programmer because in the long run it will make programming easier.

The next statement declares a new variable called **greetings** and assigns a list of greetings in different languages to it. We haven't encountered arrays before, so they need some explanation.

Arrays

So far you've used variables to store single items in memory. Those items have been numbers and strings (text). It's useful to be able to store lists of items in memory too. For example, in Minecraft, the server stores a list of players who are currently playing, a list of worlds on the server, and many other lists. Lists are useful in that they let you keep track of groups of things. In JavaScript, lists are called *arrays*. An *array* is a collection of items. For example, if you wanted to create a list (or array) of farm animals in Minecraft, you'd do so like this:

```
var farmAnimals = [ 'Sheep', 'Cow', 'Pig', 'Chicken' ];
```

An array starts and ends with square brackets ([ ]), and each item in the list is separated with a comma (,). The last item in the list should not have a comma after it. Let's do some server console experimentation with arrays. Issue the following commands at the server console prompt:

```
js var farmAnimals = [ 'Sheep', 'Cow', 'Pig', 'Chicken' ];
js console.log(farmAnimals);
```

The output should be as follows:

```
Sheep,Cow,Pig,Chicken
```

Arrays have a special property that tells you how many items are in the array. Issue the following command at the server console:

```
js farmAnimals.length
```

The output should be as follows:

```
4
```

The **length** property tells you how many items are in the array and is useful, as you'll see later. Now for the tricky part. You use the [ ] characters when constructing a new array, but it's also possible to get a particular item from the array using those same [ ] characters if you put a number between them. Let's try it. If you wanted to get the first item from the array (**Sheep**), a nonprogrammer would naturally write something like this:

```js
js farmAnimals[1]
```

Go ahead and issue that command now before reading any further.

Were you surprised by the result? If you're new to programming, you should be. The result is **Cow** and not **Sheep**. That's because in JavaScript (and many other programming languages too), indexes start at 0, not 1, so if I want to get the *first* item in the **farmAnimals** array, I say **farmAnimals[0]**. If I want to get the second item, I say **farmAnimals[1]** ; for the third item I say **farmAnimals[2]**; and so on. This can be a constant source of confusion for even experienced programmers. The reason why arrays start at 0 and not 1 harks back to the old days of computing when computer memory was not as abundant and cheap as it is today. Having arrays start at 0 rather than 1 was slightly more efficient.

Here's another question: How might you get the *last* item in an array? If you know the length of the array, you could try this:

```js
js farmAnimals[ farmAnimals.length ]
```

But that won't work. Remember, arrays begin at 0 not 1, so if you have four items in the array, then the *index* of the last item will be 3, so you need to write this:

```js
js farmAnimals[ farmAnimals.length - 1 ]
```

I told you arrays were tricky! Just remember: *Arrays begin at 0, not 1*. This is what the list of farm animals might look like with the indexes listed beside each animal:

```
[0] 'Sheep'
[1] 'Cow'
[2] 'Pig'
[3] 'Chicken'
```

Having explained the basics of how arrays work, Listing 8.1 should be a little easier to understand now. The **random()** function rolls a die (whose sides are the length of the array: 4) and then assigns the random number returned to a variable called **index**. You then use that index to get an item from the **greetings** array. You are effectively plucking a random item from the list of greetings. Try it for yourself by issuing the following commands at the in-game prompt:

```
/js refresh(); // reloads plugins
/js var greetings = require('greetings');
/js greetings.random();
/js greetings.random();
/js greetings.random();
```

You should definitely call **greetings.random()** a couple of times to verify it returns a random greeting each time. Remember, you can call up the previous command at the in-game prompt by pressing **/** and then pressing the Up arrow key.

So far you've looked only at constructing arrays and getting individual items from arrays. Arrays are powerful, and there are many things you can do with them.

Once you've constructed an array, you can add new items to the end of the array using a function called **push**. The **push()** function is used like this to add a new item:

```
/js farmAnimals.push('Horse');
```

'Horse' is added to the end of the array. After the previous command is executed, the **farmAnimals** array would look like this:

```
[0] 'Sheep'
[1] 'Cow'
[2] 'Pig'
[3] 'Chicken'
[4] 'Horse'    <-- New item appended
```

The length of the array would change from 4 to 5. You can check this by issuing the command **/js farmAnimals.length**. The **push()** function cannot be called on its own. It's a special type of function called a *method*, which means it's a function that belongs to a particular object, so it can be called only using the form **object.method()**, with **object** in this case being **farmAnimals** and **method()** being **push()**. We'll explore objects more in later chapters.

The **push()** method always *appends* items to the end of the array. If you want to insert an item into the array at a position other than the end, you'll need to use the **splice()** method instead. Here's how you insert a new animal into the **farmAnimals** array at position 2:

```
/js farmAnimals.splice( 2, 0, "Cat" );
```

This is what the array will look like after you run the previous command:

```
[0] 'Sheep'
[1] 'Cow'
[2] 'Cat'      <-- New item inserted
[3] 'Pig'
[4] 'Chicken'
[5] 'Horse'
```

You can see that the new item is inserted at position 2 and that the indexes for all the items after position 2 have changed. **'Pig'** is bumped from index 2 to index 3, **'Chicken'** from index 3 to index 4, and so on. The **splice()** method lets you insert items anywhere in an array. The first parameter is the position you want to insert the items, the second parameter is how many items you want to remove (if you're only inserting items, then leave this as 0), and the third and subsequent parameters are the items you want to insert. You can insert one or more items at a time.

```
/js farmAnimals.splice( 1, 0, "Ocelot", "Wolf" );
```

This is what the array would look like after running the previous command:

```
[0] 'Sheep'
[1] 'Ocelot'  <-- New items inserted
[2] 'Wolf'    <-- New items inserted
[3] 'Cow'
[4] 'Cat'
[5] 'Pig'
[6] 'Chicken'
[7] 'Horse'
```

Now let's say you want to remove some items from an array. The list of farm animals you've constructed so far is starting to look crowded, and there are definitely some animals in that list that shouldn't be there (wolves and farm animals don't mix). As hinted at previously, the **splice()** method can also be used to *remove* items from the array. Let's start by removing the **Cat** item from the array.

```
/js farmAnimals.splice( 4, 1 );
```

The output from the previous command will be an array of items removed, so in your display, you'll see something like this:

```
[ "Cat" ]
```

That's because the **splice()** method does not return the array it spliced; instead, it returns the items it removed from the array. Remember, the first parameter you pass to **splice()** is the index of the item, and the second parameter is always the number of items you want to remove. If no additional parameters are provided, then **splice()** will only remove items and not insert new items. To see what your **farmAnimals** array looks like now, run the **/js farmAnimals** statement. Your array will look something like this in memory:

```
[0] 'Sheep'
[1] 'Ocelot'
[2] 'Wolf'
[3] 'Cow'
[4] 'Pig'
[5] 'Chicken'
[6] 'Horse'
```

Now let's tidy up the array some more by removing the pesky ocelot and wolf.

```
/js farmAnimals.splice( 1, 2 );
```

The previous statement says "Starting at index 1, remove 2 items." The array will now look like this:

```
[0] 'Sheep'
[3] 'Cow'
[4] 'Pig'
[5] 'Chicken'
[6] 'Horse'
```

TABLE 8.1 lists a couple of other useful array methods.

You can learn more about the **Array** object and its methods and properties at **https://developer.mozilla.org/en-US/docs/Web/Javascript/Reference/Global_Objects/Array**. In later chapters you'll learn how to process all of the items in an array using JavaScript's looping statements.

TABLE 8.1 Array Methods

METHOD NAME	DESCRIPTION
.push()	Adds one or more elements to the end of an array and returns the new length of the array.
.pop()	Removes and returns the first item in the array.
.unshift()	Adds one or more elements to the beginning of an array and returns the new length of the array.
.shift()	Removes the first element from an array and returns that element. This method changes the length of the array.
.reverse()	Reverses an array in place. The first array element becomes the last, and the last becomes the first.
.splice()	Changes the content of an array, adding new elements while removing old elements.
.slice()	Returns a shallow copy of a portion of an array into a new array object.
.join()	Joins all elements of an array into a string.
.indexOf()	Returns the first index at which a given element can be found in the array, or returns -1 if it is not present.
.sort()	Sorts the elements of an array in place and returns the array. The default sort order is Alphabetic.

First Steps with Events

IMPORTANT

This new **greetPlayers.js** module should be saved in the **scriptcraft/plugins** folder, not the **scriptcraft/modules** folder, because you'll want this module to load automatically when the server starts up.

So, you have a new module **greetings.js** with a single function called **random()** that returns a random greeting. What you want is for every player who connects to be greeted with a random greeting. Let's dive right in and create a new module called **greetPlayers.js**.

Type **LISTING 8.2** into your new **greetPlayers.js** file.

Make sure to save your file and then run the JavaScript **refresh()** function to reload ScriptCraft using **/js refresh()** from the in-game prompt or **js refresh()** from the server prompt.

LISTING 8.2 Greeting Players as They Join the Server

```
var greeting = require('greetings');
function greetPlayer( event ) {
  var player = event.player;
  var message = greeting.random() + player.name;
  echo( player, message );
};
events.connect( greetPlayer );
```

Now disconnect from your server and rejoin the server. You should see something like this in your screen when you join the server:

Konnichiwa walterh

The message will of course be different for you. **FIGURE 8.1** shows where you should expect the greeting to appear when you join the server. The **echo()** function is provided by ScriptCraft as a way to send messages to players. It takes two parameters, the first being the player and the second being the message you want to send to that player.

FIGURE 8.1 Greeting players

ScriptCraft comes bundled with a built-in variable called **events**. The **events** variable is used to listen and react to events in the game. There are approximately 200 different types of events you can respond to in Minecraft. When you *register* for an *event* in your code, you are telling the server that you want to be notified when a particular type of activity occurs in the game. You register by giving the server a function that won't be called immediately but will be called only when the activity occurs. In the Listing 8.2 code, you are basically saying to Minecraft "Hey, whenever someone connects to the game, I want you (the server) to call this **greetPlayer** function."

This is the first time you've seen functions used as parameters to another function call. You call the **events.connect()** function by passing it another function as a parameter. This style of coding—passing functions as parameters to other functions—is called *functional programming*. The important thing to note here is that at no point in this module is the **greetPlayer()** function actually called. All you do is register it using the **events.connect()** function so that it will be called later each time a player connects. The **greetPlayer()** function is called an *event-handling* function because its purpose is to handle events, specifically the event that is fired by the server whenever a player connects to the game.

We'll look more closely at events and event-handling functions in a later chapter.

More on Modules

From looking at the **greetPlayers** module, you can see the first thing it does is load another module, **greetings**, which you created earlier in this chapter. If you remember, the **greetings** module in turn loads yet another module—the **dice** module you worked on in the previous chapters. This is a classic example of how programming is typically done. You start with small dedicated modules and then work on bigger and bigger modules piecing them together to solve a problem. In programming, a big part of problem solving is breaking problems down into smaller and smaller problems, solving each of these smaller problems, and then piecing together the solutions. When a program module relies on another module, we say it *depends* on the module. A module that loads another module *depends* on that module, and that module in turn will *depend* on other modules. All of the modules that are required—either directly or indirectly—by a program are called *dependencies*. You can see in FIGURE 8.2 the relationship between the **greetPlayers**, **greetings**, and **dice** modules.

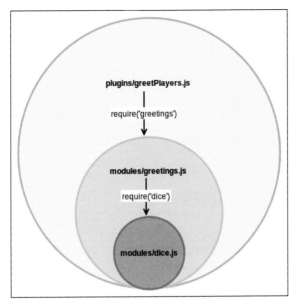

FIGURE 8.2 Encapsulation and modules

The **greetPlayers** module depends on **greetings**, but it does not know or care that **greetings**—in turn—depends on the **dice** module. This is an important principle in programming. The **greetings** module, by exporting just a single **random()** function, is defining what programmers call an *interface*. The *interface* is the contract or agreement a module has with other modules. It's a way of declaring what your module is to be used for—what its purpose is. When defining an interface, a module should hide the details of *how* it works and just say *what* it does. Modular systems work because parts can be swapped out and changed without affecting the entire program. You can think of an individual module (a JavaScript file) as working like an individual Lego brick. Modules can be pieced together to form larger modules and programs, eventually creating something truly awesome.

Minecraft is often described as "virtual Lego." Programming is similar and offers the same rewards, and it is enormously creative and can be great fun.

Greeting Players in Style

To make players feel welcome, let's add something a little more spectacular than a simple text message. Let's greet each new player with a firework that launches when and where they join the server (see **LISTING 8.3**).

LISTING 8.3 Greeting Players with Fireworks

```
var greeting = require('greetings');
var fireworks = require('fireworks');
function greetPlayer( event ) {
  var player = event.player;
  var message = greeting.random() + player.name;
  echo(player, message );
  fireworks.firework(player.location);
};
events.connect( greetPlayer );
```

You'll use the ScriptCraft **fireworks** module again in later chapters. Events and event-handling functions can be used to trigger all kinds of cool new game mechanics.

Achievement Unlocked!

Major kudos! You've created your first custom event handler and have had your first encounter with event-driven programming. Soon you'll be putting event handling to use to protect your server and add your own fun effects.

Summary

In this chapter, you learned how to create and manipulate lists of items using JavaScript arrays. You also learned about event-driven programming and wrote your first event-handling function to greet players when they connect to your server. In the next chapter, you'll explore events further and play with sounds in Minecraft.

Chapter 9

A Guessing Game

ONE OF THE GREAT THINGS about computers is that they can make decisions and take different paths through a program based on those decisions. If computer programs did the same thing every time, then they would be pretty boring. Can you imagine playing a computer game that always did the same thing? Computers make decisions all the time. When you're playing Minecraft, the server is constantly checking to see whether any players have died or whether their health or hunger levels are low. It's checking to see whether a creeper is about to explode or whether a villager will accept a trade offer. All of these decisions are made using the humbly named `if` statement. The `if` statement is such a useful statement that it's available in pretty much every programming language, including JavaScript and Java.

In this chapter, you'll create a simple number-guessing game using the `if` statement to figure out whether the player guessed correctly. Let's dive right in and write the code for the number guessing game. Type the code shown in **LISTING 9.1** into a new file called **numberGuess.js** and save it in the **scriptcraft/plugins** folder.

In this program, the **guessTheNumber()** function rolls a six-sided die and then asks the player to guess the number. If the player guesses correctly, the message **You guessed correct!** is displayed. After the player has guessed (either rightly or wrongly), the message **Thanks for playing** is displayed. You can try this code by issuing the following commands at the server console prompt:

```
js refresh();
js guessTheNumber( self )
```

LISTING 9.1 A Guessing Game

```javascript
var input = require('input');
var dice = require('dice');
var randomNumber;

function checkAnswer( answer, guesser ){
  if ( answer == randomNumber ) {
    echo ( guesser, 'You guessed correct!' );
  }
  echo( guesser, 'Thanks for playing' );
}

function guessTheNumber( player ){
  randomNumber = dice.roll(6);
  input( player,'Pick a number between 0 and 5',checkAnswer);
}

exports.guessTheNumber = guessTheNumber;
```

The `guessTheNumber()` function needs a **Player** as a parameter. The special ScriptCraft variable **self** is a variable whose type is **Player** and refers to you, the person issuing the command. That's why you pass **self** as the parameter to `guessTheNumber()`. You can try running the `guessTheNumber()` function a couple of times, and the number should be different each time.

Let's take a closer look at how this function works by first looking at how ScriptCraft asks questions of players.

Asking Questions

Most programming languages provide a function that can be used to ask a question. JavaScript runs in many different environments. The most common way to run JavaScript is in web browsers where JavaScript comes with a special `prompt()` function that can be used to ask website visitors questions by displaying a small window (known as a *dialog box*) with a question, an input field where you type the answer, and OK and Cancel buttons. This style of user interaction is called *modal* because the user cannot do anything else until they close the dialog window. You can see an example of what a modal dialog looks like in **FIGURE 9.1**.

FIGURE 9.1 A modal dialog

The problem with modal dialogs is that they interrupt the program, and the program can't resume until the user closes the dialog by clicking either OK or Cancel. This could be a problem in a fast-paced game like Minecraft where you wouldn't want such a question to appear while you were fighting off a horde of zombies. Unlike JavaScript in the browser, JavaScript in Minecraft does not have a `prompt()` function, but you *can* ask players questions using the **input** module. The questions will not appear in a modal dialog, instead appearing as a message on the player's screen. What's more, players do not have to answer the question immediately. The **input()** function takes three parameters:

- The player you want to ask a question of.
- The question you want to ask.
- The function you want to call when the player has answered the question. This function, when called, will have the answer and the player who answered as parameters.

This is the second example you've encountered of functions that take other functions as parameters—you saw an example of this in Chapter 8 when you passed an event-handling function. You can try the **input** module yourself at the server or in-game command prompt.

```js
js var input = require('input');
js function respond( answer, player ) { player.js function
respond( answer,player){ echo(player,"Wow. " + answer +
" that's old!" ) };
js input( self, 'How old are you?', respond )
```

The important thing to keep in mind when writing code that depends on asking players questions is that you can't force players to answer questions right away or even answer at all; they could be busy fighting spiders, trading with villagers, climbing, building, or simply ignoring the question altogether. In the previous commands, the **respond()** function will be called by **input()** when the player has answered the question. There's a name often used for functions that are called by other functions—they're called *callbacks*. The **input()** function when called will return immediately, and it does not return any value. Instead, it waits in the background (remember, there's a lot going on in Minecraft, so you can't stop the game in its tracks) until the player eventually answers the question and then calls the callback. A *callback* is a function that will be called back later. Callbacks are also used when writing JavaScript code for web browsers. For example, functions can be written that will be called only when a visitor clicks a button. Callback functions are super useful and part of what makes JavaScript such a flexible language.

So, you've seen how to ask a player a question. Now let's take a look at how you check to see whether the answer is correct.

The if Statement

In Chapter 3 you briefly looked at comparing numbers at the server console prompt. When you *compare* something to something else, there can be only two possible answers: **true** or **false**. For example, if I issue the command **js 5 == 3** to ask the computer if 5 is equal to 3, the answer will be **false**. If I ask the computer a different question such as **js 5 > 3**—is 5 greater than 3?—the answer will be **true**. When asking such questions, there is no **I don't know** or **Sometimes** or **Maybe**. The answer will always be **true** or **false**. When you **compare** things, you test for true or false. You can compare not only numbers but any variable. You can write code in such a way that it will execute only if some test passes. Try the following commands at the server console prompt:

```
js if ( 5 > 3 ) { console.log('test is true') }
js if ( 5 > 13 ) { console.log('test is true') }
js if ( 5 == 18 ) { console.log('test is true') }
js if ( 5 < 18 ) { console.log('test is true') }
```

The message **test is true** should be displayed only for the first and last commands. The **if** statement uses the following form:

```
if ( condition ) {
    // code to execute if condition is true
}
```

So, in the number guessing game, the following code compares two numbers—the number returned by the die roll and the number guessed by the player:

```
if ( answer == randomNumber ) {
  echo(guesser, 'You guessed correct!');
}
```

If they are equal, then the block of code between the curly brackets ({ }) is executed (the player is sent a message saying they guessed correctly). The code block will not be executed if the numbers are not the same. It's important in JavaScript when asking the question "Is something equal to another ?" that you use two equals symbols: == rather than a single equal symbol: =. The single = symbol is used when you want to assign a value to a variable. You say **name = 'steve'**, but you ask the question **name == 'steve'**?

The test is always placed between parentheses, ( ). There are many other kinds of tests you can use other than comparisons. If you use just a single number, it can be tested. Any single number except 0 will resolve to **true** when used inside an **if** test, while any nonempty text will resolve to **true**. Try issuing the following commands at the server console prompt:

```
js var gems = 5;
js if ( gems ) { console.log("you have gems"); }
js gems = 0;
js if ( gems ) { console.log("you have gems"); }
```

If **gems** is 0, then the **if** statement does not execute the code inside the **if** block (the code that appears between the curly brackets, { }). Now try the following statements to see how **String** variables are resolved to **true** or **false**:

```
js var name = "steve"
js if ( name ) { console.log("you have a name and it is " +
    → name ); }
js name = ""
js if ( name ) { console.log("you have a name and it is " +
    → name ); }
```

The last command will not output anything because a variable that is " " (an empty string) or 0 will resolve to **false** if used as a condition in an **if** statement. You can test to see whether name is equal to **steve** like this:

```
js if (name == "steve"){ console.log("Hey steve!"); }
```

What if you want to test that something is **not** true? To test that something isn't true, you **enclose** the test in **()** round brackets and put a **!** (exclamation mark) in front.

```
js if (! (name == "steve") ) { console.log("Hey, you're not
    → steve!"); }
```

The **!** operator **negates** (makes the opposite of) any boolean expression that appears after it, so all of the following expressions would return **false**:

```
js ! (5 > 2)
> false
js ! (5 < 8)
> false
js ! (8 < 5)
> true
js ! (name == "steve")
> false
```

The if-else Construct

Let's say you want the program to output one message if the player guesses correctly and a different message if the player guesses incorrectly. This is where the else statement comes in. You can see it in use in the updated LISTING 9.2 for the number-guessing game.

Change your existing numberGuess.js file to match the previous code, save it, and then issue the following commands to test it:

```
js refresh()
js guessTheNumber( self )
```

Now when you guess incorrectly, you should see the message Better luck next time appear.

LISTING 9.2 Guessing Wrong

```
var input = require('input');
var dice = require('dice');
var randomNumber;

function checkAnswer( guess, guesser ){
  if ( guess == randomNumber ) {
    echo( guesser, 'You guessed correct!');
  } else {
    echo( guesser, 'Better luck next time');
  }
  echo( guesser, 'Thanks for playing');
}

function guessTheNumber( player ){
  randomNumber = dice.roll(6);
  input( player,'Pick a number between 0 and 5',checkAnswer);
}
exports.guessTheNumber = guessTheNumber;
```

The if-else-if Construct

So far the guessing game gives players just one shot at guessing the number. In **LISTING 9.3** the code is changed further so that players get to make a couple of guesses and are told when they've guessed too high or too low. Listing 9.3 uses the **if–else–if** form, which is quite common in JavaScript.

In this revision of the number-guessing game, you're using an extra parameter called **repeat**, which is a parameter passed by the **input()** function to your input handler function **checkAnswer()**. You didn't use this parameter in the previous version of the game because you didn't need it. The **repeat** parameter is itself a function that when called will repeat the question. That's why you call it when the answer is too high or too low. The **repeat()** function when called will ask the player the same question again and, when the player answers, will call your callback function again.

Another change in the previous function is that you've given the player the option of simply quitting the game by typing **quit** as an answer to the question. You may be wondering why there's a check to see whether the guess is too low but no equivalent check to see whether the guess is too high. The reason is if the guess is not the same as or less than the **randomNumber**, then it *must* be too high—there are no other options.

How a program behaves while running is often called its *flow*. Flow diagrams help programmers sketch out how they want or expect a program to behave when it's running. In a flow diagram the start and end of the program are represented by boxes that look like capsules at the top and bottom of the diagram. Decisions that need to be made in the program are represented by diamonds and usually have two or more lines leading to other parts of the diagram. Processes are represented by plain boxes. **FIGURE 9.2** is a flowchart of how Listing 9.3 behaves while running. Flowcharts can be useful in helping to understand a program or in designing a new program.

LISTING 9.3 Too High, Too Low

```
var input = require('input');
var dice = require('dice');
var randomNumber;

function checkAnswer( guess, guesser, repeat ){
  if ( guess == randomNumber ) {
    echo( guesser, 'You guessed correct!');
  } else if ( guess == 'quit') {
    echo( guesser, 'Thanks for playing');
  } else if ( guess < randomNumber ) {
    echo( guesser, 'Too low. Guess again');
    repeat();
  } else {
    echo( guesser, 'Too high. Guess again');
    repeat();
  }
}

function guessTheNumber( player ){
  randomNumber = dice.roll(6);
  input( player,'Pick a number between 0 and 5',checkAnswer);
}
exports.guessTheNumber = guessTheNumber;
```

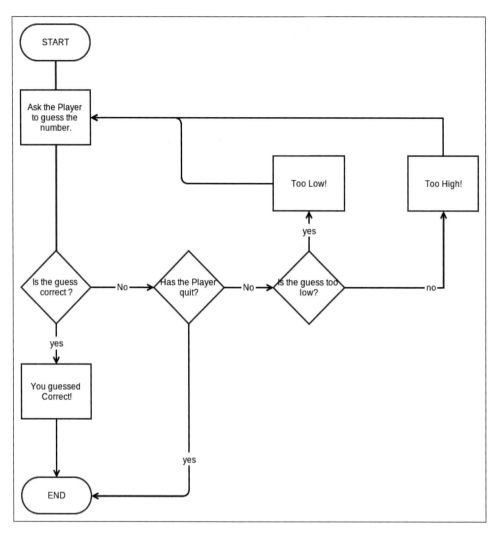

FIGURE 9.2 A flow diagram

Nested Blocks

The **if** statement is one of several **block** statements in JavaScript—that is, statements that have an accompanying block of text. Other examples of **block** statements in JavaScript are the **for** and **while** statements (which we'll explore later). Any **block** statement can have within its block other block statements. When you have one or more blocks inside another block, it's called *nesting*. The updated **numberGuess.js** file shown in **LISTING 9.4** adds a cool enhancement for players who play the game at the in-game prompt rather than at the server console window. Update your code to match Listing 9.4.

Now jump into the game and at the in-game prompt issue the commands:

```
/js refresh() // to load the changes
/js guessTheNumber( self )
```

When prompted, press the T key to start typing your guess. You may need to rerun the **guessTheNumber()** function a couple of times before you guess the right answer, but this time, when you do get it right, a firework will launch directly above your head.

Now the code checks to see whether you guessed correctly and, if so, sends a message to the guesser. Then another nested **if** statement tests to see whether the guesser is an actual player in the game (by testing to see if it has a **location** property) and launches a celebratory firework at the player's location.

Combining Conditions

If you want to check to see whether it's night or day in Minecraft, you need to get the game world's time and test it. In Minecraft, time is measured differently and is on a different scale to time in real life. A day in Minecraft lasts only 20 minutes in real time. Minecraft measures time not in hours and minutes but in *ticks*, and there are 24,000 ticks in a Minecraft day.

To test to see whether it is night or day in the game, issue the following commands at the in-game prompt:

```
/js var world = self.world;
/js if ((world.relativeTime > 13000) && (world.relativeTime <
23000)) { echo(self,'Night!') }
```

LISTING 9.4 Fireworks for Winners

```
var input = require('input');
var dice = require('dice');
var fireworks = require('fireworks');
var randomNumber;

function checkAnswer( guess, guesser, repeat ){
  if ( guess == randomNumber ) {
    echo( guesser, 'You guessed correct!');
    if ( guesser.location ) {
      fireworks.firework( guesser.location );
    }
  } else if ( guess == 'quit') {
    echo( guesser, 'Thanks for playing');
  } else if ( guess < randomNumber ) {
    echo( guesser, 'Too low. Guess again');
    repeat();
  } else if ( guess > randomNumber ) {
    echo( guesser, 'Too high. Guess again');
    repeat();
  }
}

function guessTheNumber( player ){
  randomNumber = dice.roll(6);
  input( player,'Pick a number between 0 and 5',checkAnswer);
}
exports.guessTheNumber = guessTheNumber;
```

Logical AND

You can combine one or more tests to perform more complex tests. In the previous statements, you check to see whether the time is greater than 13000 *and* less than 23000. If both of these conditions are true, you know it's night. If you are combining tests like this, it's a good idea to enclose each test in its own parentheses. That's why you write this:

```
( world.relativeTime > 13000 ) && ( world.relativeTime <
23000 )
```

rather than just this:

```
world.relativeTime > 13000 && world.relativeTime < 23000
```

The **&&** operator combines the expressions on the left and right of it, and if both are true, then it evaluates to **true**. If either the left-side or right-side expressions evaluate to **false**, then the whole test is false. When you combine tests using the **&&** (AND) operator, the test passes only when *all* of the expressions evaluate to **true**.

Logical OR

There's more than one way to combine tests. You can use the || (OR operator) to test whether any *one* of two or more conditions are true. Let's say you want to add a new rule to the game. The rule is this:

```
if a player breaks a block while either sneaking OR flying then
    the block yields 2 cookies.
```

How would you write such a rule in JavaScript? Well, let's refine the previous statement. Remember, Minecraft is event-driven, so you want your rule to be enforced whenever any block is broken. The statement might be better written in English as follows:

```
when a block is broken
    if the player is flying or the player is sneaking then
        the block yields 2 cookies.
```

In JavaScript you write it like **LISTING 9.5**.

LISTING 9.5 Cookies for Ninjas

```javascript
var items = require('items');

function dropCookiesIfSneakingOrFlying(event){
  var breaker = event.player;
  var broken = event.block;

  if ( breaker.sneaking || (! breaker.onGround ) ) {
    broken.world.dropItem( broken.position, items.cookie(2));
  }
}
events.blockDestroy( dropCookiesIfSneakingOrFlying );
```

If you like, you can save the previous code into a file called **stealthCookies.js** in your **scriptcraft/plugins** folder, reload your plugins (using **/js refresh()**), and try breaking some blocks while flying or sneaking to see the code in action.

The test **breaker.sneaking || ! breaker.onGround** checks to see whether the player who broke the block is either sneaking or flying, and if so, the broken block will give up a cookie. You use the **items** module here, which includes functions for all the possible items you might keep in your inventory in the game. You can see a list of all the **items** functions in the appendixes.

Complex Logic

So, you've seen the use of the **&&** (logical AND) operator and the **||** (logical OR) operator. These two operators can be combined to form even more complex logic. Let's say, for example, you want to refine the earlier rule so that cookies will be given up only when the player breaks a block of sand. In English, you might write such a rule like this:

```
when a block is broken:
  if the block is and AND the player is flying OR
    the player is sneaking then:
      the block yields 2 cookies.
```

To you and me, that rule might look clear enough, but the computer would be confused. There are actually two possible ways to interpret the previous rule, as shown in **FIGURE 9.3**.

You have to be careful when writing test conditions in JavaScript. It's easy to write a test condition that seems clear but results in unexpected behavior when executed. You need to use parentheses inside the **if** condition to tell the computer exactly how the rule should be interpreted. So, you would need to write the JavaScript code shown in **LISTING 9.6**.

Notice the additional parentheses around the test **breaker.sneaking ||** **!breaker.onGround**. These are needed so that you can phrase the rule so the computer will read it the same way you do.

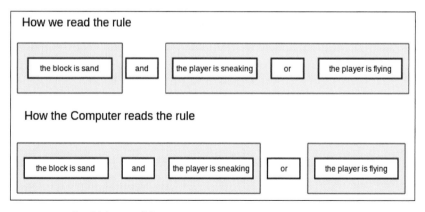

FIGURE 9.3 Combining conditions

LISTING 9.6 If X and (Y or Z)

```
var items = require('items');

function dropCookiesIfSneakingOrFlying( event ){
  var breaker = event.player;
  var broken = event.block;
  var isSand = items.sand(broken.type);
  if ( isSand && ( breaker.sneaking || (! breaker.onGround) ) ) {
    broken.world.dropItem(broken.position, items.cookie(2));
  }
}
events.blockDestroy( dropCookiesIfSneakingOrFlying );
```

Summary

In this chapter, you learned how to use the **if** statement to make decisions and make your program do different things based on tests. You also learned about combining different tests for true and false and about ScriptCraft's **input** function, which is used for asking for input from players.

Chapter 10

Animal Sounds

IN THIS CHAPTER, you'll create a simple program to ask players a question and play back sounds based on the answer given. You'll learn about JavaScript's `switch` statement and ScriptCraft's `sounds` module. The new program will ask players what their favorite animal is and play back that animal's sound.

The switch Statement

In Chapter 9 you learned how to get input from players and how to test the input using JavaScript's **if** statement. JavaScript provides an additional statement for testing values: the **switch** statement. The **switch** statement is useful when you want to make decisions by testing a single value. The **switch** statement is best explained by example. Create a new file called **animalSounds.js** in the **scriptcraft/plugins/** folder and type the code shown in LISTING 10.1.

Save your file and then issue the **js refresh()** command to reload all the JavaScript code. Then at the in-game prompt, issue the following command:

```
/js animalSounds( self );
```

You will be prompted to type the name of your favorite animal. Press the T key to enter text and then type in any of the following: cat, chicken, cow, pig, sheep, wolf. When you hit Enter, you should hear an appropriate sound—a wolf bark, cow moo, and so on. If you give any other answer, the program responds with a message saying it never heard of such an animal.

LISTING 10.1 Animal Sounds

```javascript
var sounds = require('sounds');
var input = require('input');
function onInput( animal, player ) {

  switch (animal) {
    case 'cat':
      echo( player, "A cat says 'meow'");
      sounds.catMeow(player.location);
      break;
    case 'chicken':
      echo( player, "A chicken says 'cluck'");
      sounds.chickenSay(player.location);
      break;
```

continued...

LISTING 10.1 *continued*

```
    case 'cow':
      echo( player, "A cow says 'moo'");
      sounds.cowSay(player.location);
      break;
    case 'pig':
      echo( player, "A pig says 'oink'");
      sounds.pigSay(player.location);
      break;
    case 'sheep':
      echo( player, "A sheep says 'baa'");
      sounds.sheepSay(player.location);
      break;
    case 'wolf':
      echo( player, "A wolf says 'woof'");
      sounds.wolfBark(player.location);
      break;
    default:
      echo( player, "I never heard of a " + animal);
  }
};
function animalSounds( player ){
  input( player,
    "What's your favorite animal" +
    " - cat, chicken, cow, pig, sheep or wolf?",
    onInput );
}
exports.animalSounds = animalSounds;
```

The **switch** statement works much like the **if-else-if** construct you used in Chapter 9 . You could have written the **animalSounds.js** module using an **if-else-if** form.

```
if (animal == 'cat') {
    sounds.catMeow(player.location);
} else if (animal == 'chicken') {
    sounds.chickenSay(player.location);
} else if (animal == 'cow') {
    sounds.cowSay(player.location);
...
```

But since every test is on the same **animal** variable, it makes more sense to use a **switch** statement instead. Here are some things to note about the **switch** statement:

- The **switch** statement is used for testing a single expression against many possible values.
- It has one or more *case* labels, each of which must be followed by a value and the : symbol (also known as a *colon*).
- The block of code after the colon (**:**) is executed only if the value matches. All code up to the special **break** statement will be executed.
- If no case matches, then the **default** case is executed.

The **default** case is executed when you enter an animal that isn't one of cat, chicken, cow, pig, sheep, or wolf.

A common pitfall when using the **switch** statement is forgetting to include the **break** statement at the end of each case. As an exercise, try commenting out the **break** statement inside the block for **sheep**. Remember, to *comment out* a line of code, just put **//** at the start of the line. Save and reload and then run the program again (**/js animalSounds(self);**) and this time enter **sheep** as your favorite animal. What happens? The following output will appear in your screen:

```
A sheep says 'baa'
A wolf says 'woof'
```

And you will hear both a sheep bleat *and* a wolf bark! That's because in a case block, the code will keep executing until it hits a **break** statement, and if it doesn't hit one, it carries right on through to the next **case** statement.

The sounds Module

There are many sounds in Minecraft, and the list of sounds available in the game changes with each new release. ScriptCraft provides a **sounds** module that makes it easy to play any of the in-game sounds. At the time of writing, there are approximately 160 sounds in Minecraft, and the **sounds** module provides a function for each one. Each of the functions in the **sounds** module takes up to three parameters.

- The location where you want to play the sound. This parameter is optional; if omitted, the sound will be played for all online players to hear.

- The volume at which you want to play the sound. This parameter is optional; if omitted, it defaults to 1.0 (full volume). Volume is in the range 0 to 1, with 0 being no sound at all and 1 being maximum volume. For example, if you wanted to play a Cat's Meow at half volume, you would write **sounds.catMeow(location, 0.5);**.

- The pitch at which you want to play the sound. The parameter is also optional and if left out will default to 1.0 (moderate pitch). Pitch can vary between 0 and 4.

TABLE 10.1 shows all the possible sound functions available at the time of writing. This list may not be up to date because new sounds are added on an ongoing basis, while some sounds may also be removed.

The **sounds** module is not a built-in variable in ScriptCraft, so you'll need to load the module first so you can use it. At the in-game prompt, you play various sounds like this:

```
/js var sounds = require('sounds');
/js sounds.catMeow( self.location );
/js sounds.burp( self.location );
```

In Minecraft, players, blocks, monsters, animals, and villagers all have a **location** property that can be passed to any of the **sounds** module functions.

TABLE 10.1 Sound Functions

sounds.ambienceCave()	sounds.ambienceRain()	sounds.ambienceThunder()
sounds.anvilBreak()	sounds.anvilLand()	sounds.anvilUse()
sounds.batDeath()	sounds.batHurt()	sounds.batIdle()
sounds.batLoop()	sounds.batTakeoff()	sounds.blazeBreath()
sounds.blazeDeath()	sounds.blazeHit()	sounds.bow()
sounds.bowHit()	sounds.breath()	sounds.burp()
sounds.catHiss()	sounds.catHit()	sounds.catMeow()
sounds.catPurr()	sounds.catPurreow()	sounds.chestClosed()
sounds.chestOpen()	sounds.chickenHurt()	sounds.chickenPlop()
sounds.chickenSay()	sounds.chickenStep()	sounds.click()
sounds.cowHurt()	sounds.cowSay()	sounds.cowStep()
sounds.creeperDeath()	sounds.creeperSay()	sounds.digCloth()
sounds.digGrass()	sounds.digGravel()	sounds.digSand()
sounds.digSnow()	sounds.digStone()	sounds.digWood()
sounds.doorClose()	sounds.doorOpen()	sounds.drink()
sounds.eat()	sounds.enderdragonEnd()	sounds.enderdragonGrowl()
sounds.enderdragonHit()	sounds.enderdragonWings()	sounds.endermanDeath()
sounds.endermanHit()	sounds.endermanIdle()	sounds.endermanPortal()
sounds.endermanScream()	sounds.endermanStare()	sounds.explode()
sounds.fallBig()	sounds.fallSmall()	sounds.fire()
sounds.fireIgnite()	sounds.fizz()	sounds.fuse()
sounds.ghastAffectionateScream()	sounds.ghastCharge()	sounds.ghastDeath()
sounds.ghastFireball()	sounds.ghastMoan()	sounds.ghastScream()
sounds.glass()	sounds.hurt()	sounds.hurtFlesh()
sounds.irongolemDeath()	sounds.irongolemHit()	sounds.irongolemThrow()
sounds.irongolemWalk()	sounds.itemBreak()	sounds.itemPickup()
sounds.lava()	sounds.lavaPop()	sounds.levelUp()
sounds.liquidSplash()	sounds.magmacubeBig()	sounds.magmacubeJump()

TABLE 10.1 *continued*

sounds.magmacubeSmall()	sounds.minecartBase()	sounds.minecartInside()
sounds.noteBass()	sounds.noteBassAttack()	sounds.noteBassDrum()
sounds.noteHat()	sounds.notePiano()	sounds.notePling()
sounds.noteSnare()	sounds.orb()	sounds.pigDeath()
sounds.pigSay()	sounds.pigStep()	sounds.pistonIn()
sounds.pistonOut()	sounds.play()	sounds.portal()
sounds.portalTravel()	sounds.portalTrigger()	sounds.sheepSay()
sounds.sheepShear()	sounds.sheepStep()	sounds.silverfishHit()
sounds.silverfishKil()	sounds.silverfishSay()	sounds.silverfishStep()
sounds.skeletonDeath()	sounds.skeletonHurt()	sounds.skeletonSay()
sounds.skeletonStep()	sounds.slimeAttack()	sounds.slimeBig()
sounds.slimeSmall()	sounds.spiderDeath()	sounds.spiderSay()
sounds.spiderStep()	sounds.splash()	sounds.stepGrass()
sounds.stepGravel()	sounds.stepLadder()	sounds.stepSand()
sounds.stepSnow()	sounds.stepStone()	sounds.stepWood()
sounds.stepWool()	sounds.swim()	sounds.water()
sounds.witherDeath()	sounds.witherHurt()	sounds.witherIdle()
sounds.witherShoot()	sounds.witherSpawn()	sounds.wolfBark()
sounds.wolfDeath()	sounds.wolfGrowl()	sounds.wolfHowl()
sounds.wolfHurt()	sounds.wolfPant()	sounds.wolfShake()
sounds.wolfStep()	sounds.wolfWhine()	sounds.woodClick()
sounds.zombieDeath()	sounds.zombieHurt()	sounds.zombieInfect()
sounds.zombieMetal()	sounds.zombiePigAngry()	sounds.zombiePigDeath()
sounds.zombiePigHurt()	sounds.zombiePigIdle()	sounds.zombieRemedy()
sounds.zombieSay()	sounds.zombieUnfect()	sounds.zombieWood()
sounds.zombieWoodbreak()		

Improving the Code

When running the `animalSounds()` function, what happens if you enter **Cow** instead of **cow**? Try it and see.

If you enter **Cow** or **COW**, the function says it hasn't heard of a **Cow** or **COW**. To you and me, a *Cow* is a *COW* is a *cow*, but to a computer they are three different strings. That's because computers are *case-sensitive*—they don't see the word *Cow* and know that whether it's spelled with capital letters or lowercase letters, it means the same thing. The computer sees only a sequence (or list) of letters, and as far as the computer is concerned, *C* and *c* are completely different. You can see this for yourself by issuing these commands at the in-game prompt:

```
/js 'COW' == 'cow'
> false
/js 'Cow' == 'cow'
> false
```

How do you make the `animalSounds()` function understand that when a player types COW it should be treated the same as cow? Fortunately, there's a **String** function that helps solve this problem. Issue the following command at the in-game prompt:

```
/js 'COW'.toLowerCase() == 'cow'
> true
```

The **String.toLowerCase()** function will convert any string to its lowercase equivalent so COW becomes *cow*, and Cow also becomes *cow*. This can be really useful when you want to test **String** values but don't care whether they're uppercase or lowercase. Let's look at the improved **animalSounds** module (see **LISTING 10.2**).

The only change to this module is this new statement just before the **switch** statement:

```
animal = animal.toLowerCase();
```

This statement ensures that the **animal** parameter is converted to lowercase first so the program won't report silly messages about not knowing what a Cow or SHEEP is.

LISTING 10.2 Case-Insensitive Animal Sounds

```
var sounds = require('sounds');
var input = require('input');
function onInput( animal, player ) {
  animal = animal.toLowerCase();
  switch (animal) {
    case 'cat':
      echo( player, "A cat says 'meow'");
      sounds.catMeow(player.location);
      break;
    case 'chicken':
      echo( player, "A chicken says 'cluck'");
      sounds.chickenSay(player.location);
      break;
    case 'cow':
      echo( player, "A cow says 'moo'");
      sounds.cowSay(player.location);
      break;
    case 'pig':
      echo( player, "A pig says 'oink'");
      sounds.pigSay(player.location);
      break;
    case 'sheep':
      echo( player, "A sheep says 'baa'");
      sounds.sheepSay(player.location);
      break;
```

continued...

LISTING 10.1 *continued*

```
    case 'wolf':
      echo( player, "A wolf says 'woof'");
      sounds.wolfBark(player.location);
      break;
    default:
      echo( player, "I never heard of a " + animal);
  }
}
function animalSounds( player ) {
  input( player,
         "What's your favorite animal" +
         " - cat, chicken, cow, pig, sheep or wolf?",
         onInput);
}
exports.animalSounds = animalSounds;
```

More on Strings

All strings in JavaScript also have a **toUpperCase()** function that returns an UPPERCASE version of the string. Note that neither the **toLowerCase()** nor the **toUpperCase()** function changes the original string; these functions just return a new string, which is why I need to assign the **animal** variable to the returned value. If I simply used this:

```
animal.toLowerCase();
```

...the **switch** cases would still fail for **COW** because the value of **animal** does not change when you call its **toLowerCase()** function. If you use the toLowerCase(), toUpperCase(), or *any of the string* methods, none of them changes the original string. In JavaScript any string is *immutable*, meaning none of its methods change it in any way. In Chapter 8 you saw that you could add a new item to an array by calling its **push()** method. Arrays are *mutable* objects: The methods can change the object on which they're called. Let's see an example at the in-game prompt:

```
/js var animals = ['cow','pig'];
/js animals.push('sheep');
/js animals[2]
> sheep
```

The previous statement—animals.push('sheep');—actually *changes* the animals value. With strings, this never happens. None of the string methods (and there are quite a few) changes the value for which they are called. For example, here is a **String.concat()** function that adds another string:

```
/js var name = "steve ";
/js name.concat("crafter");
> steve crafter
/js name
> steve
```

You can see that while **name.concat("crafter");** returns the value **steve crafter**, the original **name** variable remains unchanged. If you wanted to change the **name** variable, you'd have to do it like this:

```
/js var name = "steve ";
/js name = name.concat("crafter");
> steve crafter
/js name
> steve crafter
```

TABLE 10.2 shows the most common string methods.

A full reference of all String methods is available at *https://developer.mozilla.org/en-US/docs/Web/Javascript/Reference/Global_Objects/String*.

TABLE 10.2 Commonly Used String Methods

METHOD NAME	DESCRIPTION
`.charAt(index)`	Returns the character at index from the string.
`.concat(text1, text2)`	Combines the text from one or more strings and returns a new string.
`.indexOf(text)`	Returns the first position where text was found or returns -1 if the text is not in the string. For example, `"Ice Cream".indexOf("Cream")` returns 4.
`.lastIndexOf(text)`	Returns the last position where text was found.
`.replace(regex, replacement)`	Returns a new string with some or all matches of a pattern replaced by a replacement. Here's an example: `"I hate Creepers".replace(/Creepers/, "Spiders")`.
`.split(separator)`	Splits a string into an array of strings. Here's an example: `"I hate creepers".split(" ")` returns `["I", "hate", "creepers"]`.
`.substring(indexA,[indexB])`	Extracts characters starting at `indexA` and continuing to `indexB` (or end of string if `indexB` is not provided). Here's an example: `"I hate creepers". substring(7)` returns `"creepers"`.
`.toLowerCase()`	Returns a new string with all characters in lowercase.
`.toUpperCase()`	Returns a new string with all characters in uppercase.
`.trim()`	Returns a new string with whitespace removed from both ends of the string. Here's an example: `" I hate Creepers ".trim()` returns `"I hate creepers"`.

Summary

In this chapter, you learned how to use the **switch** statements to make decisions. You also learned how to play sounds using ScriptCraft's **sounds** module. Later in the book, you'll learn how to simplify this module even further using objects.

Chapter 11

Leaderboards: More Fun with Arrays

ONE OF THE REALLY COOL THINGS about arrays in JavaScript is that they can be sorted. *Sorting* is the process of looking at each item in an array and deciding whether it is greater than or less than another item in the same array. When all of the items in an array are sorted, the array is like a leaderboard—a ranked list of items. In this chapter, you'll create a ranked list of players based on who has jumped most.

Array.sort()

The `Array.sort()` method is used to sort items in an array. Let's see it in action. Issue the following commands at the server console prompt:

```
js var animals = ['pig','wolf','cow','cat','sheep'];
js console.log( animals );
> pig,wolf,cat,cow,sheep
js animals.sort();
js console.log( animals );
> cat,cow,pig,sheep,wolf
```

You can see from the output that `Array.sort()` will sort a list of strings alphabetically (in other words, the order the letters appear in the alphabet). So, `cat` is moved to the first position in the array, while `wolf` is moved to the last position in the array. All of the animals in between are sorted alphabetically too. What happens if you try to sort an array of numbers?

```
js var luckyNumbers = [ 9, 23, 5, 40, 21 ];
js luckyNumbers.sort();
js console.log( luckyNumbers );
> 21, 23, 40, 5, 9
```

Well, that makes no sense! In JavaScript, the default way to sort items in an array is alphabetically. It even does this when the items in an array are all numbers. In JavaScript, arrays can contain *anything*, such as numbers, strings, objects, other arrays, and even a mixture of all of these types. If you want the `Array.sort()` method to sort by any way other than alphabetically, you have to tell it how. For example, issue the following commands at the server console prompt:

```
js function numerically( a, b ) { return a - b };
js luckyNumbers.sort( numerically );
js console.log( luckyNumbers );
> 5, 9, 21, 23, 40
```

Now the `luckyNumbers` array is sorted in the correct order. The `numerically()` function you created in the first command in the previous code is a function that takes two parameters, **a** and **b**, and subtracts them. This function is then passed to the `Array.sort()` method and will be called many times by `Array.sort()` because it plucks two items from the array and asks the numerically() function the question, "Which item is bigger—a or b?" You can see that your numerically() function will get called many times if you add a console.log() statement.

```js
function numerically( a, b ) { console.log('a = ' + a + ',
b = ' + b); return a - b }
```
```js
luckyNumbers.sort( numerically );
> a = 9, b = 5
> a = 21, b = 9
> a = 23, b = 21
> a = 40, b = 23
```

The exact output you see probably won't be the same, but the point of adding the console.log() statement is to illustrate that the numerically() function will be called many times during the course of an array sort.

How to Compare Items in an Array

The numerically() function you created earlier is called a *comparator* function because its only job is to *compare* things to one another. The rules that Array.sort() uses when sorting are simple. The Array.sort() method plucks two items from the array and calls the comparator (the comparing function) passing the two items. It repeats this process until all of the items in the array have been compared to each other. Comparator functions typically just name their parameters a and b.

- If the function returns the number 0, then it means that a and b are the same (in ranking at least).
- If it returns a number less than 0, then it means that a *is less than* b, so a should appear before b in the array.
- If it returns a number greater than 0, then it means that a is *greater than* b, so a should appear after b in the array.

Let's look at these rules and see how they're used in the numerically() function.

```js
function numerically( a, b ) { return a - b ; }
```

TERM **Java Collection**

A Java collection is like a JavaScript array—it is a collection of items. However, it does not have the same methods or functions and can't be used the same way you use a JavaScript array. For example, in JavaScript, you can find out how many items are in an array using the **length** property. A Java collection has no such property. To find out how many items are in a Java collection, you need to call a **size()** method instead. Many of the objects you'll use in your plugins are Java objects. As a general rule, the **server** variable and any of its properties are Java objects. Similarly, events and players and block objects are also Java objects, so any of their properties will be Java objects too. If you want to sort a Java collection, it's easier to first convert it to a JavaScript array. ScriptCraft comes with a **utils** module that has an **array()** function to do just that.

Sorting numerically is relatively easy. For numeric sorts, you just need to subtract one number from another to give the **Array.sort()** method the information it needs to sort. So, plucking any two numbers from the array and passing them to the **numerically()** function should give the correct order.

- 21 – 40 is -19, which is less than 0, meaning 21 will be listed *before* 40 in the array.

- 21 – 9 is 12, which is greater than 0, meaning 21 will be listed *after* 9 in the array.

- 5 – 9 is -4, which is less than 0, meaning 5 will be listed *before* 9 in the array, and so on.

The **Array.sort()** method takes the results of all these calculations to move each item into its correct position in the array. At first glance, it might seem that the **Array.sort()** method is pretty dumb (after all, it doesn't even understand how to sort numbers and has to be explicitly told how to do so) but actually it's pretty flexible and powerful. **Array.sort()** can sort anything really; you just need to tell it what rules to use for sorting.

Let's look at a slightly more complex example. Typically, your server will have three worlds created when it starts up. The worlds are usually called **world**, **world_nether**, and **world_the_end**. If you wanted to sort these worlds based on their populations (how many living entities—animals, mobs, and players—are present), you could do so by creating a new **byPopulation()** function that would look something like this:

```js
js function byPopulation(a,b){
    return a.entityLivingList.size() -
        b.entityLivingList.size();
}
```

The **byPopulation()** function takes two parameters, called **a** and **b**, both of which it assumes are Minecraft worlds. Each Minecraft world object has an **entityLivingList** property that is a *Java collection* of living things. The entityLivingList property in turn has a **size()** function, so if you want to find out how many living beings are on a world, you call the world's **entityLiv-ingList.size()** method. You can compare the populations by subtracting one population size from another.

The code to use your new **byPopulation()** function would look like this:

```js
js var utils = require('utils');
js var worlds = utils.worlds();
js worlds.sort( byPopulation );
js console.log( worlds );
```

The **utils.worlds()** function returns an array of all the worlds on the server. It is sorted, and the results are printed to the console. The previous example demonstrates how you can apply whatever rules you like to sorting items in an array. Now let's talk about sorting players.

Sorting Players by Name

One way to sort players is by name. This isn't strictly a leaderboard in the truest sense of the word, but it does demonstrate how to sort based on a player's attribute—his name. Create a new file called **playerSort.js** in the **scriptcraft/modules** folder and type in the code shown in LISTING 11.1.

LISTING 11.1 Sorting Players by Name

```
function byName( a, b ) {
  if (a.name == b.name) {
    return 0;
  } else if (a.name > b.name) {
    return 1;
  } else {
    return -1;
  }
};
exports.byName = byName;
```

The **byName()** function performs a couple of comparisons of the name of each player. When comparing two strings using the < and > operators, the comparison is always based on the alphabetic sequence of characters, so **'cat'** < **'cow'** will return **true** while **'cat'** > **'cow'** will return **false**. However, you don't want the comparator function **byName()** to return **true** or **false**; you want it to return a number. This is a common mistake even experienced programmers make when writing functions for use in sorting. They forget that the comparing function must return a number, not simply **true** or **false**.

To try this module, issue the following commands at the server console prompt. Make sure there's at least two players on your server or the results won't be very interesting.

```
js var utils = require('utils');
js var playerSort = require('playerSort');
js var players = utils.players();
js players.sort( playerSort.byName );
js console.log( players );
```

Sorting Players by Experience

Let's face it, a leaderboard based on player names would be both boring and unfair. Instead, let's try one based on a player's experience points. Update your **playerSort.js** file, adding a new **byExp()** function (**Exp** is short for experience), as shown in LISTING 11.2.

The new **byExp()** function just does a numeric sort, meaning it returns the result of subtracting player **a**'s **experience** from player **b**'s **experience**. One thing to note is that although there is only a single function used for sorting by experience, you *export* it twice—under the name **byExp** and also under the longer name **byExperience**. This gives programmers who use this module the option of using the short name or long name for that function; whichever name they use, it will be the same function being called. Issue the following commands to see this function in action again; it helps if there's more than one player on your server:

```
js var sortPlayers = require('playerSort');
js var utils = require('utils');
js var players = utils.players();
js players.sort( sortPlayers.byExp );
js console.log( players );
```

LISTING 11.2 Sorting Players by Experience

```
function byName( a, b ) {
  if (a.name == b.name) {
    return 0;
  } else if (a.name > b.name) {
    return 1;
  } else {
    return -1;
  }
};

exports.byName = byName;

function byExp( a, b ) {
  return a.experience - b.experience;
};

exports.byExperience = byExp;
exports.byExp = byExp;
```

When I ran this code with just two players, I got the following output:

```
[walterh, sean_higgins]
```

The actual experience points at the time were as follows:

```
Player       Total Experience
---------------------------
walterh          52
sean_higgins     103
```

You should be surprised by the results. In any leaderboard based on player experience, the *most* experienced players—that is, the players with the highest experience number—should be placed first ahead of lesser experienced players. However, the `byExp()` function sorts in *ascending* order (that is, from lowest to highest), so the `players` array will list least-experienced players first. That's not what you want for a leaderboard.

Reversing Arrays

You can easily reverse an array by calling the `reverse()` method.

```js
js players.reverse()
```

The `reverse()` method reverses an array in place. The first array element becomes the last, and the last becomes the first. This is exactly what you want for a leaderboard where the highest score (that is, the larger numeric value) should be first in the array.

There is another way you can sort players for inclusion in a leaderboard without using the `reverse()` method. You can change the sort order in the comparing function itself. To sort items numerically, you compare the first parameter (usually called **a**) to the second parameter (usually called **b**) by subtracting **a** from **b**. When you say `return a - b`, you are sorting in *ascending* order from lowest to highest. If you want to sort in *descending* order (most leaderboards are presented in descending order), then you say `return b - a` instead. For now, you can continue to write comparing functions using ascending order and use the `reverse()` function to change the order from ascending to descending.

Sorting Players by Other Rules

You can use many different player statistics for sorting players. You can have a leaderboard of players who have jumped the most, have flown the most, have caught the most fish, have spent the most time riding horses, have crafted the most items, or have mined the most blocks. In short, there are plenty of statistics to use for display in leaderboards.

Player Statistics

In Minecraft each player is an *object* in the game. *Objects* in JavaScript are variables that have both data and behavior. A player has a name (data) and among other things can chat (behavior). You can see this by issuing the following commands at the in-game prompt:

```
/js self.name
/js self.chat('Hello World!')
```

The first command will display your name. The second command will make you say "Hello World!" to everyone in the game. In the first command, you access a *property* of the object called `self`, and in the second command you call a *method* on the object called `self`. *Properties* are just variables that belong to objects. *Methods* are just functions that belong to objects. In later chapters I'll show you how to discover all of the properties and methods of the **Player** object and other in-game objects. For now, you're going to use another player method called `getStatistic()` that returns a statistic for a player. You use it like this:

```
/js var utils = require('utils');
/js self.getStat( utils.stat.JUMP );
```

This command calls the `.getStat()` method on the `self` object, which refers to your in-game character and displays the number returned by that method. Now jump again and issue the same command once more (remember, you can issue the previous command by pressing / and then the Up arrow key). The number returned should be greater by 1. You're going to use each player's JUMP statistic to display a leaderboard of players who have jumped the most. Open your **playerSort.js** file in the editor and update it adding the **byJumps()** function, as shown in LISTING 11.3.

Save the file and then issue the **/js refresh()** command to reload Script-Craft. Test your new function by issuing the following commands at the server console prompt:

```
js var playerSort = require('playerSort');
js var utils = require('utils');
js var players = utils.players();
js players.sort( playerSort.byJumps );
js console.log( players );
```

LISTING 11.3 Sorting Players by Number of Jumps

```
var utils = require('utils');
function byJumps( a, b ) {
  var aJumps = a.getStat( utils.stat.JUMP );
  var bJumps = b.getStat( utils.stat.JUMP );
  return aJumps - bJumps;
};
exports.byJumps = byJumps;
```

The output from the previous command doesn't look much like a leaderboard; it simply prints all of the **Player** objects on a single line with a comma (**,**) between each player. Let's make it look better.

Displaying the Leaderboard

So far, you've just been using the **console.log()** function to display the entire contents of the array on a single line. The output when displaying the array of players using **console.log()** might look something like this:

```
Player{name=abcdefg}, Player{name=hijklmn}, Player{name=opqrst}
```

For a leaderboard display you'll want something a little more sophisticated. Let's create a function that displays each player's name and the number of jumps on a single line. To do that, you'll need to process each item in the array one at a time. One of the ways you can process items in an array is using *loops*. Computers are good at repeating the same thing over and over. In programming, repeating the same thing over is called *looping*. There are two *looping* statements in JavaScript: the **for** statement and the **while** statement.

The for Loop

The **for** loop is usually used to process each item in an array. For example, if you have an array of animals like `['cat','cow','pig','sheep','wolf']`, you could print out each animal using the following code:

```js
js var animals = ['cat','cow','pig','sheep','wolf'];
js console.log( animals[0] ); // <-- 'cat'
js console.log( animals[1] ); // <-- 'cow'
js console.log( animals[2] ); // <-- 'pig'
js console.log( animals[3] ); // <-- 'sheep'
js console.log( animals[4] ); // <-- 'wolf'
```

This would get really repetitive and tiring to type. Fortunately, there's an easier way to print out each item in the array on its own line. The best way to see how the **for** statement works is with an example. Issue the following commands at the server prompt and see what happens:

```js
js var animals = ['cat','cow','pig','sheep','wolf'];
js for (var i = 0; i < animals.length; i++ ) { console.log(
animals[i] ); }
```

The **for** loop is used for repeating a block of statements over and over. Did you notice how quickly the array of animals was printed? Let's try using the **for** statement again, this time just to print all of the numbers from 0 to 99.

```js
js for (var i = 0; i < 100; i++ ) { console.log(i); }
```

On a modern computer, those 100 numbers are printed in the blink of an eye. If you're curious, try running the command again, this time changing the number from 100 to 1 million (that's 1 with six zeros after it). It should take a good deal longer but will still complete before you or I could count to 100. Computers are fast, and now you're starting to get a feel for just how fast! Let's take a closer look at the first **for** statement you used.

```js
js for (var i = 0; i < animals.length; i++ ) { console.log(
animals[i] ); }
```

The part of the **for** statement in parentheses—(**var i = 0; i < animals. length; i++**)—sets up some rules for the **for** loop. Each rule is separated by a semicolon (**;**).

- The first rule (**var i = 0**) is called the *initialize* expression and is run only once before the loop begins.

- The second rule (**i < animals.length**) is called the *test* expression and is run at the *start* of each time through the loop to see whether the loop should end.

- The third rule (**i++**) is called the *increment* expression and is run at the *end* of each time through the loop.

After the **for** statement, you have a block of one or more statements enclosed by curly braces (**{ }**). These statements will be executed each time through the loop. Let's put **for** loops to use to create a more pleasing leaderboard display of players who jump the most. Create a new file called **leaderboard.js** in the **scriptcraft/modules** folder and type in the code shown in LISTING 11.4.

To try the new module save it, issue the **js refresh()** command to reload ScriptCraft and then issue the following commands at the in-game prompt:

```
/js var leaderboard = require('leaderboard');
/js leaderboard.jumps( self );
```

The list of all players on the server and the number of times they've jumped should be displayed in descending order, meaning the players who have jumped the most will be at the top of the list. In a later chapter, you'll revisit this module to display the leaderboard using an onscreen scoreboard as seen on popular player-versus-player servers.

The **jumps()** function takes a single parameter called receiver, which is short for **MessageReceiver**. A **MessageReceiver** is anything in the game capable of receiving messages. For example, players are message receivers since they can receive messages (and send them using the in-game prompt). What you want to do in this function is send output to the player who issued the command. That's why you use **echo(receiver, ...)** instead of **console.log()** to display the leaderboard. If you used **console.log()**, then players would not see the leaderboard because **console.log()** writes messages only to the server console window, not to players. In the previous **jumps()** function, you sort the players by how many times they've jumped, then reverse the array so that the higher numbers are at the front of the array, and finally *loop* over the array using the **for** loop. Inside the **for** loop, you have a block of statements.

LISTING 11.4 A Simple Jumps Leaderboard: for Loop

```
var playerSort = require('playerSort');
var utils = require('utils');

function jumps( receiver ) {
  var players = utils.players();
  players.sort( playerSort.byJumps );
  players.reverse();

  for (var i = 0; i < players.length; i++ ) {

    var player = players[i];
    var playerJumps = player.getStat(utils.stat.JUMP );
    echo( receiver, player.name + '_____' + playerJumps);


  }

};

exports.jumps = jumps;
```

```
var player = players[i];
var jumpStats = player.getStatistic( bukkit.stat.JUMP );
echo( receiver, player.name + ' ' + jumpStats);
```

The previous block of code gets executed a number of times—the number depends on how many players are connected to the server. The variable **i** is the current position in the **players** array. This variable's value will change each time through the loop. The first time through the loop it will be 0, then 1, then 2, and so on, until it reaches the end of the array and there are no more players to process. The first statement gets the player at the current position (**players[i]**) and assigns it to a variable called **player**. You then get this player's jump count and name and then display them onscreen.

The while Loop

The second kind of loop is called the **while** loop. The **for** loop is useful for *iterating* (a fancy word for looping) over arrays or for when you know in advance how many times you need to loop. Sometimes you won't know how many times you need to loop, and you'll want to keep looping until some condition is met. A **while** loop is also called a *conditional* loop—it's like the **if** statement except it will keep repeating the same block of code over and over until a *test condition* is no longer true. The best way to understand this is by example. Let's look at the leaderboard module again—this time it's been written using a **while** loop instead of a **for** loop (see LISTING 11.5). The code behaves *exactly* the same; it just uses **while** instead of **for**.

Breaking Out of Loops

Sometimes you'll want to break out of a loop early. Let's say you want to display only the players who have actually jumped—in other words, players whose jump count is greater than zero. You can break out of a loop early using the JavaScript **break** statement. Take a look at LISTING 11.6 to see an example of the **break** statement.

In the previous code, the **while** loop will stop when it encounters the first player who has not jumped.

Skipping a Turn in a Loop

The **break** statement will break out of a loop, effectively ending the loop so that the block of code in the loop won't be executed again. Sometimes you just want to skip an iteration (a turn) on the loop. Let's say you have an *unsorted* list of players and want to display only players who have jumped. The **continue** lets you skip to the next iteration of the loop. In LISTING 11.7, only players who have jumped will be displayed. This isn't a leaderboard because players are displayed in no particular order.

LISTING 11.5 A Simple Jumps Leaderboard: while Loop

```
var playerSort = require('playerSort');
var utils = require('utils');
function jumps( sender ) {
  var players = utils.players();
  players.sort( playerSort.byJumps );
  players.reverse();

  var i = 0;
  while ( i < players.length ) { // start of loop

    var player = players[i];
    var jumpStats = player.getStat( utils.stat.JUMP );
    echo( sender, player.name + ' ' + jumpStats);

    i++;

  } // end of loop

};

exports.jumps = jumps;
```

LISTING 11.6 Breaking Out of Loops

```
var playerSort = require('playerSort');
var utils = require('utils');
function jumps( sender ) {
  var players = utils.players();
  players.sort( playerSort.byJumps );
  players.reverse();

  var i = 0;
  while ( i < players.length ) { // start of loop

    var player = players[i];
    var jumpStats = player.getStat(utils.stat.JUMP );
    if ( jumpStats == 0 ) {
      break;
    }
    echo( sender, player.name + ' ' + jumpStats);

    i++;

  } // end of loop

};

exports.jumps = jumps;
```

LISTING 11.7 Skipping a Loop Iteration

```
var utils = require('utils');
function jumps( sender ) {
  var players = utils.players();

  var i = 0;
  while ( i < players.length ) { // start of loop

    var player = players[i];
    var jumpStats = player.getStat( utils.stat.JUMP );
    if ( jumpStats == 0 ) {
      continue;
    }
    echo( sender, player.name + ' ' + jumpStats);

    i++;
  } // end of loop

};

exports.jumps = jumps;
```

Infinite Loops

Within any loop block there must be a statement that will affect the loop's condition. For example, in Listing 11.7 you check the value of the i variable each time round the loop. If you never changed the i variable, what do you think would happen? If i never changed, then the test `i < players.length` would always be true (unless of course there were no players on the server, in which case the code inside the `while` block would never execute). A loop that keeps running and never stops is called an *infinite loop*. Infinite loops usually happen because a programmer forgot to increment a counter variable or because the loop condition is wrong. An infinite loop is usually a sign that something went wrong—that there's a bug in the code.

There are infinite loops that aren't accidental. Most games and programs that have a user interface (windows, buttons, and so on) have an *event loop*, which is a loop that's constantly running and listening for incoming events from the user or other parts of the system. A game's event loop might listen for key presses from the user, check to see whether any collisions between objects in the game have occurred, check the player's health, and so on. The Minecraft server has just such a loop.

Creating a New Command for Players

So far in this chapter you've been creating JavaScript functions that can be invoked by anyone on the server who is an operator. Only operators can and should be able to execute JavaScript code at the in-game or server prompts. *The ability to execute code is potentially dangerous, so you definitely don't want to grant that permission to everyone on your server.* The `js` command will take any JavaScript code and try to execute it. There's another command provided by ScriptCraft, and that's the `jsp` command. The `jsp` command is available for *everyone* to use. Unlike the `js` command, the `jsp` command *does not execute* JavaScript code, so it can be used safely by players without operator privileges. The `jsp` command lets you create your own custom commands that can be used by all players.

You want *all* players to be able to call up the leaderboard with a simple in-game command, and you want them to be able to do so without them needing to know JavaScript. In the next part of this chapter, you're going to change the **leaderboard.js** file so that anyone can call up the leaderboard using this command:

```
jsp leaderboard
```

When a player issues this command at the in-game prompt, a leaderboard of players who have jumped most will be displayed to the player who issued the command. Don't try this just yet—you haven't created the **leaderboard** command yet.

The **jsp** Command

The **jsp** command by itself doesn't do much. It's just a placeholder, which is a "dummy" command that can be extended to support new types of commands. In the Minecraft server, commands have a *name* and one or more arguments. For example, in the following command, **gamemode** is the name of the command and **creative** and **walterh** are the command's arguments:

```
/gamemode creative walterh
```

The purpose of the **jsp** command is to make it easy to create your own custom commands using JavaScript. The **jsp** command name was made deliberately short because it's really just a prefix for custom commands. You want to be able to create custom commands with a **jsp** prefix so that your custom commands don't conflict with commands provided by other plugins.

In ScriptCraft you create new commands for use by everyone using the **command()** function. The best way to see how the **command()** function works is with a simple example.

```
/js function boo( params, sender ) { echo( sender, 'Boo!') }
/js command( boo );
```

In the first statement I create a new function called **boo()**, which will simply say "Boo!" In the second statement, I call the ScriptCraft **command()** function, passing the newly created function **boo()**, which will be called whenever any player issues this command:

```
/jsp boo
> Boo!
```

Here are the important points to note:

- Any player can now issue this new **jsp boo** command and will see a message on their screen. They don't have to be operators to do so.

- The **command()** function lets you—the JavaScript programmer—safely provide new commands for use by all players.

Now let's dive in and create a new **jsp leaderboard** command. Create a new file called **leaderboardCmd.js** in the **scriptcraft/plugins** folder and type in the code shown in LISTING 11.8.

This file must be saved in the **scriptcraft/plugins** folder so that it will be automatically loaded and run at startup. This module loads the **leaderboard** module created earlier, creates a new **leaderboard()** function, and calls Script-Craft's **command()** function, passing the new **leaderboard()** function that will be run whenever any player invokes the command.

You may have noticed there's no **exports** in this new module. That's because you don't need to export anything for this particular module—you provide a new command for use by all players through the **command()** function instead. Now let's see this new command in action. Issue the **js refresh()** command to reload ScriptCraft; then at the in-game prompt issue the following command:

```
/jsp leaderboard
```

LISTING 11.8 Adding a Custom Command for All Players

```
var lboard = require('leaderboard');

function leaderboard( params, sender ) {
  lboard.jumps( sender );
};

command( leaderboard );
```

The list of player names and jump counts should appear as messages onscreen. Now try the following: Type /jsp le and then press the Tab key. Pressing the Tab key should fill in the rest of the command name for you just as it does with regular Minecraft commands! The jsp command makes use of Tab completion: the ability to fill in the remaining parts of a command or cycle through command argument values by just pressing Tab repeatedly.

Achievement Unlocked!

You've just learned how to provide new custom commands in Minecraft!

Summary

In this chapter, you learned how to loop over each item in an array using **for** loops and **while** loops. You also learned how to sort and reverse arrays and how to provide new custom commands using ScriptCraft's **command()** function.

Chapter 12

Building a Skyscraper

IN THIS CHAPTER, you'll build a 10-story skyscraper using just a couple of lines of code and **loop** statements. You'll use **for** and **while** loops and ScriptCraft's **Drone** functions to build large structures in Minecraft.

Building Using Drones

In Minecraft, building by hand is fun but can be tedious when you want to build big structures such as towers, castles, and fortresses. ScriptCraft includes a module for building large structures in Minecraft using JavaScript. The **Drone** module has many functions for use in building. You can use the **Drone** module at the in-game prompt to build right within the game, or you can create a *blueprint* for a more complex structure by using the **Drone** functions in a JavaScript file. It's useful to think of the drone as an invisible remote control plane that can place blocks anywhere and that you control using JavaScript. Let's start by creating a simple structure at the in-game prompt. The first thing you should do when building using the **Drone** module is look at (also known as *target*) a block. In **FIGURE 12.1**, the targeted block is outlined in a slightly darker color than the surrounding blocks.

Once you've targeted a block—pick any block you like but preferably one just above ground level—issue the following command at the in-game prompt:

```
/js box( blocks.gold, 1, 3);
```

The targeted block will disappear, and a column of gold blocks one block wide and three blocks high will instantly appear in its place, as shown in **FIGURE 12.2**.

The **box()** function is used to place blocks in the game. It takes four parameters:

- **Material**: The type of material you want the blocks to be made from.
- **Width**: How wide you want the box to extend. The box will extend from the targeted block to the right.
- **Height**: How high you want the box to extend. The box will extend from the targeted block upward.
- **Length**: How far away you want the box to extend. The box will extend from the targeted block away from you.

The **box()** function is used to create cubes and cuboids of any size (see **FIGURE 12.3**). A cube is a three-dimensional shape whose sides are all the same length. A cuboid is a three-dimensional shape whose width, height, and length can differ.

Let's try a couple of more examples. While targeting the original block (it's gold now), issue the following command to turn the column from Gold to Iron:

```
/js box( blocks.iron, 1, 3)
```

FIGURE 12.1 Targeting a block in Minecraft

FIGURE 12.2 A gold column

If you are unsure which material to use, you can use Tab completion to fill in the material. Just type **box (blocks.** and then press Tab to see a list of possible materials. Now target a different block—this time one that is at ground level preferably—and create a stone path 2 blocks wide and 10 blocks long by issuing the following command:

```
/js box( blocks.stone, 2, 1, 10)
```

This will create a stony path that extends 10 blocks away from you (see **FIGURE 12.4**).

If you leave out any of the width, height, and length parameters, they will default to 1. So, **box(blocks.gold, 5, 3)** will create a box five blocks wide, three blocks high, and one block long; **box(blocks.gold, 5)** will create a box five blocks wide, one block high, and one block long; and **box(blocks.gold)** will create a gold box one block wide, high, and long. For the first parameter—the material—you can use any of the values in the special **blocks** variable. **TABLE 12.1** lists all of the possible block materials that can be used for building.

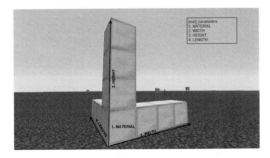

FIGURE 12.3 Box function parameters

FIGURE 12.4 A stone path 2 x 1 x 10

TABLE 12.1 Building Materials

blocks.air	blocks.anvil	blocks.beacon
blocks.bed	blocks.bedrock	blocks.bookshelf
blocks.brewing_stand	blocks.brick.chiseled	blocks.brick.cracked
blocks.brick.mossy	blocks.brick.red	blocks.brick.stone
blocks.button_wood	blocks.cactus	blocks.cake
blocks.carpet.black	blocks.carpet.blue	blocks.carpet.brown
blocks.carpet.cyan	blocks.carpet.gray	blocks.carpet.green
blocks.carpet.lightblue	blocks.carpet.lightgray	blocks.carpet.lime
blocks.carpet.magenta	blocks.carpet.orange	blocks.carpet.pink
blocks.carpet.purple	blocks.carpet.red	blocks.carpet.white
blocks.carpet.yellow	blocks.carrots	blocks.cauldron
blocks.chest	blocks.chest_locked	blocks.chest_trapped
blocks.clay	blocks.coal_block	blocks.coal_ore
blocks.cobblestone	blocks.cobblestone_wall	blocks.cobweb
blocks.cocoa	blocks.command	blocks.crafting_table
blocks.dandelion	blocks.daylight_sensor	blocks.dead_bush
blocks.detector_rail	blocks.diamond	blocks.diamond_ore
blocks.dirt	blocks.dispenser	blocks.door_iron
blocks.door_wood	blocks.double_plant	blocks.dragon_egg
blocks.dropper	blocks.emerald	blocks.emerald_ore
blocks.enderchest	blocks.endportal	blocks.endportal_frame
blocks.endstone	blocks.farmland	blocks.fence
blocks.fence_gate	blocks.fire	blocks.flower_red
blocks.flower_yellow	blocks.flowerpot	blocks.furnace
blocks.furnace_burning	blocks.glass	blocks.glass_pane
blocks.glowstone	blocks.gold	blocks.gold_ore
blocks.grass	blocks.grass_tall	blocks.gravel
blocks.hardened_clay	blocks.hay	blocks.hopper
blocks.ice	blocks.iron	blocks.iron_bars
blocks.iron_ore	blocks.jackolantern	blocks.jukebox
blocks.jungle	blocks.ladder	blocks.lapis_lazuli_block
blocks.lapis_lazuli_ore	blocks.lava	blocks.lava_still
blocks.leaves	blocks.lever	blocks.lily_pad
blocks.melon	blocks.melon_stem	blocks.mobhead

TABLE 12.1 *continued*

blocks.monster_egg	blocks.monster_spawner	blocks.moss_stone
blocks.mushroom_brown	blocks.mushroom_brown_huge	blocks.mushroom_red
blocks.mushroom_red_huge	blocks.mycelium	blocks.nether
blocks.nether_fence	blocks.netherportal	blocks.netherquartzore
blocks.netherrack	blocks.netherwart	blocks.note
blocks.oak	blocks.obsidian	blocks.packed_ice
blocks.piston	blocks.piston_extn	blocks.potatoes
blocks.powered_rail	blocks.pressure_plate_stone	blocks.pressure_plate_weighted_heavy
blocks.pressure_plate_weighted_light	blocks.pressure_plate_wood	blocks.pumpkin
blocks.pumpkin_stem	blocks.quartz	blocks.rail
blocks.rail_activator	blocks.redeston_repeater_active	blocks.redstone
blocks.redstone_comparator	blocks.redstone_comparator_active	blocks.redstone_lamp
blocks.redstone_lamp_active	blocks.redstone_ore	blocks.redstone_ore_glowing
blocks.redstone_repeater	blocks.redstone_wire	blocks.rose
blocks.sand	blocks.sandstone	blocks.sapling
blocks.sapling.birch	blocks.sapling.jungle	blocks.sapling.oak
blocks.sapling.spruce	blocks.sign	blocks.sign_post
blocks.slab.birch	blocks.slab.brick	blocks.slab.cobblestone
blocks.slab.jungle	blocks.slab.netherbrick	blocks.slab.oak
blocks.slab.quartz	blocks.slab.sandstone	blocks.slab.snow
blocks.slab.spruce	blocks.slab.stone	blocks.slab.stonebrick
blocks.slab.wooden	blocks.slab.upper.birch	blocks.slab.upper.brick
blocks.slab.upper.cobblestone	blocks.slab.upper.jungle	blocks.slab.upper.netherbrick
blocks.slab.upper.oak	blocks.slab.upper.quartz	blocks.slab.upper.sandstone
blocks.slab.upper.spruce	blocks.slab.upper.stone	blocks.slab.upper.stonebrick
blocks.slab.upper.wooden	blocks.snow	blocks.soulsand
blocks.sponge	blocks.spruce	blocks.stained_clay.black
blocks.stained_clay.blue	blocks.stained_clay.brown	blocks.stained_clay.cyan
blocks.stained_clay.gray	blocks.stained_clay.green	blocks.stained_clay.lightblue

continued...

TABLE 12.1 *continued*

blocks.stained_clay.lightgray	blocks.stained_clay.lime	blocks.stained_clay.magenta
blocks.stained_clay.orange	blocks.stained_clay.pink	blocks.stained_clay.purple
blocks.stained_clay.red	blocks.stained_clay.white	blocks.stained_clay.yellow
blocks.stairs.birch	blocks.stairs.brick	blocks.stairs.cobblestone
blocks.stairs.jungle	blocks.stairs.nether	blocks.stairs.oak
blocks.stairs.quartz	blocks.stairs.sandstone	blocks.stairs.spruce
blocks.stairs.stone	blocks.sticky_piston	blocks.stone
blocks.stone_button	blocks.sugar_cane	blocks.table_enchantment
blocks.tnt	blocks.torch	blocks.torch_redstone
blocks.torch_redstone_active	blocks.trapdoor	blocks.tripwire
blocks.tripwire_hook	blocks.vines	blocks.water
blocks.water_still	blocks.wheat_seeds	blocks.wood
blocks.wool.black	blocks.wool.blue	blocks.wool.brown
blocks.wool.cyan	blocks.wool.gray	blocks.wool.green
blocks.wool.lightblue	blocks.wool.lightgray	blocks.wool.lime
blocks.wool.magenta	blocks.wool.orange	blocks.wool.pink
blocks.wool.purple	blocks.wool.red	blocks.wool.white
blocks.wool.yellow		

Moving Your Drone

TERM Axis

When drawing on paper, you draw in two dimensions. The two dimensions are width, which is along what's called the x-axis, and height, which is along the y-axis. In real life there is a third dimension, length, which is along the z-axis. The x-axis, y-axis, and z-axis make up the three dimensions.

A drone that doesn't move about and is built on only one location wouldn't be very interesting. You can direct the drone to move and even turn and place blocks in any direction. There are a couple of functions that you can use to move the drone along any axis.

Let's get familiar with some of the movement functions by using them first at the in-game prompt. To place a block of gold and then move two places to the right and place another block of gold, target a block and then issue the following command:

```
/js box(blocks.gold).right(2).box(blocks.gold)
```

The previous statement might look odd, but it's perfectly valid JavaScript. This style of calling functions one after another is called *chaining* because each period (.) forms a link in a chain of function calls. You can't call all functions in JavaScript like this, but you can call all of the drone's functions this way. Another term used by programmers to describe this style of function calling is *fluency*. As you'll see later, you can extend the abilities of the drone by adding your own functions that can be called in the same fluent way.

In the previous statement, there are three different function calls being made; the first call—**box(blocks.gold)**—creates a gold block. The **box()** function returns a **Drone** object that can be used to call other **Drone** functions. The next call—**.right(2)**—moves the drone right two blocks, and it too returns the same **Drone** object. The last call—**.box(blocks.gold)**—creates another gold block. If you were to plot this out on graph paper, it would look like **FIGURE 12.5**.

You could also write the previous code as three distinct statements like this:

```
/js var drone = box(blocks.gold);
/js drone.right(2);
/js drone.box(blocks.gold);
```

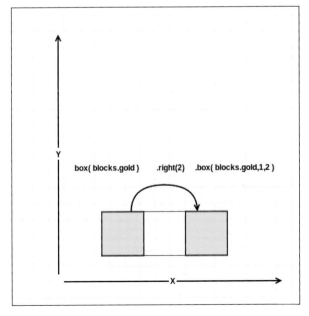

FIGURE 12.5 Moving the drone, graph paper plot

I personally prefer to write it using a single statement, `box(blocks.gold).right(2).box(blocks.gold)`, because it fits on one line and is slightly shorter than the three separate statements. Be careful, though, when writing such statements because the in-game command prompt accepts only a maximum of 100 letters for each command.

THE CORNERSTONE

If building just above ground level, it's a good idea to always place a block where you would like to build and then target that block before issuing any **Drone** functions. Think of the targeted block as the cornerstone of your building. If building on a flat world, you will first need to manually place a cornerstone block or else your building will begin in the ground instead of just above ground level (see **FIGURE 12.6**).

Let's use more chaining to create a series of three jumping platforms, each of which are two blocks apart. Target a block and then issue the following command:

```
/js box(blocks.gold).fwd(2)
  →.box(blocks.gold,1,2).fwd(2)
  →.box(blocks.gold,1,3)
```

This statement will create three platforms. The first platform will be one block high, the second platform will be two blocks high, and the third will be three blocks high. Since each platform is two blocks away, they are perfect for in-game jumping practice.

In **FIGURE 12.7** you can see how the pillars are constructed, and **FIGURE 12.8** shows how the jumping platforms look in the game.

FIGURE 12.6
A cornerstone

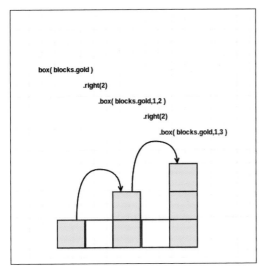

FIGURE 12.7 Jumping platforms on graph paper

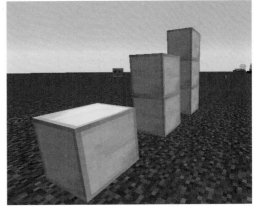

FIGURE 12.8 Jumping platforms

Turning Your Drone

In addition to moving your drone, you can make your drone change direction too. To change direction, use the **turn()** function. When turning, you always turn right 90 degrees. To turn around so you're facing the opposite way, turn twice **turn(2)**. To turn left, you need to turn right three times: **turn(3)**. You can combine turning, movement, and building in a single chained statement like this:

```
/js box(blocks.gold,1,1,4).fwd(4).turn()
  →.box(blocks.iron,1,1,3).fwd(3).turn()
  →.box(blocks.ice,1,1,2)
```

This command creates three small walls of gold, iron, and ice. In **FIGURE 12.9** you can see how the walls are constructed using a combination of **box()**, **turn()**, and **fwd()** function calls.

FIGURE 12.10 shows the result in Minecraft.

All of the drone's functions return the drone itself, so each function can chain directly onto another. If you want to find out more about the **Drone** object and its functions, you can refer to the **Drone** API Reference online at *http://scriptcraftjs. org/api#drone-plugin.*

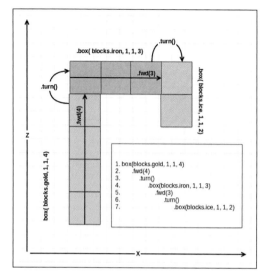

FIGURE 12.9 Three walls on graph paper

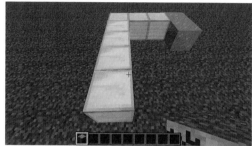

FIGURE 12.10 Turning and movement while building

Blueprints

A *blueprint* is a technical drawing of a building. Blueprints are created by architects when designing buildings. They are visual instructions used by the construction team to make sure they build what the architect designed. You can think of the code you write as a blueprint for the computer to execute. You are the designer of your program, and the computer must use those instructions to execute it. When we talk about building in Minecraft using a drone, your code is a blueprint the drone uses to build. How do you create a blueprint for a drone? A drone blueprint is just a JavaScript module. LISTING 12.1 is an example blueprint for a pyramid. You can see that it's not very different from the modules you've already been writing

Listing 12.1 will let you create pyramids by simply targeting a block in the game and issuing this command at the in-game prompt:

```
/js pyramid()
```

You can what the result looks like in FIGURE 12.11.

You'll dive deeper into drone blueprints in the next exercise—blueprint basics.

LISTING 12.1 A Blueprint for a Pyramid

```
var Drone = require('../drone').Drone;
var blocks = require('blocks');

function pyramid ( side ) {
  if ( !side ) {
    side = 30;
  }
  var i = side;
  this.chkpt('pyramid');

  while ( i > 0 ) {
    this.box( blocks.sandstone, i, 1, i)
      .up()
      .right()
      .fwd();
    i = i - 2;
  }

  this.move('pyramid');
}

Drone.extend( pyramid );
```

FIGURE 12.11 A pyramid

Blueprint Basics

Before designing your skyscraper, let's start with something a little smaller so you can better understand the basics of adding new blueprints for building in Minecraft. You'll start with a simple structure I'll call *monolith*. It will be a large black slab four blocks wide by nine blocks high by one block long. The monolith is from an old movie called *2001: A Space Odyssey*. In the movie, astronauts discover this large black slab of stone on the moon. I use it as an example here because it can be created using a single call to **Drone**'s **box()** method.

You've seen already that the drone has many functions for building, moving, and turning and that these functions can be chained together to perform complex building operations. What you haven't yet seen is that the drone can be extended; that is, new functions can be added to the drone and combined with existing functions. For example, wouldn't it be cool if once you have created a blueprint for a monolith, you could build a couple of them side-by-side using a single command? Well, the **Drone** API has a function called **extend()** that lets you do just that. Once you've created the monolith blueprint, you should be able to perform any of these commands (don't try to execute these right now—you haven't yet defined the **monolith()** function):

```
/js monolith()
/js monolith().fwd(4).monolith().fwd(4).monolith().fwd(4).
monolith()
```

In the first example you just call **monolith()** because any function that belongs to the **Drone** API is a global function, meaning it can be called without

LISTING 12.2 A Blueprint for a Monolith

```
var Drone = require('../drone').Drone;
var blocks = require('blocks');

function monolith( ) {
  this.box( blocks.wool.black, 4, 9, 1);
}
Drone.extend( monolith );
```

first calling **require()**. In the second example, you can see that once you've created the **monolith()** function you'll be able to use it in a drone building chain that forms part of a series of building commands. The second command sets up a series of monoliths like a line of dominoes. I'll explain how this works, but first let's create a new module called **monolith.js** and save it to the **scriptcraft/ plugins/drone/contribs** folder (see LISTING 12.2).

Once you've saved the file, issue the **js refresh()** command to reload your plugins. Then find a nice clear parcel of land in the game, place a cornerstone, and issue this command:

```
/js monolith()
```

In a very short time, an imposing black monolith will appear (see **FIGURE 12.12**). Now let's take a closer look at the **monolith.js** source code.

FIGURE 12.12 An imposing black monolith

Modules Needed for Blueprints

The first two lines of the `monolith.js` module load both the **Drone** and **blocks** modules. You may be wondering why I required `'../drone'` and not simply `'drone'`. The `../` part specifies to look for the **Drone** module in the folder above this one (also known as the *parent folder*). Remember, the `monolith.js` module is saved in the `scriptcraft/plugins/drone/contrib` folder. The **Drone** module is located in the `scriptcraft/plugins/drone` folder, so `require('../drone')` effectively says "Load the `drone.js` module from the parent folder `scriptcraft/plugins/drone`." The `../` part of the string means this is a *relative path*. A relative path is a file path in relation to where the module is located. In this instance, you're saying you want to load a module from the parent folder.

The other thing to note about the first `require()` statement is the trailing `.Drone` just after the call to `require()`. Every call to `require()` returns a module object with zero or more properties and methods. If you're interested in only one of the returned object's properties or methods, then you can just grab that one property using the dot-notation (adding a `.` and getting the property or method by name). The following statement is how all blueprints usually begin and access the **Drone** API, so if you're creating a blueprint of your own, you'll want to do this too:

```
var Drone = require('../drone').Drone;
```

The second `require()` call loads the **blocks** module, which provides useful names for all of the possible materials used for building—without the **blocks** module, you would need to memorize all of the data values for the building materials in Minecraft. There are online resources on the Minecraft wiki, but it's nice to be able to use memorable names in your code.

The next section of the code is the `monolith()` method. I call it a *method* because this function is not going to be a stand-alone function; instead, it will be attached to a drone. A method is just a function that belongs to an object. How does a method know what it belongs to? In JavaScript there is a special keyword—`this`—that refers to the object a function belongs to. I've mentioned objects previously, and you'll explore them in more detail in Chapter 14. For now, all you need to remember is that when you create a new function for building stuff in Minecraft, your function will in fact be a method and has privileged access to the **Drone** object.

```
this.box( blocks.wool.black, 4, 9, 1);
```

Inside the body of the `monolith()` method, you see the `this` keyword. Inside a **Drone** method, the `this` keyword always refers to a **Drone** object. To build a monolith, you need to be able to manipulate and control an existing **Drone** object just as you've already done in the command-prompt examples earlier. The difference is that within a method you must use the `this` keyword at the start of each **Drone** function call. It's important that inside the method you don't simply use `box()` but instead use `this.box()`. A call to the global `box()` function will actually return a new **Drone** object. When inside of a **Drone** method, you work under the assumption that a **Drone** object is already present, and you access it using the `this` keyword. When you use any of the **Drone** methods at the in-game prompt, you are controlling the drone from outside, whereas when you use the drone inside your method, you are effectively in the cockpit piloting the drone from within. That's why you need to use the `this` keyword.

```
Drone.extend( monolith );
```

Having declared the `monolith()` function, you turn it into a **Drone** method using the `Drone.extend()` function, which takes a function and turns it into a method, effectively attaching that function to itself so it can form part of a chain of calls. The drone is extensible—it is capable of taking on new blueprints and building using those blueprints. When you add a new function to the drone using the `extend()` method, it is as if the function were an integral part of the drone. As if by magic, the function becomes global and chainable and can be chained with any other **Drone** methods.

```
/js box(blocks.gold).fwd(2).monolith().fwd(4).turn().fwd(4).
monolith()
```

So, now you can see how easy it is to extend the drone to build new, interesting things in Minecraft. Let's build a skyscraper!

A Blueprint for a Skyscraper

You're going to create a blueprint for a skyscraper so that you can place skyscrapers anywhere in your world with just a single JavaScript function call. Let's create a new module called **skyscraper.js** and save it to the **scriptcraft/plugins/ drone/contribs** folder (see **LISTING 12.3**).

Once you've saved the file, issue the **js refresh()** command to reload your plugins. Then find a nice clear parcel of land in the game, place a cornerstone, and issue this command:

```
/js skyscraper()
```

LISTING 12.3 A Blueprint for a Skyscraper

```
var Drone = require('../drone').Drone;
var blocks = require('blocks');

function skyscraper( floors ) {
  var i = 0;
  if ( typeof floors == 'undefined' ) {
    floors = 10;
  }
  this.chkpt('skyscraper');
  for ( i = 0; i < floors; i++ ) {
    this
      .box( blocks.iron, 20, 1, 20)
      .up()
      .box0(blocks.glass_pane, 20, 3, 20)
      .up(3);
  }
  this.move('skyscraper');
}
Drone.extend( skyscraper );
```

In a short time, a 10-story skyscraper will appear. Impressive, no? You might already be thinking of new and wonderful buildings and structures to add to Minecraft, but before you start coding, let's take a closer look at the skyscraper code.

The `skyscraper()` Method

The first few lines of the `skyscraper()` method declare a variable `i` and check to see whether the `floors` parameter is set. If it isn't, then a default of 10 floors will be created. Next you see the first occurrence of the `this` keyword in the method. The `.chkpt()` method—which is short for "checkpoint"—bookmarks the drone's current location so it can return there later. It's a good idea to bookmark the drone's current location at the start of any method and to return to that location at the end of your method because—ideally—your method should be used only for building and not moving or turning the drone. You can of course turn and move the drone within your method, but you should return the drone to where it was before your method was called. The `.chkpt()` and `.move()` pair of functions will respectively save a drone's location before it goes on an excursion and return to the location when the excursion is done.

The next section of the method is a `for` loop that repeatedly does the following (for each floor):

1. Builds an iron floor 20 blocks wide by 1 block high by 20 blocks long

2. Moves up one block

3. Builds a glass-pane wall three blocks high on all four sides

4. Moves up another three blocks

These four steps are repeated for each floor so that when the `for` loop is done, an entire skyscraper has been constructed. You can see what just one floor of the skyscraper (one pass through the `for` loop) looks like in FIGURE 12.13.

At the end of the method, an entire skyscraper is constructed. FIGURE 12.14 shows what the result looks like in the game.

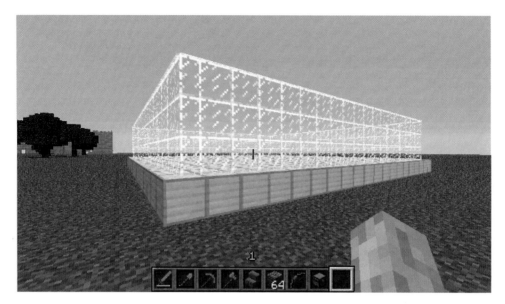

FIGURE 12.13 A single floor of the skyscraper

FIGURE 12.14 The complete skyscraper

Chaining in Source Files

At the in-game prompt you are limited to a single line for your code, so when chaining together a couple of **Drone** method calls, you need to write code like this:

```
/js box(block.iron, 20,1,20).up().box0(blocks.glass_pane, 20, 3, 20).up(3)
```

This can be difficult to read and understand. Fortunately, you have no such limits when writing code in source files and can have statements that span more than one line like this:

```
this
  .box( blocks.iron, 20, 1, 20)
  .up()
  .box0(blocks.glass_pane, 20, 3, 20)
  .up(3);
```

This is actually a single statement—notice that there's only a semicolon after the last line. The previous code could also be written on a single line, but breaking up the statement as shown earlier makes the code more readable. The previous code can also be written using multiple statements:

```
this.box( blocks.iron, 20, 1, 20);
this.up();
this.box0(blocks.glass_pane, 20, 3, 20);
this.up(3);
```

Since each of the **Drone** methods returns the **drone** object, it's possible to chain methods using the dot (**.**) character. It's largely a matter of personal taste which style you use. What's important is that your code is readable and understandable.

The box0() Method

The **box0()** method is another method provided by the drone; it's similar to **box()** except it creates only four walls and does not fill in the four walls. The **box0()** method is especially useful for constructing dwellings. It takes the same parameters as the **box()** method.

Achievement Unlocked!

Congratulations, Master Builder! You've just discovered how to build massive structures using JavaScript and some object extension magic.

Summary

In this chapter, you learned how to build large and complex buildings in Minecraft using ScriptCraft's **Drone** functions. You used JavaScript's **for** statement to construct a skyscraper with many floors. I touched on the topic of objects and methods, as well as JavaScript's **this** keyword and what it means when used inside a method.

Chapter 13

Create a Fireworks Show

IN THIS CHAPTER, you'll write code to create a spectacular fireworks show in Minecraft. You'll learn about ScriptCraft's built-in `fireworks` module and the `setTimeout()` function, and you'll use a powerful programming technique called *recursion*. You'll begin by writing code to launch a single firework after a delay of two seconds and then build on that code to launch many fireworks.

The fireworks Module

ScriptCraft includes a **fireworks** module that can be used to launch a single firework at a given location. You can use the **fireworks** module directly at the in-game command prompt like this:

```
/js var fireworks = require('fireworks')
/js fireworks.firework( self.location )
```

The **fireworks** module's **firework()** function takes a single parameter—a location—and launches a firework at that location. A location in Minecraft is any place in the game. Most objects, such as players, animals, blocks, and so on, have a location. When I pass the parameter **self.location**, I am passing my own location, meaning the firework will launch from where I am in the game. I urge you to run the previous commands and then look directly up to see the firework explode.

Deferred Execution

In the commands you just executed at the in-game prompt, the firework launches immediately. What you'd like to do is delay the launch by a couple of seconds so that you can move to a safe position with a better view. Fortunately, there's a way to delay the execution of a function. Create a new file called **scriptcraft/plugins/fireworkshow.js** and type in the code shown in LISTING 13.1.

Save the file and then issue the **js refresh()** command to reload your JavaScript plugins. Now issue this command to launch a firework:

```
/js fireworkshow( self.location )
```

Move back a couple of steps so you can better see the firework. Did you notice the firework did not launch immediately? There was a delay of two seconds.

LISTING 13.1 A Short Fireworks Show

```
var fireworks = require('fireworks');
function fireworkshow (location){
  function launch(){
    fireworks.firework(location);
  }
  setTimeout(launch, 2000);
}

exports.fireworkshow = fireworkshow;
```

The `setTimeout()` Function

The `setTimeout()` function lets you delay calling of a function. It takes two parameters.

- A function that it should eventually call.
- A delay. The delay is measured in milliseconds. There are 1,000 milliseconds in a second, so a delay of 2,000 is equal to 2 seconds.

`setTimeout()` returns a value that can be used to stop the timed function from executing. To stop a function you've scheduled to execute, you need to store the value returned by `setTimeout()` in a variable and pass this value to the `clearTimeout()` function like this:

```
js function later(){ console.log('I ran!') };
js var scheduled = setTimeout( later, 30000 );
js clearTimeout( scheduled );
```

The `later()` function in the previous code won't execute because the *scheduled* task for running that function is canceled when you call `clearTimeout( scheduled )`.

Although `setTimeout()` is not part of the JavaScript language, it is provided with web browsers and Node.js, and it's implemented in ScriptCraft too. A common mistake when using `setTimeout()` is to assume that the delay is in seconds rather than milliseconds.

A Fireworks Show

I promised you a fireworks show at the start of this chapter. A single firework that launches isn't much of a show, is it? Let's fix that. The next step is to change your code so that it launches many fireworks with a two-second gap between each launch. Change your **fireworkshow.js** file so it matches **LISTING 13.2**.

Then issue the **/js refresh()** command and at the in-game command prompt issue the following command:

    /js fireworkshow(self.location, 5)

Move back a couple of steps and watch the show as five fireworks are launched one after another. The show should end after the fifth firework has launched. You can change the number of fireworks launched by changing the second parameter.

LISTING 13.2   A Longer Fireworks Show

```
var fireworks = require('fireworks');
function fireworkshow( location, count ) {

  function launch( ){
    fireworks.firework( location );
    count = count - 1;
    if ( count > 0 ) {
      setTimeout( launch, 2000 );
    }
  }

  setTimeout( launch, 2000 );
}


exports.fireworkshow = fireworkshow;
```

Me, a Name I Call Myself

A function that calls itself is called a *recursive* function. Recursive functions can be powerful. They can be used for visiting all files and folders on a disk or drawing pretty fractal diagrams. Recursion is beyond the scope of this book, so I won't go into great detail. To get a taste for what recursion is about, imagine a computer program that controls a robot arm that opens a Russian doll and keeps opening any Russian dolls inside that until there are no more Russian dolls inside. The code for such a program might read like this:

```
function openRussianDoll( doll ){
  console.log( doll.size );
  if ( doll.inner ) {
    openRussianDoll( doll.inner );
  }
}
```

The **openRussianDoll()** function wouldn't be called just once or twice but would be called every time a new doll was uncovered. This is the power of recursion. If you're curious about recursion, a few people have created some very cool fractals in Minecraft using recursion. Malin Christersson has some example code at *https://github.com/malinc/MinecraftFractals*. You can see an example of one of Malin's fractal creations in **FIGURE 13.1**.

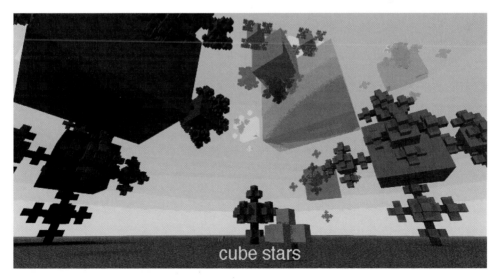

FIGURE 13.1 Malin Christersson's Fractal Cube Stars

Canceling the Fireworks Show

Let's say you kicked off a long-running fireworks show and after a while you get bored and want to *cancel* the show. There are two ways to schedule a repeating task in JavaScript. One way is to use **setTimeout()** *and have* a function that calls itself. You've already seen this in the earlier example. Another way is to use the **setInterval()** function, which is like **setTimeout()** except it will keep executing the task after each delay instead of executing only once after the delay. Let's take a look at an example of using **setInterval()** at the server console prompt.

```
js function askQuestion(){ console.log('Are we there yet?') }
js var scheduled = setInterval( askQuestion, 1000 )
```

Run the previous commands, and you will see an "Are we there yet?" message appear every second.

```
[19:24:00 INFO]: [scriptcraft] Are we there yet?
[19:24:01 INFO]: [scriptcraft] Are we there yet?
[19:24:02 INFO]: [scriptcraft] Are we there yet?
[19:24:03 INFO]: [scriptcraft] Are we there yet?
[19:24:04 INFO]: [scriptcraft] Are we there yet?
[19:24:05 INFO]: [scriptcraft] Are we there yet?
[19:24:06 INFO]: [scriptcraft] Are we there yet?
```

The message will keep printing out for as long as the server is running. Fortunately, there's a way to cancel this scheduled function. At the server console prompt, issue the following command:

```
js clearInterval( scheduled )
```

The messages will stop appearing. Phew! The **setInterval()** function is useful for scheduling tasks that you want the computer to do every so often. Let's update the **fireworkshow.js** module so that it looks like LISTING 13.3.

In Listing 13.3 you no longer rely on recursion to repeatedly launch fireworks. Instead, you use the **setInterval()** function to repeatedly call **launch()**. Inside the **launch()** function, you subtract 1 from the count, and if count is zero, then you cancel the show using the **clearInterval()** function. The difference between this version of the **fireworkshow** module and the previous version is that now you can cancel the show earlier than planned because the **fireworkshow()** function returns the scheduled task, which you can cancel at any time. Save Listing 13.3 and issue the **/js refresh()** command to reload

LISTING 13.3 Using **setInterval()** and **clearInterval()** to Create a Fireworks Show

```
var fireworks = require('fireworks');
function fireworkshow( location, count ) {

  function launch( ) {
    fireworks.firework( location );
    count = count - 1;
    if ( count == 0 ) {
      clearInterval(scheduled);
    }
  }
  var scheduled = setInterval( launch, 2000 );
  return scheduled;
}

exports.fireworkshow = fireworkshow;
```

your plugins. Then at the in-game prompt issue the following command to launch an extended fireworks show:

```
/js var show = fireworkshow( self.location, 300 );
```

The previous statements start a fireworks show in which there will be 300 launches each two seconds apart. The show will go on for about 10 minutes if left alone, but you're going to cancel the show early. Issue the following command to cancel the show:

```
/js clearInterval( show );
```

The fireworks will cease. If you ever schedule tasks using the **setInterval()** or **setTimeout()** function, it's always a good idea to keep the value returned by these functions so that you have the option of canceling the task using **clearInterval()** and **clearTimeout()**, respectively.

Summary

In this chapter, you learned about the **setTimeout()** function and how to use it to delay or "defer" execution of your code. You also learned how to make a function call itself and how to schedule repeating tasks using the **setInterval()** function.

Chapter 14

Animal Sounds Revisited

IN THIS CHAPTER, you'll revisit the Animal Sounds plugin from earlier, but this time, instead of using a `switch` statement, you'll use a lookup table.

Objects

It's time to take a closer look at objects. An *object* in JavaScript is something that can hold both data and functions. You've already been using objects throughout this book. You used the **console** object to log messages to the Minecraft server log and console window. You used the **exports** object to provide new properties and functions for others to use. You used array objects to sort arrays with **sort()**. Last but not least, you used some of Minecraft's built-in objects such as **Player** and **Event** to respond to events that happen in the game.

Objects are useful in programming. Java—the language Minecraft is written in—is an *object-oriented* language. This means in Java *everything* is an object—players, worlds, blocks, tools, recipes, and so on. Objects let you group related *properties* and *functions*. For example, a player:

- Has a food level (how much food they have)
- Can have a bed
- Has an experience level
- Can perform commands
- Can fly
- Can sneak

...and so on. In programming terms, something that the player *has* is called a *property*, while something that the player *does* is called a *method*. Methods are just functions that belong to an object.

How to Make an Object

In JavaScript creating a new object is easy. Here's an example you can try at the in-game prompt:

```
/js var myFirstObject = { name: 'steve', job: 'minecrafter' }
```

To create an object in JavaScript, you start with the curly brace ({) followed by a *key*, which is followed by a colon (:) and then a value. You can separate each key-value pair using the comma (,). You finish the object definition with a closing curly brace (}). The object example shown previously has two key-value pairs. It has a *name* and a *job*. You can find out what's inside an object if you know its keys.

```js
/js myFirstObject.name
> "steve"
```

```js
/js myFirstObject.job
> "minecrafter"
```

JavaScript is quite a flexible language. You've already seen how you can use square brackets ([ ]) to access items in an array. You can use the same square bracket notation to get object values.

```js
/js myFirstObject["name"]
> "steve"
```

```js
/js myFirstObject["job"]
> "minecrafter"
```

This means you can also access object keys using variables rather than string literals.

```js
/js var key = "name";
/js myFirstObject[key]
> "steve"
```

Even if you don't already know what keys an object has, you can find out using a special form of **for** loop.

```js
/js for (var key in myFirstObject){ self.sendMessage( key ) }
```

You can even use this form of **for** loop to process all the keys *and values* of an object.

```js
function displayObject ( object ) {
  var value = null;
  var key = null;
  for ( key in object ) {
    value = object[ key ];
    console.log( key + ' = ' + value );
  }
}
```

When you create an object like this, this is known as an *object literal.*

```
/js var myFirstObject = { name: 'steve', job: 'minecrafter' }
```

There are other ways to create objects in JavaScript, but in this book we'll focus on object literals only. You can add a new key to an existing JavaScript object easily.

```
/js myFirstObject.toolOfChoice = 'Axe'
```

You can also delete a key from an object using the **delete** keyword.

```
/js delete myFirstObject.toolOfChoice
```

There are no rules about what keys you can add or remove from a JavaScript object because JavaScript does not enforce strict rules about such things. JavaScript is a *dynamically typed* language, which means you can create new objects on the fly and add and remove keys from them and change the key's value types while your program is running.

Two Kinds of Objects

When programming plugins using ScriptCraft, you have two different types of objects available to you. ScriptCraft uses a special version of JavaScript that is available from within any Java program. This means that from within your JavaScript plugins, you not only can use JavaScript objects but can also access and use all of the *Java* objects available via the *CanaryMod* API. Unlike JavaScript, Java *does* have strict rules about what you can and cannot do with Java objects. Java is *strictly typed*—it does not let you add or remove properties from Java objects, and it enforces strict rules about types and variables. For example, the **self** object that you've used for some command-prompt examples in this book is a *Java* object, so while you can access the object's keys like this:

```
/js self.isOnGround
> true
```

...you could not *add* new keys to the object like this:

```
/js self.favoriteFood = 'Pizza'
```

This would display a Java error, while attempting to delete a key from a Java object, like so, will fail silently:

```
/js delete self.isOnGround
```

The key will *not* be deleted.

Objects as Lookup Tables

In JavaScript it's easy for programmers to create objects, and JavaScript can *look up* object keys quickly. A lookup table is anything you *look up* to find information. For example, you look up a word in a dictionary to find out what the word means, or you look up a name in a phone book to find out that person's phone number.

In the following example, you're going to change the **animalSounds.js** module from Chapter 10 and use an object instead of a **switch** statement. Open the **animalSounds.js** file located in the **scriptcraft/plugins** folder and edit it so it matches **LISTING 14.1**.

Listing 14.1 creates a new object called **noises**.

LISTING 14.1 A Lookup Table of Animal Sounds

```
var sounds = require('sounds');
var input = require('input');

var noises = {
  cat: sounds.catMeow,
  chicken: sounds.chickenSay,
  cow: sounds.cowSay,
  'ender dragon': sounds.enderdragonGrowl,
                        continued...
```

Let's take a look at the **noises** variable declared near the top of this module.

```
var noises = {
  cat: sounds.catMeow,
  chicken: sounds.chickenSay,
  cow: sounds.cowSay,
  'ender dragon': sounds.enderdragonGrowl,
  pig: sounds.pigSay,
  sheep: sounds.sheepSay,
  wolf: sounds.wolfBark
};
```

LISTING 14.1 *continued*

```
    pig: sounds.pigSay,
    sheep: sounds.sheepSay,
    wolf: sounds.wolfBark
};
function onInput( animal, player ) {
    var makeNoise = null;
    animal = animal.toLowerCase();

    if ( animal in noises ) {

        makeNoise = noises[ animal ];
        makeNoise( player.location );

    } else {

        echo( player, "I never heard of a " + animal);

    }
};


exports.animalSounds = function( player ) {
    input( player,
            "What's your favorite animal" +
            " - cat, chicken, cow, ender dragon, pig, sheep or wolf?",
            onInput );
};
```

■

There are a few points to note about this statement:

- The statement creates a single object. Like many statements in JavaScript, it can span more than one line. Having the object definition span more than one line makes the code more readable.

- The `noises` object has the following keys: `cat`, `chicken`, `cow`, `ender dragon`, `pig`, `sheep`, `wolf`. Keys are always on the left side in an object literal.

- The keys do not need to have quote marks around them, but if the key contains whitespace—for example `'ender dragon'`—then it should be enclosed in either single or double quotes.

- You cannot use JavaScript keywords as keys in an object, so the literal values `true`, `false`, `default`, and so on, can't be used.

- Keys must be of type number or string. You cannot have another object as a key in an object; you can, however, have another object as a value in an object.

- Values in objects *can* be of any type—even functions and other objects! When an object contains another object as a value, that value is called a *nested object*. You'll see an example of a nested object later.

- Every key-value pair must be separated with a single comma (`,`). Try to avoid putting an extra comma at the end of the last key-value pair. There is no comma after the last key-value pair `wolf: sounds.wolfBark` because it is not needed and some versions of JavaScript will report an error if they see an extra comma just before the closing curly brace (`}`).

Having created the `noises` lookup table, you use it in the `onInput()` function to see whether the animal the player typed is in the `noises` object. The following `if` statement checks to see whether the animal is in the `noises` table:

```
if ( animal in noises ) {
```

This *key in object* construct will look up the object and return `true` if `key` is in it. If the animal is not in the lookup table, the function reports it hasn't heard of that animal. If it is in the lookup table, it gets the appropriate `noise` function.

```
makeNoise = noises[ animal ];
```

Each value in the `noises` table is a function, so when you look up an animal in the `noises` table, what you get back is a function that, when called, will emit that animal's noise. So, `makeNoise` is a variable that will point to a function that emits an animal noise. This is yet another example of the use of functions as data. In this case, the functions are values in a lookup table. This is a powerful idea in computer programming. In the next statement in the function, you invoke the function you've just found in the lookup table, passing in the player's location as the place where you want the sound to play.

```
makeNoise( player.location );
```

The remaining parts of the module are unchanged from the previous version.

Why Use a Lookup Table Instead of a `switch` Statement?

There are a few reasons why you should use a lookup table instead of a `switch` statement.

■ Adding new sounds is easier if you need to change only the data in the lookup table, not the code in the `onInput` function.

■ Changing code is error prone. Every time you have to change the `onInput` function because you want to support a new sound, you run the risk of introducing errors into the code.

■ There are many sounds in Minecraft. If you were to support each sound using a `switch` statement, you'd need to add a case for every sound. The `switch` statement would grow quite large. On the other hand, adding a single key-value pair to the lookup table is comparatively easier. Because it's data, you could expose the lookup table for use outside of this module and allow other modules or parts of the program to add and remove sounds. The `onInput()` function no longer needs to concern itself with what's in the lookup table, making the function shorter and more maintainable.

Objects and References

One thing to note about objects and variables is that when you assign a new variable to an existing object, you don't make a copy of the object. For example, in ScriptCraft, when you execute JavaScript statements at the in-game or server prompt, there's a special variable called `self`, which refers to the player (or console operator) who is currently executing the statement. If you assign a new variable to be the same as `self`, then you are really only adding a new name for the same thing. You're not making a copy. So, for example, the following does not create a clone of the player:

```
/js var me = self;
```

It merely adds a new JavaScript name for the player object. You are adding a new *reference* to the player. The variables `me` and `self` both point to the same thing. The same is true no matter how many variables you add.

If I have more than one variable that refers to the same object, then I can control or change that object through any of the variables that refer to it (also known as *references*). This means if I have three variables (`me`, `self`, and `walter`), all of which refer to the same player (see **FIGURE 14.1**), I can make that player chat by using any of the following statements:

```
/js me.chat('Hi!');
```

or

```
/js self.chat('Hi!');
```

or

```
/js walter.chat('Hi!');
```

This is an important point to remember when passing around variables that refer to objects. When you change the `.flying` property for *any* of the `me`, `self`, and `walter` variables, you effectively change it for *all* of them because they all refer to the same object. As an example, execute each of the following commands and make a note of the results:

```
/js player.displayName;
/js self.displayName;
/js player.displayName = 'steeeeve';
/js player.displayName
/js self.displayName
```

When you change the **player** object or call any of its methods, the changes are reflected in all of the variables that refer to the object.

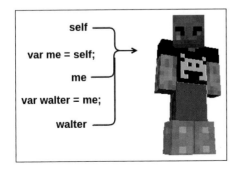

FIGURE 14.1 Objects and references: `Player`

Objects as Parameters

In JavaScript, when you pass an object as a parameter to a function, the object is passed *by reference*. This means a reference to the original object is passed, not a copy of the object. To illustrate this, let's imagine you have a function that will restore a player's health. Try this yourself at the in-game prompt. Make your game mode creative by issuing the `/gamemode survival` command and then issue the following command:

```
/js self.health = 20;
```

Your health is fully restored. Now let's create a function called **boost** that you can use to boost a player's health. The first draft of the function will look like this:

```
/js function boost( health ) { health = 20; }
```

Now try to run this function (while your health is low) by issuing the following command:

```
/js boost( self.health );
```

Did anything happen?

The reason nothing happens when you call the **boost()** function is because in this first draft of the function, you only change the boolean value passed in as a parameter. Setting the **health** parameter to **20** has no effect on the object because you haven't passed the object as a reference. Instead, you've passed the object's **health** property. Let's revisit the **boost()** function, this time changing it so that it takes an object instead.

```
/js function boost( player ) { player.health = 20; }
```

You're also going to change how you call the **drop()** function. This time you'll pass the **self** variable instead.

```
/js boost(self);
```

Now the **boost()** function works because you've passed a reference to the object, so any changes to the object inside the function act upon the object. This is an important point to remember: If you want to change an object within a function, you must accept the object as a parameter, not just the object's property you want to change.

Nested Objects

Objects in JavaScript can contain *any* kind of data, even—as previously mentioned—other objects! Recall the Russian doll code from Chapter 13 when I talked about recursion. If you were to *model* the data for a Russian doll, it might look something like this:

```
var largeDoll = {
    size: 'large',
    inner: {
        size: 'Medium',
        inner: {
            size: 'Small',
            inner: {
                size: 'Tiny',
                inner: null
            }
        }
    }
};
```

This is an example of an object that has objects *nested* within it, just like a Russian doll has other dolls inside it. In this example you have a **Large** doll housing a **Medium** doll housing a **Small** doll and so on. The innermost **Tiny** doll has an *inner* property of **null**, meaning there's nothing inside. The previous code could also be written as a series of statements, each creating a distinct object like this:

```
var tinyDoll = { size: 'Tiny', inner: null };
var smallDoll = { size: 'Small', inner: tinyDoll };
var mediumDoll = { size: 'Medium', inner: smallDoll };
var largeDoll = { size: 'Large', inner: mediumDoll };
```

Regardless of how the **largeDoll** object is created, its structure will be the same in both cases. You could use this **largeDoll** object as a parameter to the **openRussianDoll()** recursive function you defined earlier in Chapter 13. To put this to the test, create a new file **russiandoll.js** in the **scriptcraft/plugins** folder and type the code in **LISTING 14.2**.

Save the file and issue the **js refresh()** command to reload your plugins; then at the server console issue the following command:

```
js openDoll()
```

LISTING 14.2 A Russian Doll

```javascript
var tinyDoll = { size: 'Tiny', inner: null };
var smallDoll = { size: 'Small', inner: tinyDoll };
var mediumDoll = { size: 'Medium', inner: smallDoll };
var largeDoll = { size: 'Large', inner: mediumDoll };

function openRussianDoll( doll ){
  console.log( doll.size );
  if ( doll.inner ) {
    openRussianDoll( doll.inner );
  }
}

function openDoll(){
  openRussianDoll( largeDoll );
}
exports.openDoll = openDoll;
```

You should see the following output on your screen:

```
> Large
> Medium
> Small
> Tiny
```

Try changing the value passed to **openRussianDoll** from **largeDoll** to **mediumDoll**, **smallDoll**, or **tinyDoll** and see what happens.

JSON

I can't talk about objects in JavaScript without mentioning JSON. JSON is short for JavaScript Object Notation and refers to how objects are constructed using the object literal style you've already seen. JSON has become popular among web programmers because it is an efficient way to send data back and forth between a web browser and a web server. Any time you see an object literal like this, you're looking at JSON:

```
var steve = { "name": "steve", "occupation": "miner" }
```

There is also a built-in `JSON` module that provides methods to do the following:

- Let programmers print out an object in a way which is *somewhat* readable by humans
- Read a string of JSON output and convert it from a string back into an object

You'll learn more about JSON and loading and saving data later in the book.

Achievement Unlocked!

Congratulations! You've discovered the power of objects in JavaScript and how to create efficient lookups. Your plugin development apprenticeship is complete!

Summary

In this chapter, you learned how to create objects and how to access and lookup objects based on property names. You also learned about nested objects. This is the final chapter in the "Basic Modding" part of the book. Next, you move on to advanced modding.

Part III

Advanced Modding

THIS PART OF THE BOOK will focus on event-driven programming and using CanaryMod's API. The Minecraft game is very customizable because CanaryMod provides so many ways to change the game. The CanaryMod API is a collection of functions and data types that let plugin developers create exciting new additions to Minecraft. In the following chapters, you'll learn how to explore the extensive CanaryMod API using the online documentation and how to better understand the types of data provided by CanaryMod.

Chapter 15

Saving Player Preferences

IN THIS CHAPTER, you'll learn how to load and save player preferences. You'll create a new command that lets players choose which color they would like to use for in-game chat. The color they choose will be saved so that when the player disconnects or the server is restarted, the player's choice of text color is restored.

A Day in the Life of a Minecraft Plugin

Minecraft plugins lead a busy life behind the scenes. A typical large public server might have many Minecraft plugins installed, and some or all of those plugins might be turned on or off while the server is running. All plugins are *loaded* automatically when the server starts up, and all plugins are *unloaded* automatically just before the server shuts down. Plugins are executable code that add behavior and settings to the game. Plugins often have to manage *data*, player preferences, settings, and so on. What happens to that data when the plugin is loaded and unloaded? This is the question I'll answer in the coming sections.

Chat Colors

In this chapter you're going to add a new command to the game so that players can choose the color they'd like to use in chat messages. Players will be able to choose from more than a dozen colors. You want the player's choice of color to be saved so that when the server shuts down and is started up again, the same color is chosen for that player. The new command will be called `/jsp chatcolor` and will support tab completion so that when the player hits the Tab key, a list of colors will be displayed. You encountered the `/jsp` command in Chapter 11. This command is a prefix (something that is added at the start) for new custom commands.

Tab Completion for Custom Commands

One of the nice things about issuing commands at the in-game or server console prompt in Minecraft is *tab completion*—the ability to have the program fill in the remaining parts of a command without you having to type the entire command yourself. You can create your own custom commands that support tab completion quite easily in JavaScript. Let's create an example command at the in-game prompt that avails of tab completion. This custom command will be called `jsp icecream` and will prompt the player to enter a flavor when the Tab key is hit.

The first thing you need to do is say what the possible flavors can be. You'll do this by creating an array called **flavors**.

```
/js var flavors = ['chocolate','strawberry','vanilla'];
```

Next you create a new function that will be executed when a player issues the command. (Although presented here as multiple lines, the following code should be entered on a single line.)

```
/js function icecream( args, player ){
      echo(player,'Yum ! ' + args[0] )
    }
```

And finally you create a new custom command that will allow players to issue an **icecream** command that prompts them to choose flavors.

```
/js command( icecream, flavors );
```

Now try it and see what happens when you type the following and hit the Tab key:

```
/jsp ice
```

Hitting the Tab key should complete the first part of the command, so now your command prompt input looks like this:

```
/jsp icecream
```

Now press the spacebar and then press the Tab key once more; you'll see a list of possible flavors to choose from. You can cycle through the list of flavors by repeatedly pressing the Tab key. How did you do this? The secret is in how you created the new **/jsp icecream** command using the **command()** function. The **command()** function takes two parameters:

- The function that will be executed when a player issues the command. This function in turn takes two parameters: **args**, which is an array of strings, and **player**, which is the player who issued the command. The function *must* have a name because the function's name is used by the **command()** function to present a new command name for players with a prefix of **jsp** followed by a space. So, while the name of the command you define is **icecream**, players must use **jsp icecream** when issuing the command.

- A list of possible options for the command. This is the list of strings used by Minecraft's tab completion feature.

In upcoming sections you're going to create a new command that provides a list of colors as possible options that will display when the player hits the Tab key.

Choosing Chat Color

The color of text messages in Minecraft can be changed by using a special § symbol known as the Section symbol. This symbol can't be entered in Minecraft itself; it's used only internally by Minecraft and plugin developers. There are 16 different colors you can use for chat messages, and each color must use a special *code*. For example, to say "Hello" using yellow text, you would need to put the special code \xa7a in front of the message. You can try this by issuing the following command at the in-game prompt:

```
/js echo(self,'\xa7aHello');
```

The text \xa7 is just another way of writing the § symbol in JavaScript. The first character following \xa7 should be a number between 0 and 9 *or* a letter in the range *a* through *f*.

How You Count

We typically count in what's called *base 10*, which means numbers start at 0 and go all the way up to 9. If you want to write a number bigger than 9, then you add another digit on the left. So, the number 475 is as follows:

4 times 100 +

7 times 10 +

5 times 1

We count in base 10 because that's the numbering system the Romans used. Why did they use base 10? It might be because of how many digits we have on our hands, but I don't know for sure. There are other ways to count. Base 2—also known as *binary*—has just two numbers, 0 and 1. How would you count to 5 with just two numbers? When you reach 1, you can add a digit on the left. Here's an example:

- 0 in binary is equal to 0 in decimal.
- 1 in binary is equal to 1 in decimal.
- 10 in binary is equal to 2 in decimal.
- 11 in binary is equal to 3 in decimal.
- 100 in binary is equal to 4 in decimal.
- 101 in binary is equal to 5 in decimal, and so on.

Another base that's more commonly used by programmers is hexadecimal, or base 16. In hexadecimal (often shortened to just *hex*), the numbers 10 through 15 are substituted with the letters *a* through *f*, so the sequence of numbers 0 through 32 looks like **TABLE 15.1**.

Character Codes

The characters displayed in Minecraft and in other programs on your computer have a *code* that the computer uses internally. The letter *A* has the character code 65, *B* is 66, and so on. The lowercase alphabet starts at number 97, so *a* is character code 97, *b* is 98, and so on. You can see a full list of characters and their codes at *http://en.wikipedia.org/wiki/ISO/IEC_8859-1*.

Text Colors in Minecraft

The special § symbol has the character code 167, and Minecraft uses this special character at the start of a string to mean the string should be displayed in a certain color. The exact color is one of the 16 possible colors listed in **TABLE 15.2** (also available at *http://minecraft.gamepedia.com/Formatting_codes*).

In the first part of this chapter, you'll create a module that will be used to provide a list of color names, and you'll create a **colorize()** function that will add color to any chat message. In your editor, create a new file called **textcolors.js** in the **scriptcraft/modules** folder and type in the code in **LISTING 15.1**.

Once you've saved this file and reloaded the plugin using **js refresh()**, test it by issuing the following commands at the in-game prompt to display a message in gold (see **FIGURE 15.1**):

```
/js var textcolors = require('textcolors');
/js var goldText = textcolors.colorize( 'gold', 'I am gold!' );
/js echo(self, goldText);
```

FIGURE 15.1 Creating gold text

TABLE 15.1 Hexadecimal Numbers and Their Decimal Equivalents

HEXADECIMAL	DECIMAL
0	0
1	1
2	2
3	3
4	4
5	5
6	6
7	7
8	8
9	9
a	10
b	11
c	12
d	13
e	14
f	15
10	16
11	17
12	18
13	19
14	20
15	21
16	22
17	23
18	24
19	25
1a	26
1b	27
1c	28
1d	29
1e	30
1f	31
20	32

TABLE 15.2 Text Colors and Their Hexadecimal Equivalent

COLOR	HEX CODE
Black	0
Dark Blue	1
Dark Green	2
Dark Aqua	3
Dark Red	4
Dark Purple	5
Gold	6
Gray	7
Dark Gray	8
Blue	9
Green	a
Aqua	b
Red	c
Light Purple	d
Yellow	e
White	f

LISTING 15.1 Text Colors Module

```
var names = [
  'black',
  'darkblue',
  'darkgreen',
  'darkaqua',
  'darkred',
  'darkpurple',
  'gold',
  'gray',
  'darkgray',
  'blue',
  'green',
  'aqua',
  'red',
  'lightpurple',
  'yellow' ,
  'white'
];

function colorize( color, text ) {
  var index = names.indexOf( color );
  if (index >= 0){
    return '\xa7' + index.toString(16) + text;
  } else {
    return text;
  }
}

exports.names = names;
exports.colorize = colorize;
```

The module in Listing 15.1 exports the **names** array and the **colorize()** function for use by others. The **names** array will be used later to provide hints to players who want to change their chat color using tab completion. The **colorize()** function will take a color name and text and add the necessary color codes to the start of the text so that it will be displayed in color in the chat window. It does this by searching for the color in the **names** array using the **Array.indexOf()** method, which will return the position of the matching color in the array. For example, **names.indexOf('darkgreen')** would return 2. Remember, arrays begin at index 0, not 1, so **'black'** is at index 0, **'darkblue'** is at index 1, and so on. The **Array.indexOf()** method will return –1 if the item is not found in the array. If the **colorize()** function is passed a color that does not exist in the **names** array, then the text is unchanged—no color code will be added to the text.

The index of the color is important because that number is converted to a hexadecimal value using the **Number.toString(16)** method. This value along with the special § symbol, which is written as **\xa7**, combine to form the color code that is inserted in front of the original text. The **colorize()** function is a perfect example of how functions can be used to package up tricky code that you don't want to have to write more than once. It's much easier to simply write **colorize('gold','I am gold!')** than to write **\xa76I am gold!'**. Having to memorize all 16 color codes and the special **\xa7** prefix code every time you wanted to write colored text would be difficult. That's why you wrap up this code inside an easy-to-use function and *export* it so other modules and plugins can use it.

The following are the next steps in writing the Chat Color plugin:

1. Provide a new command so players can choose their color.

2. Add an event handler so that chat messages are colored according to a player's preferences.

In your editor, create a new file called **chatcolor.js** in the **scriptcraft/plugins** folder and type the code in LISTING 15.2.

LISTING 15.2 Setting and Applying Player Chat Color Preferences

```
var textcolors = require('textcolors');
var preferences = { };

function chatcolor ( args, player ) {
  var color = args[0];
  preferences[ player.name ] = color;
}
command( chatcolor, textcolors.names );

function onChat( event ) {
  var player = event.player;
  var playerChatColor = preferences[ player.name ];
  if ( playerChatColor ) {
    event.message = textcolors.colorize( playerChatColor,
                                         event.message );
  }
}
events.chat( onChat );
```

In this plugin you use the **textcolors** module you created earlier, and you create a new **preferences** variable that is an empty object, { }. This **preferences** object will be used to store each player's preferred color. Let's say you have a server with three players who have chosen custom chat colors. In such a scenario the **preferences** object might look something like this:

```
{
    "steve1901": "blue",
    "jane1908": "gold",
    "john1911": "red"
}
```

...where **steve1901** is the name of a player and **blue** is his chosen chat color, **jane1908** is the name of another player and her chosen chat color is **gold**, and so on. The **preferences** object is a lookup table of player names and their colors. If I wanted to find out what player **jane1908**'s chosen color was, I'd do so using the expression **preferences["jane1908"]**, which would return "gold."

The **chatcolor()** function is a *callback* that will be called when a player issues the **jsp chatcolor** command. The name of the player who issued the command and the color they chose are stored in the **preferences** object using the following statement:

```
preferences[ player.name ] = color;
```

You can add any property you like to an object by using the square brackets (**[ ]**) and putting the property name inside the square brackets. The property name does not have to be an object literal like **'age'** or **'address'**; it can be any JavaScript expression that evaluates to a string. So in this case, the player's name becomes a new property of the preferences object—a key by which the preferences can be looked up.

The **command()** function creates a new **/jsp chatcolor** command, which will invoke the **chatcolor()** function and which will provide the **textcolors.names** array as a list of color names as hints when the player hits the Tab key.

The first section of Listing 15.2 up to and including the call to **command()** sets up the preferences and a command to set color preferences. The next section of the module is concerned with what happens when a player chats in Minecraft and ensures that player color preferences are applied to any chat messages.

```
function onChat( event ) {
  var player = event.player;
  var playerChatColor = preferences[ player.name ];
  if ( playerChatColor ) {
    event.message = textcolors.colorize( playerChatColor,
                                         event.message );
  }
}
events.chat( onChat );
```

The **onChat()** function is another callback function. This function is invoked whenever a player chats in the game. The function gets the player who is chatting, checks to see whether they have a preferred color, and, if they *do* have a preferred color, changes the event's message property (the **.message** property of the event is the text of the message that the player is about to send) by adding the player's chosen color using the `textcolors.colorize()` function you wrote earlier.

Once you've saved the `chatcolor.js` file, reload the plugins using `/js refresh()` and at the in-game prompt type the following:

```
/jsp chatcolor
```

Press the spacebar and then the Tab key, and you should see a list of possible colors to choose from. You can cycle through the list of colors by repeatedly pressing Tab. Choose a color and then press T to begin chatting. Type a message, and the message should appear in the color you've chosen.

Cool! You've just created a useful new command that a lot of players are going to like. Plugins like the one you've just created are popular on multiplayer servers. Try changing the chosen color a few times using the `/jsp chatcolor` command to make sure all the colors work.

What happens if you issue the `js refresh()` command?

Right now, your plugin does not save the chat color preferences, so when the plugin is reloaded or the server shuts down, the color preferences for each player are lost. The player's chat colors will revert to the default color. It would be nice if it was possible to load and save preferences for your plugin so color preferences weren't lost when the server stops. Not only is it possible, it's super easy too!

Plugin Data

For any Minecraft JavaScript plugin, you want to be able to load plugin data when the plugin is loaded and automatically save plugin data when the plugin is unloaded. That way, you can be sure that plugin-specific data is never lost when the server is shut down. Let's look first at loading data.

Loading Plugin Data

ScriptCraft provides a `persist()` function that handles saving and loading data. Let's take a look at the `chatcolor.js` file again. The only data in that file you'd like to *persist* is the `preferences` object declared near the top of the file and assigned a value of `{ }`, which means it is an empty object.

```
var preferences = { };
```

The previous code *initializes* the plugin's data to an empty object. What you'd like to do instead is the following:

1. Check to see whether there is saved data in a file.

2. Do one of the following:

   ■ Load the data from the file if a save file is present.

   ■ Or, initialize the data to a default value defined by the plugin.

This is where the `persist()` function helps—it performs all the previous functions (and more). To understand how to call the `persist()` function, let's look at an example. Open the `chatcolor.js` function in your editor and change the following line:

```
var preferences = { };
```

...to the following:

```
var preferences = persist('chatcolor-prefs', { } );
```

The `persist()` function takes up to three parameters, but only the first parameter is required. The parameters are as follows:

■ A unique filename to use when loading or saving data. The filename should be unique, so avoid using generic names such as **data** or **preferences**. The example uses the name **chatcolor-prefs**.

■ An object that will be used as the initial value for the data. If no object is provided, then the default value is **{ }** (empty object).

■ A write flag. The write flag indicates whether the data should be written to the file right now. The write flag should be **true** or **false**. If no write flag parameter is provided, then the default is **false**, meaning data will be read, not written.

The `persist()` function returns an object that will be either of two things:

■ **If the file exists**: The data loaded from the file merged with the data provided in the second parameter

■ **If the file does not exist**: The data in the second parameter

The statement `var preferences = persist('chatcolor-prefs', { } )` in plain English says, "Set the preferences variable to whatever is in the `chatcolor_prefs` file or an empty object if there's no file."

Save the `chatcolor.js` file and reload your plugins using the `/reload` command. At this point you'll notice that the chat color preferences still have not been preserved. Change your color preferences at the in-game prompt using the following command:

```
/jsp chatcolor yellow
```

Type a message or two to verify the chat messages appear in the chosen color and then issue the /reload command and type another message. You'll notice that the chat color preferences have been preserved.

Saving Plugin Data

At this point you might be wondering how chat color preferences were preserved after the server plugins were unloaded and reloaded. The persist() function, in addition to loading data, marks data for saving when the plugin is unloaded. This means that any data returned by the persist() function is *automatically* saved when the plugin is unloaded. As a JavaScript plugin developer, you don't need to worry about saving your plugin's data because it will be saved automatically once you load it using the persist() function. Any changes you make to the object returned by persist() will be saved. You can verify this at the in-game prompt by trying the following commands:

```
/js var test = persist('testpers', {});
/js test.name = 'Your name here';
/js refresh();
```

The refresh() function will cause ScriptCraft to reload. Now issue the following commands:

```
/js var test = persist('testpers', {});
/js test.name
```

The name you entered earlier should display. It's important to note that only changes to the object returned by persist() will be saved. In the previous example, if you were to later reassign the test variable to another object and make changes, then those changes would not be saved. The following code *would not work*:

```
/js var test = persist('testpers', {});
/js test = { name: 'Your name here' }; // changes to test will
not be saved.
```

You may be wondering "Where is the plugin data saved to?" Let's take a look.

Saved Data

ScriptCraft saves plugin data in the **scriptcraft/data** folder. If you open the folder in your editor, you'll notice there's now a **chatcolor-prefs-store.json** file already present. Open this file in your editor, and you'll see something like this:

```
{
    "walterh": "blue"
}
```

The **.json** at the end of the filename means this is a JSON file. JSON is short for JavaScript Object Notation and is just a way to load, store, and send JavaScript data. When you call **persist()**, it takes the filename parameter (for example, **chatcolor-prefs**), appends **-store.json** to the filename, and saves the file. The data is saved in JSON format because that's the easiest way for JavaScript to store and load data.

More on JSON

When you create a new object in JavaScript with name and value pairs, you can do so like this:

```
var player = { name: "steve" }
```

...or like this:

```
var player = { "name": "steve" }
```

That is, you can do so with or without quotes around the **name** property. However, when saving data, the built-in JSON module will write out **player** by adding double quotes around each of the object's keys.

```
{ "name": "steve" }
```

The built-in JSON module has two important functions that are used by ScriptCraft's **persist()** function:

- **JSON.parse(string)**: Takes a string and tries to convert it to a JavaScript object. For example, **JSON.parse("[9,5,3]")** will take the string **"[9,5,3]"** and return an array with three items: 9, 5, and 3.
- **JSON.stringify(object)**: Does the opposite of **JSON.parse()**. It takes a JavaScript object and converts it to a string; for example, **JSON.stringify([9, 5, 3])** takes an array and returns the string **"[9,5,3]"**.

If the `JSON.parse()` function encounters an object key without surrounding quotes, it complains and refuses to try to convert the string to an object.

JSON, Persistence, and Java Objects

If the data you want to save includes references to Java objects, then saving and loading data will not work using the standard **persist()** function, which is provided by ScriptCraft. The **persist()** function uses JSON's **stringify()** and **parse()** functions to save and load data, and these functions *work only with native JavaScript objects*. If you want to save Java objects, consider instead saving a unique identifier for that object. For example, instead of storing the **net.canarymod.api.entity.living.humanoid.Player** object, store only the player's name. If you want to save a **Location** object, then consider using the **utils** module's **locationToJSON()** and **locationFromJSON()** pair of functions for converting the **Location** Java object to and from JSON.

```
var utils = require('utils');
// convert from Java to JSON
var locationAsJSON = utils.locationToJSON(player.location);
// convert from JSON to Java
var locationObject = utils.locationFromJSON(locationAsJSON);
```

Summary

In this chapter, you learned about providing tab completion hints for your own custom commands and about persistence—saving and restoring state. Persistence is a useful feature to have in your own plugins. Many plugins allow players to set preferences, and it's useful to be able to save and restore player preferences and other settings when your plugin is loaded and unloaded.

Chapter 16

Add New Recipes: The Ender Bow

ALL FUN MINECRAFT PLUGINS begin with a simple question: What if...? Minecraft has become such a popular game because the possibilities are endless. For Minecraft plugin developers, it's even more fun because the programming API allows for endless creativity in customizing the game. In this chapter, you'll use the CanaryMod API to create a new crafting recipe—one that will produce a new in-game item—the *ender bow*. What's an ender bow? It's a bow that shoots arrows that teleport the player to wherever the arrow lands! This could be a handy tool if you're in a tight spot surrounded by monsters on all sides and need to make a quick getaway. With an ender bow in hand, you just draw your bow, aim at where you want to teleport, and shoot. As soon as the arrow hits, you'll be teleported.

In this chapter, you'll add a new crafting recipe that will construct an *ender bow*, you'll explore the CanaryMod API in more detail, and I'll explain how to go about exploring and discovering features of the API that you can use in your own plugins. You'll learn about Java *classes* and *inheritance* and how these ideas help you figure out the CanaryMod API's capabilities. In Chapter 17, you'll add teleporting behavior to the bow.

Before you get into the "how" of adding the new crafting recipe to the game, let's first consider the "what"—what ingredients will be required for the new recipe and how you go about choosing them.

Crafting an Ender Bow

A regular bow in Minecraft is crafted using three bits of stick and three bits of string. By arranging each piece in a certain formation in the crafting grid, a bow is crafted. The ender bow you'll add to the game is special, though. It will require some extra ingredients to add teleporting magic to the bow. I call this new item the *ender bow* after the EnderMan monster type in Minecraft. An EnderMan can teleport from one location to another at random, which is what makes him such a terrifying and unpredictable opponent. If you're lucky enough to defeat an EnderMan in battle, they drop *ender pearls*, which can be thrown by hand to teleport a short distance. The range of the ender bow will obviously be longer than throwing by hand, and—unlike throwing ender pearls—it won't deal any damage to the shooter when they are teleported. FIGURE 16.1 shows what the crafting grid for a regular bow looks like in Minecraft.

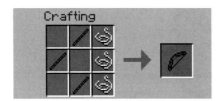

FIGURE 16.1 Crafting recipe for a bow

In the next section, you'll look at how you can use this information to craft a new type of bow.

Choosing What Materials Should Be Used

It's a good idea to base a new crafting recipe on an existing recipe. Server plugins cannot add new graphics to the Minecraft client. For example, you couldn't add a completely new item like a portal gun because even if you were a graphics whizz, the CanaryMod API provides no way to add new item graphics to the client. Another reason to base new crafting recipes on existing items is that players are already familiar with many of the crafting recipes, and if you add a new recipe that is just a little twist on an existing recipe, it makes the recipe and the resulting item easier to remember and master.

For the ender bow recipe, you'll base your new recipe on the existing bow recipe but add some ingredients to give the bow its special powers. You'll notice that for a standard bow recipe, there are three empty slots in the grid. You're going to use these slots, adding a new ingredient to each of the three empty slots to craft an ender bow.

The ingredient you're going to add is an *ender pearl*. These are obtained from teleporting EnderMan monsters, so it makes sense they should be ingredients for an ender bow. You could, of course, choose whatever material you like. You could, for example, decide that an extra block of grass in the middle is all that's needed to create an ender bow. For players, that might not make the new item very interesting. Any new item you add to the game should be interesting both in what it does *and* in how it's constructed. New items should not be *too* easy to make, especially if they're powerful like the ender bow. Ender pearls are difficult to obtain in survival mode, so they make for good ingredients for the ender bow. So, your ender bow will be constructed using the recipe shown in **FIGURE 16.2**.

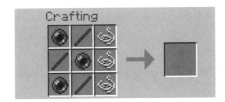

FIGURE 16.2 Crafting recipe for a bow

You'll notice in Figure 16.2 that no item appears in the right side. That's because you haven't yet instructed the server to recognize that recipe. Now that you've figured out what you want your new crafting recipe to look like from a player's point of view, let's dive in to how you'll program this new behavior into the game.

Exploring the CanaryMod API

So, we've answered the question of "what" we want to do, and now we'll consider "how" we are going to do it. This is a list of what we want to do:

1. Add a new crafting recipe to the game.

2. Add new teleporting behavior for arrows fired from an ender bow.

We'll tackle the second item in the next chapter, so let's look at how you add a new crafting recipe to the game.

CanaryMod has a community of developers who have been using the API and posting questions and answers on the CanaryMod forums. If there's something you want to do, a good place to start is by searching online.

Often such results can be useful when starting down the path of creating your own plugin.

What's even more useful is the comprehensive API reference available at *https://ci.visualillusionsent.net/job/CanaryLib/javadoc/*. This API reference is a set of interlinked web pages that are generated automatically from comments in the CanaryMod source code. The reference lists all of the *classes*, *packages*, and *methods* in the CanaryMod API. A Java *class* is much like a JavaScript module, while a Java *method* is much like a JavaScript method or function. A Java *package* is a folder of Java *classes*; it's just another way of organizing large numbers of source files. Java programs can be quite large, much larger than their JavaScript equivalents, so the source files must be organized in folders and subfolders. Each folder and subfolder is known as a *package* in Java terms.

For example, in Minecraft there are hundreds of different types of *events* (or "hooks") that can occur in the game. It would be difficult for the CanaryMod development team and for plugin developers if all of the event source code was in a single folder called **hooks**, so it makes sense to create subfolders for categories of events.

If you visit *https://ci.visualillusionsent.net/job/CanaryLib/javadoc/*, you'll see a web page with three distinct areas (see **FIGURE 16.3**).

The area on the top left is the list of packages. This area provides a high-level overview of the entire API. You can quickly move from one package to another by clicking any of the packages listed in this area.

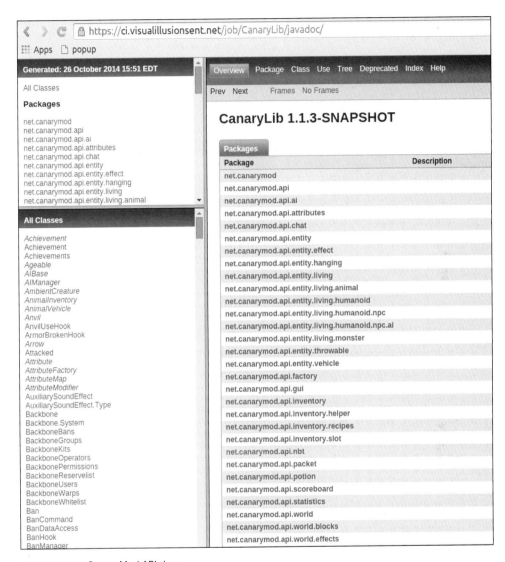

FIGURE 16.3 CanaryMod API docs

The area on the bottom left is the list of classes in the current package (the package selected in the top-left pane). Clicking any of the items in this area will display more details about the chosen item in the main display pane on the right (see **FIGURE 16.4**).

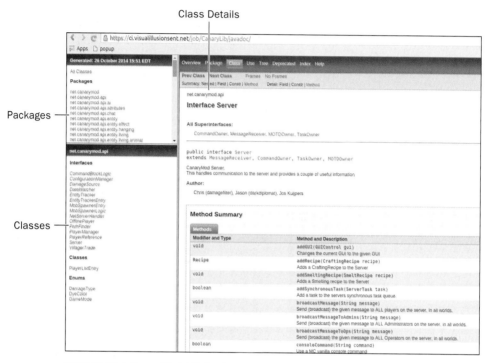

FIGURE 16.4 CanaryMod API doc layout

Clicking any of the method links in the right side of the page will take you to more information about the method.

You can call any of the Java classes and methods from within JavaScript; in fact, that's what you've been doing throughout this book.

One of the key differences between Java and JavaScript is that Java is *strictly typed*. That means it has no **var** keyword. Instead, when variables are declared, their type must also be declared. So, while in JavaScript, you could write the following:

```
var myString = "Hello World";
```

In Java you would have to write the following:

```
String myString = "Hello World";
```

You'll notice when browsing the CanaryMod API that many methods include both the types of parameters they expect and the type of data they return. For example, the **Server** class found in the **net.canarymod.api** package has an **addRecipe()** method whose method summary looks like this:

```
Recipe addRecipe(CraftingRecipe recipe)
```

Let's look at this piece by piece. The **Recipe** to the left of the method name is the type of data the method returns. The **CraftingRecipe recipe** inside the round brackets says that the method takes one parameter named **recipe** of type **CraftingRecipe**. This is the conventional way that Java methods are defined: The parameter type is shown along with the parameter name.

Every type name in the Java documentation page is a link to more information about the type. So if I want to find out more information about the **CraftingRecipe** Java type, I just click that link.

Interfaces, Classes, Enums, Exceptions, and Annotations

Java has a couple of different object types, but you don't have to worry too much about the differences. Still, it's useful to know what the different terms mean.

INTERFACES

A Java interface is an *abstract* type. That is, it says what the object *should* do but not *how* it should be done. Interfaces are used quite a lot in Java and throughout the CanaryMod API. For example, the **Recipe** type is an *interface*. It has an empty method called **getResult()** that should return the item crafted by the recipe. The **Recipe** type has subtypes called **ShapedRecipe** and **ShapelessRecipe**, each of which provide their own **getResult()** method implementations.

In Java, if a method takes an **Interface** type as a parameter, it will also take any subtypes too. That's one of the nice features of Java and object-oriented programming.

CLASSES

Classes are like interfaces except they are *concrete* types; they have methods that are not empty. A Java class is much like a module in JavaScript; it is a way to package up a collection of related functions and variables into a single logical unit.

ENUMS

Enums are like classes except they are usually just a collection of named properties. For example, the `net.canarymod.api.GameMode` enum has three possible values that correspond to the supported game modes in Minecraft:

- ADVENTURE
- CREATIVE
- SURVIVAL

Another example of an enum is the `net.canarymod.api.world.World.Difficulty` enum that has the following values:

- EASY
- HARD
- NORMAL
- PEACEFUL

EXCEPTIONS

Exceptions are error types in Java. They work much like errors in JavaScript. In both Java and JavaScript, you can *throw* an exception when some unexpected condition occurs in your code.

ANNOTATIONS

You don't need to worry about annotation types when calling Java code from JavaScript.

The Code

That's just enough Java for now. Before you explore the CanaryMod API further, let's fire up the programming editor and write some code. Create a new folder in the `plugins/scriptcraft/plugins` folder and call the new folder `enderbow`. Then inside the `enderbow` folder create a new file called `recipe.js` and add the code in LISTING 16.1.

LISTING 16.1 The Ender Bow Recipe

```javascript
var items = require('items');
var recipes = require('recipes');
var cm = Packages.net.canarymod;
var cmEnchantment = cm.api.inventory.Enchantment.Type;
var cmItemFactory = cm.Canary.factory().itemFactory;
var cmEnderBow, cmLuck;

cmEnderBow = items.bow(1);
cmLuck = cmItemFactory.newEnchantment(cmEnchantment.
                                LuckOfTheSea,3);
cmEnderBow.addEnchantments( [ cmLuck ] );

var enderBowRecipe = new Object();
enderBowRecipe.result = cmEnderBow;

enderBowRecipe.shape = [ 'ESW',
          'SEW',
          'ESW' ];

enderBowRecipe.ingredients = {
    E: items.enderPearl(1),
    S: items.stick(1),
    W: items.string(1)
  };

var recipe = recipes.create( enderBowRecipe );
server.addRecipe( recipe );
```

Save the file, reload using the /js refresh() command, and then bring up the crafting grid by right-clicking a crafting table. When you place ender pearls, string, and sticks in the grid, you should see a shimmering bow appear in the right side (see **FIGURE 16.5**).

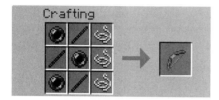

FIGURE 16.5 Crafting recipe for a bow

Put the crafted ender bow in your inventory, but don't try using it just yet. It will still behave just like a regular bow. You'll add the teleportation magic in the next chapter.

Using CanaryMod Classes and Enums in JavaScript

Near the start of Listing 16.1, you declare some variables.

```
var cm = Packages.net.canarymod;
var cmEnchantment = cm.api.inventory.Enchantment.Type;
var cmItemFactory = cm.Canary.factory().itemFactory;
```

The names of classes in Java can be quite long-winded because you have to include the package name and the class name. Java programmers call this the *fully qualified name*. Java programmers will often save themselves the need to use fully qualified names by *importing* packages. The JavaScript engine that runs inside Java has an **importPackage()** function, but this function is not supported in newer versions of JavaScript for Java. I personally like to avoid using fully qualified names throughout JavaScript code, which is why whenever I need to refer to a CanaryMod Java type, I declare a short-named variable at the top of the module that refers to the longer fully qualified name of the CanaryMod type. I also put a **cm** at the front of the variable name so I know I'm working with a CanaryMod object and not a regular JavaScript object. This is just a personal preference. I've found it helps me when I'm writing plugins in JavaScript. It may be useful to you too.

Enchantments

One way you can mark an item as having special powers is to add an enchantment to it. Enchanted items shimmer and glow in the game. An ender bow should shimmer so that players know they're not holding a regular bow. For most of the activities you can do in the game, there are equivalent classes and methods in the CanaryMod API. For example, in the game players can *add enchantments* to *items*. If you browse the CanaryMod API reference, you see there's an *inventory* package that has a couple of classes, one of which is called `Item`. The `Item` interface represents a collection of one or more *items* that can be placed in one of the player's inventory slots or held in the player's hand. This `Item` interface has an `addEnchantments()` method that you can use to add special powers to items in the game. With this knowledge, let's figure out what you want to do.

1. You want to *enchant* the item created from the recipe so that it shimmers and is visually distinct from a regular bow.

2. You're going to use a `ShapedRecipe` object. The ScriptCraft `recipes` module provides a function called `create()`, which creates a new ShapedRecipe object.

3. You know (from browsing the API reference) that you can add a new recipe to the game using `Server.addRecipe()`.

The first thing you do is load ScriptCraft's `items` module. This module simplifies the creation of Java `Item` objects. If you want to create an `Item` consisting of one bow, you call `items.bow(1)`, and it will return a Java `Item` object to which enchantments can be added. The `items` module has roughly 450 different functions—one for each of the materials in Minecraft. You can call each of these functions in three different ways. Let's take the `items.bow()` function as an example.

- `items.bow()` when called without parameters will return the value `net.canarymod.api.inventory.ItemType.Bow`. This is a `ItemType` object that is used throughout the CanaryMod API.

- `items.bow()` when called with a number as a parameter, as in `items.bow(2)`, will return a `net.canarymod.api.inventory.Item` object of two bows. The `Item` type is also used throughout the CanaryMod API.

- `items.bow()` when called with a *material* as a parameter, will compare the material to the material for this function (each function has its own material) and return `true` if it's the same or `false` if it isn't. You saw an example of this in Listing 9.6 when you wanted to check whether a broken block was of type `SAND`.

There are many different *enchantments* in Minecraft, some of which are designed for use with bows. You want to use an enchantment that is not already designed for a bow because you don't want to interfere with existing enchantment rules. If you look at the list of possible *enchantments* in the CanaryMod API docs, there are no obvious teleportation-related enchantments, so I chose the **LuckOfTheSea** enchantment because it's normally for use with fishing rods.

Adding a level-three **LuckOfTheSea** enchantment to a bow minimizes the risk that this particular configuration of item, enchantment, and level will conflict with existing item/enchantment game rules.

The Recipe

Having created and enchanted the item that will be "cooked" every time the player uses the recipe, the next step is to set up the ingredients for the recipe.

A new Way to Create Objects

In JavaScript you can create objects using *object literals* like this:

```
var myNewObject = { name: 'ender bow' }
```

But there's another way to create objects I haven't mentioned yet. The **new** keyword in JavaScript can be used to create a new JavaScript object. For example, JavaScript has a **Date** function that when called like this returns the current date and time as a string. In Java 7 for Linux, the following code throws an exception, but the official JavaScript specification says you should be able to call **Date()** as follows:

```
var today = Date();
```

However, when you add the **new** keyword in front of the call to **Date()**, it behaves differently. When called like this, the **Date()** function returns a new object of type **Date**.

```
var today = new Date();
```

The **new** keyword in JavaScript means the **Date()** function becomes a *constructor*. A constructor is any function that returns a new object. In *Java* there are only limited ways to create objects using object literals, so the most common way to construct a new object in *Java* is using the **new** keyword. The following statement creates a new JavaScript object:

```
var enderBowRecipe = new Object();
```

We'll set properties on this object to specify what the recipe looks like.

The Crafting Grid

The crafting grid in Minecraft is what appears onscreen when you right-click a crafting table. The grid consists of three rows, each of which have three slots. You need to be able to define—in code—what combination of ingredients will result in a new ender bow. Fortunately, this is relatively easy. The in-game grid can be mapped to an array of JavaScript strings that substitute each letter for a material. FIGURE 16.6 shows the crafting grid with letters superimposed on each cell.

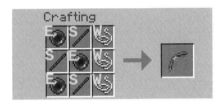

FIGURE 16.6 Crafting grid with material codes

E is for ender pearl, S is for stick, and W is for string (web). If you were to imagine the recipe using just E, S, and W as shorthand, the recipe might look like this:

```
E S W
S E W
E S W
```

This is how you define the layout of a new shaped recipe in code too. You specify the shape of the recipe using an array of three strings.

```
enderBowRecipe.shape = [
  'ESW',
  'SEW',
  'ESW'
];
```

Calling Variable-Argument Java Methods from JavaScript

In the Item reference page at *https://ci.visualillusionsent.net/job/CanaryLib/javadoc/net/canarymod/api/inventory/Item.html*, the information about the .addEnchantments() method is presented as follows:

```
void    addEnchantments(Enchantment... enchantments)
    Adds enchantments to this item.
```

The `Enchantment... enchantments` within the parameters section means that the `.addEnchantments()` method takes one *or more* Enchantment objects as parameters. In Java, this style of parameter passing is called **varargs**, which is short for "*a variable number of arguments.*" When you see a Java method that uses this style of argument passing, the `...` tells you there can be one or more parameters of that type. When calling such methods from JavaScript, you need to pass the parameters as an array instead. That's why you call the `.addEnchantments()` method like this:

```
cmEnderBow.addEnchantments( [cmLuck] );
```

Notice the opening [and closing] array brackets around the `cmLuck` parameter. This says that we are passing an array as a parameter. In this case the array has just a single enchantment but the array could contain more if you wanted to add more. If you try to call the `.addEnchantments()` method as follows, it will fail:

```
cmLuck = cmItemFactory.newEnchantment(cmEnchantment.
    LuckOfTheSea,3);
cmInfinity = cmItemFactory.newEnchantment(cmEnchantment.
    Infinity,1);
cmEnderBow.addEnchantments( cmLuck, cmInfinity );
```

You must instead enclose the parameters (even if it's only one) inside an array like this:

```
cmLuck = cmItemFactory.newEnchantment( cmEnchantment.
    LuckOfTheSea, 3);
cmInfinity = cmItemFactory.newEnchantment( cmEnchantment.
    Infinity, 1);
cmEnderBow.addEnchantments( [ cmLuck, cmInfinity ] );
```

Whenever you see a method that uses the `...` notation for a parameter, pass an array in its place.

Setting Ingredients

Now you've defined the shape of the recipe, you need to say what each of the letters E, S, and W mean. You do this by setting the *ingredients* property.

```
enderBowRecipe.ingredients = { E: items.enderPearl(),
  S: items.stick(),
  W: items.string()};
```

Inheritance

Finally, having set up the rules for the new recipe, you can add it to the game using the `server.addRecipe()` method. Let's look at this method again in the online documentation.

1. Go to *https://ci.visualillusionsent.net/job/CanaryLib/javadoc/*.

2. Click the `net.canarymod.api` link in the top-left pane.

3. Click the *Server* link in the bottom-left pane.

4. Click the *addRecipe* link in the right (main) pane.

The details in the right pane will look something like this:

```
Recipe addRecipe(CraftingRecipe recipe)
  Adds a CraftingRecipe to the Server.
  Parameters:
    recipe - the recipe to add
  Returns:
    A Recipe object from the Created Recipe
```

If the `server.addRecipe()` function expects a **Recipe** but you give it a **ShapedRecipe** (that's what **enderBow** is), why does no error occur? No error occurs because **ShapedRecipe** is a subtype of **Recipe**. In Java programming, we say that **ShapedRecipe** *inherits* from **Recipe** or is a *subclass* of it.

Inheritance is an important principle in programming. It's useful to understand inheritance because it will make navigating and using the CanaryMod API easier. If you click the Recipe link at *https://ci.visualillusionsent.net/job/CanaryLib/javadoc/*, you will be taken to the Recipe details page where you'll find the following information in the heading:

```
net.canarymod.api.inventory.recipes
  Interface Recipe


    All Known Implementing Classes:
      ShapedRecipe, ShapelessRecipe
    public interface Recipe
    Represents some type of crafting recipe.
```

Under `All Known Implementing Classes:` is a list of *subclasses*, or specialized types of **Recipe**. You can think of these classes as *children* of **Recipe**. Each of the classes **ShapedRecipe**, and **ShapelessRecipe** is also a **Recipe** object, and they *inherit* all of the parent class's methods and properties, much like people inherit some of the characteristics of their parents: eye color, hair color, and so on. Since the parent class **Recipe** has a method **.getResult()**, you can infer that there's a **ShapelessRecipe.getResult()** method, and a **ShapedRecipe.getResult()** method. You can click the **ShapedRecipe** link to verify this. **ShapedRecipe** does indeed have a **.getResult()** method along with many other of its own methods.

In programming, inheritance diagrams like the one shown in FIGURE 16.7 are useful for understanding inheritance.

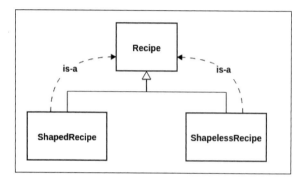

FIGURE 16.7
Recipe inheritance diagram

From this diagram you can see that **ShapedRecipe** and **ShapelessRecipe** share a common ancestor.

Ultimately the **server.addRecipe()** method *doesn't care* what type of **Recipe** is added; all the **server** object cares is that it *is* a **Recipe** object so it can call the **Recipe.getResult()** method (which is common to all three subclasses) when someone uses the recipe in a crafting grid. You'll revisit this topic in the following chapter.

Summary

In this chapter, we covered a lot of ground. You learned how to explore the CanaryMod API reference documentation, how to use the **new** keyword, and about inheritance and how to use it when calling Java code. In the next chapter, you'll build upon what you've done here to add teleporting behavior to the ender bow.

Chapter 17

Arrows That Teleport You

IN THE PREVIOUS CHAPTER, you learned how to add a new crafting recipe to the game. In this chapter, you'll expand upon the work done previously by adding event-handling code that will listen for *projectile hit* events and teleport the player who shot the arrow, if it was fired from an ender bow. You'll also learn more about inheritance and how to use the CanaryMod API reference documentation.

Making the Ender Bow Work

The ender bow crafted from your new crafting recipe doesn't do much right now. If you fire an arrow using the ender bow, it behaves just like an arrow fired from a regular bow. You're going to change that.

What you'd like is for players to be able to use the ender bow to shoot arrows that teleport them to wherever the arrow lands. To do this, you'll need to follow these steps:

1. Write a function that will listen for the *projectile hit* event and when it receives such an event continues with the next steps.

2. Get the player who shot the arrow.

3. Get the item the player is currently holding.

4. If it's an ender bow, remove the arrow.

5. Teleport the player to the arrow's location.

Exploring Events

There are more than 100 possible events that you can listen for in Minecraft. Event-driven programming means you can write functions that will automatically be called by the game when an event occurs. Such functions are called *callback* functions because the programmer does not call them directly; the program does. It's a case of "Don't call me. I'll call you!" To have your callback function be executed when an event occurs, you must *register* the function. ScriptCraft makes registering your callback function easy by providing a registration function for each of type of event. You can register your own callback function to listen for *projectile hit* events by issuing the following commands at the in-game prompt:

```
/js function ouch( event ) { echo(event.projectile.owner,
    →'ouch!') }
/js events.projectileHit( ouch );
```

Now every time you throw any projectile such as a snowball or an egg or fire an arrow, you'll see "Ouch!" appear on your screen. We'll dig deeper into how this code works later.

You can see a list of all events functions online at *http://scriptcraftjs.org/ api#events-helper-module*. Each function of the **events** module corresponds to a type of event in the game. There are so many types of events in Minecraft that they need to be grouped into these Java packages:

- `net.canarymod.hook.command`
- `net.canarymod.hook.entity`
- `net.canarymod.hook.player`
- `net.canarymod.hook.system`
- `net.canarymod.hook.world`

In each of these packages you'll find dozens of event types, and each event type is different. So, when you register for an event using one of the **events** module's functions, you can be guaranteed that when that type of event occurs in the game, your callback will be invoked with the event as a parameter.

The events Module and Event Packages

The **events** module has hundreds of functions—one for each event type—and was designed to make event registration discoverable at the server or in-game prompt using tab completion. If you type **events.** and then press Tab at the server prompt, you will see all 100+ event registration functions. Each function lets you register for one type of event.

The **events.projectileHit()** function lets you register for events of type **net.canarymod.hook.entity.ProjectileHitHook**, the **events.connection()** function lets you register for events of type **net.canarymod.hook.player.ConnectionHook**, and so on. The **events.projectileHit()**, **events.connection()**, and most other **events** functions are shorthand functions. The function names are *deliberately* short to save typing and to make playing with events at the command prompt easier. There's another function you should know about if you ever need to register for events that are not part of the standard CanaryMod API (for example, events provided by other plugins).

The events.on() Function

The events.on() function lets you register for an event of *any* type. It takes two parameters:

- **eventType**: This must be a fully qualified event type. This is better explained by the following examples.

- **callback**: A function that will be invoked when the event occurs. This callback behaves exactly as it would when using one of the events module's shorthand functions.

So, there are two possible ways in which a *projectile hit* event can be listened for. Imagine you have a listening function called **onProjectileHit** that looks something like this:

```
function onProjectileHit( event )
  { console.log('projectile hit') }
```

The first way to register is using the shorthand **events.projectileHit()** function, like this:

```
events.projectileHit( onProjectileHit );
```

The second way is to use the **events.on()** function passing a fully qualified event type name:

```
events.on( net.canarymod.hook.entity.ProjectileHitHook,
    onProjectileHit );
```

It doesn't really matter which of the two approaches you use, but in the rare case you find you need to listen for nonstandard events, you should choose the second way and pass the event type's fully qualified name to **events.on()**.

Of the two ways to register for events, using one of the **events** module's shorthand functions is probably the easiest. Visit *http://scriptcraftjs.org/api#events-helper-module* for a full list of event registration functions.

Types of Events and Event Properties

Once you register for an event, the callback you provide will be executed whenever that event type occurs in the game. The callback is passed a parameter—the event that was fired. Typically, in your callback function you'll want to do something with the event. The event your callback receives as a parameter will usually have information you'll want to look at and use in your callback. How do you know what information is inside a given event? It's time to revisit a topic touched on in the previous chapter—inheritance.

Digging Deeper into Inheritance

Every event callback function takes a single argument. You can call the parameter anything you like—**event** or **evt** or even just **e**. You'll want to do something with the parameter in the function callback. In the case of the ender bow, you'll need to get some crucial information from the event so you can teleport the player. This is where—yet again—the CanaryMod API reference documentation, and the ability to browse it, is essential.

In this particular instance, you're interested in exploring the properties and methods of the **net.canarymod.hook.entity.ProjectileHitHook** type in the online CanaryMod reference at *https://ci.visualillusionsent.net/job/CanaryLib/javadoc/*. Visit the link in a web browser, click the **net.canarymod.hook.entity** link in the top-left pane, then click the ProjectileHitHook link in the bottom pane; information about this type of event will appear in the right pane. The information you're interested in is the method summary:

```
Entity getProjectile()
    Gets the Entity projectile
```

The **getProjectile()** method returns an object of type **Entity**. If you click the Entity link you'll see one of its sub-types is *Projectile*; click on the *Projectile* link and you're taken to the information page for this type where you find the hierarchy (see **FIGURE 17.1**).

```
package: net.canarymod.api.entity
Interface Projectile
All Superinterfaces:  EntityAll Known Subinterfaces:
  Arrow, ChickenEgg, EnderPearl, EntityPotion,
EntityThrowable, Snowball, XPBottle…
```

net.canarymod.api.entity

Interface Projectile   Parent Types

All Superinterfaces: Child Types
  Entity

All Known Subinterfaces:

  Arrow, ChickenEgg, EnderPearl, EntityPotion, EntityThrowable, Snowball, XPBottle

FIGURE 17.1 Projectile API hierarchy

The pieces of information that are useful here are the *superinterfaces*—that is, the parents of this type and the *subinterfaces* or children of this type. **FIGURE 17.2** shows you the relationship better. In this diagram, only some of the **Projectile** subtypes are shown for sake of clarity.

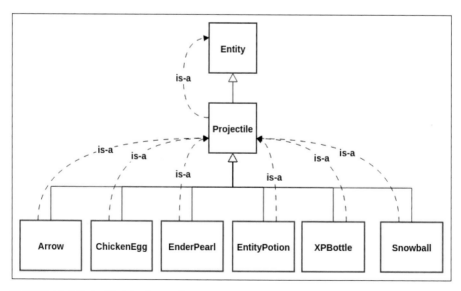

FIGURE 17.2 Projectile inheritance diagram

The superinterfaces and subinterfaces are important when browsing the CanaryMod API types because they tell you about the type's *ancestry*. The *ancestry* of a type is important because anything a type's parent can do, the type can do too. The same goes for the type's children; they *inherit* the properties and methods of the type.

If you look at the **Entity** type you'll find a treasure trove of useful properties and methods. For example, you can find out where the projectile is by calling the parent type's **.getLocation()** method. You can also *destroy* the projectile by calling the parent type's **.destroy()** method. Note that neither the **.getLocation()** method nor the **.destroy()** method appears on the information page for the **Projectile** type. You need to click the type's parent link **Entity** to see all these useful methods. Remember, because **Projectile** is a *child*, or subtype, of the **Entity** type, it *inherits*, or has, all of these properties and methods too! That's the power of inheritance in Java, and it's useful to keep this rule in mind when browsing the CanaryMod API reference. Anything the parent type can do, the type can do too! Anything an **Entity** type can do, the **Projectile** type and **Arrow** type can do too!

If you browse around the CanaryMod API and find a type (such as **Arrow**) that appears to have only a handful of methods, look at the ancestry—visit the parent-type links under **extends** or **Superinterface**. If you don't find what you're looking for there, look at the parent's parent, and so on. There are lots of useful properties and methods in the CanaryMod API, but it's often a matter of knowing where and how to look for them. Understanding inheritance helps you dig deeper into the CanaryMod API documentation.

The Code

You're going to put what you learned about inheritance to use in the following code, which will add teleporting behavior to arrows fired by the ender bow. Launch your programming editor and create a new file called **arrow.js** in the **enderbow** folder you created in the previous chapter; then enter the code in **LISTING 17.1**.

Save this code and then reload the plugins using **'/js refresh()**. Then with ender bow in hand, fire an arrow to teleport!

LISTING 17.1 Teleporting Arrows

```javascript
var items = require('items');
var cm = Packages.net.canarymod;
var cmEnchantment = cm.api.inventory.Enchantment.Type;
var cmArrow = cm.api.entity.Arrow;
var cmPlayer = cm.api.entity.living.humanoid.Player;

function onArrowHit( event ) {
  var projectile = event.getProjectile();
  if (! (projectile instanceof cmArrow) ) {
    return;
  }
  var shooter = projectile.getOwner();
  if (! (shooter instanceof cmPlayer) ) {
    return;
  }
  var itemInHand = shooter.getItemHeld();
  var arrowLocation = projectile.getLocation();
  if ( isEnderBow( itemInHand ) ) {
    projectile.destroy();
    shooter.teleportTo( arrowLocation );
  }
}
events.projectileHit( onArrowHit );

function isEnderBow( item ){
  if (item && ( item.getType() == items.bow() ) ) {
    var enchantment = item.getEnchantment();
    if (enchantment &&
        enchantment.getLevel() == 3 &&
        enchantment.getType() == cmEnchantment.LuckOfTheSea){
      return true;
    }
  }
  return false;
}
```

Now let's look at the previous code in more detail. As in the previous chapter, you load the **items** module because it has functions for comparing Minecraft items. Next you declare three variables that refer to CanaryMod Java classes. I use the same naming convention as in the previous chapter: **cmEnchantment** is short for **net.canarymod.api.inventory.Enchantment.Type**, and **cmArrow** is short for **net.canarymod.api.entity.Arrow**. Having the names begin with **cm** is a reminder to myself that these are CanaryMod classes.

The **onArrowHit()** function is a callback that will be executed by the server whenever a projectile strikes something. In this function, you need to do the following:

1. Get the event's projectile, the thing that was fired.

2. Get the projectile's shooter, the person or thing that fired the arrow.

3. Get the shooter's item held, the thing the shooter is currently holding.

4. Check whether the item held is an ender bow, and if it is, then teleport the player.

Like all event-handling callback functions, **onArrowHit()** takes a single parameter: **event**. Because you register using the **events.projectileHit()** function, this **event** will be of type **net.canarymod.hook.entity.ProjectileHitHook**, and if you browse the online reference at *https://ci.visualillusionsent.net/job/CanaryLib/javadoc/*, you'll see there's a **.getProjectile()** method that returns the projectile for this event. For the rest of this function, every piece of information you need can be obtained via the **Projectile** object.

You can test to see whether the **projectile** variable is of type **cmArrow**, and if it is not, the function returns—this function is concerned only with arrows, not eggs or snowballs.

Next you need to get the shooter—the person or thing that fired the arrow. The **Arrow.getOwner()** method returns an object of type **Entity**, which is an abstract type; that is, there can be many possible subtypes. If you browse the online reference and look at **net.canarymod.api.entity.Entity**, you see it has many subinterfaces or subtypes: **AnimalVehicle**, **Arrow**, **Player**, and so on. You test to see whether **shooter** is a **Player**, which is a specific type of **Entity**. Again, you're interested only in teleporting players.

Then you get the item currently held by the player by calling the **.getItemHeld()** method. This is yet another example where you need to use inheritance rules to find out what methods a **Player** object has. If you look at the online reference for the **net.canarymod.api.entity.living. humanoid.Player** object, you will see that the **Player** object itself does not have a **.getItemHeld()** method but one of its ancestry types does. A **Player** is a subtype of **Human**, which has a **.getItemHeld()** method. Because there's a **Human.getItemHeld()** method and **Player** is a subtype of **Human**, you can call the **.getItemHeld()** method on **Player** too! The inheritance diagram for the **Player** type shown in FIGURE 17.3 shows just *some* of the player's ancestry.

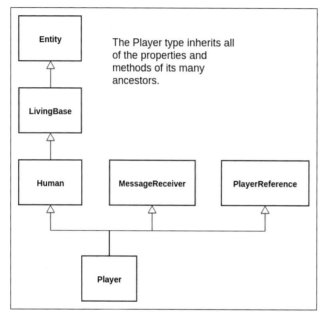

FIGURE 17.3 Player ancestry

As you can see in Figure 17.3, each type in Java can have more than one direct ancestor. Every type inherits all of the properties and methods of its ancestry. So, a **Player** object can, for example, use any of the **MessageReceiver** or **Entity** methods. The **Player** type in Minecraft is one of the most versatile object types because of its rich ancestry.

Once you have the item the player is currently holding, you pass it to a function you define called **isEnderBow()**. This function checks to see whether the item is of type **Bow** and whether it has a level-three **LuckOfTheSea** enchantment.

Finally, if the item held is an ender bow, you remove the projectile because you don't want the arrow left behind (it makes sense that an arrow that teleports you should disappear), and then you teleport the shooter to the arrow's location.

More on Types

The `instanceof` operator is an operator common to both Java and JavaScript. It's used to test the type of an object. It can be useful when calling the CanaryMod API from JavaScript when you want to identify the exact type of an object. In Listing 17.1 you use the operator to check whether the projectile fired was an arrow. It could be any type of projectile—an egg, fireball, snowball, and so on—but you're interested in handling the event only if it was an arrow. The `instanceof` operator is used to test whether something is of a given type. You can test this at the command line.

```
/js self instanceof net.canarymod.api.entity.living.animal.
  →Horse
> "false"
/js self instanceof net.canarymod.api.living.humanoid.Player
> "true"
```

The `instanceof` operator also lets you test a generic type against a specific type. Note that because of the way Java inheritance works, it's possible for an object to be an instance of more than one type. For example, both of these JavaScript expressions will return true because a player is an instance of both types, `MessageReceiver` and `LivingBase`.

```
/js self instanceof net.canarymod.chat.MessageReceiver
> "true"
/js self instanceof net.canarymod.api.entity.living.
  →LivingBase
> "true"
```

The `instanceof` operator is most commonly used to narrow down an object to a specific type, so you can be confident that you can call methods for that type without exceptions being thrown. For example, if you wanted to be sure that a given object was an actual **Player** and not just any **LivingBase** (all creatures and villagers are also of type **LivingBase**), you would do so by testing like this:

```
/js self instanceof net.canarymod.api.entity.lving.humanoid.
  →Player
```

The `net.canarymod.api.entity` package is where you'll find all of the entity types. The `instanceof` operator can be used for testing *any* type of object in Java or JavaScript.

JavaBeans

The type of functions you used to get information about the event, projectile, and shooter in Listing 17.1 are called *getters*. They're called *getters* because they each *get* some property of the object they're called for; `event.getProjectile()` gets the event's projectile property, `projectile.getOwner()` gets the projectile's owner property, and so on. As you can probably guess, there's also a family of functions called *setters*, which are functions whose job is to *set* the property for an object. For example, you can *get* your current food level using the `.getHunger()` method:

```
/js self.getHunger()
```

And you can *set* your current food level using the `.setHunger()` method:

```
/js self.setHunger(20)
```

Java classes that use the convention of having *getters* and *setters* methods to get and set properties are known as JavaBeans. JavaScript enables you to treat getter and setter methods in JavaBeans as equivalent JavaScript properties. The name of the property is the name of the JavaBean method without the **get** or **set** suffix and starts with a lowercase letter. For example, you can call the `getHunger()` and `setHunger()` methods in a **Player** object using the **hunger** property as follows:

```
/js self.hunger
> "17"
```

To set the **hunger** property, just assign a value to it.

```
/js self.hunger = 20
```

This is a nice convenience when writing JavaScript code that uses Java types. Let's revisit the code from earlier, this time using just property names instead of `get()` methods (see Listing 17.2).

I prefer using just the property names rather than the **get** and **set** methods because I think the resulting code is more readable, but it's a matter of personal taste. If you feel more comfortable sticking to the Java convention of using `getX()` and `setX()` (where **X** is some property) when working with Java types from within JavaScript, then by all means use those methods.

LISTING 17.2 Accessing JavaBean Properties Directly

```
var items = require('items');
var cm = Packages.net.canarymod;
var cmEnchantment = cm.api.inventory.Enchantment.Type;
var cmArrow = cm.api.entity.Arrow;
var cmPlayer = cm.api.entity.living.humanoid.Player;

function onArrowHit( event ) {
  var projectile = event.projectile;
  if (! (projectile instanceof cmArrow) ) {
    return;
  }
  var shooter = projectile.owner;
  if (! (shooter instanceof cmPlayer) ) {
    return;
  }
  var itemInHand = shooter.itemHeld;

  if ( isEnderBow( itemInHand ) ) {
    projectile.destroy();
    shooter.teleportTo( projectile.location );
  }
}
events.projectileHit( onArrowHit );

function isEnderBow( item ){
  if (item && ( item.type == items.bow() ) ) {
    var enchantment = item.enchantment;
    if (enchantment &&
        enchantment.level == 3 &&
        enchantment.type == cmEnchantment.LuckOfTheSea){
      return true;
    }
  }
  return false;
}
```

A Note on Style

At the start of this chapter I suggested running the following code and said I'd explain how it works:

```
/js function ouch( event ) {
    →echo(event.projectile.owner,'ouch!') }
/js events.projectileHit( ouch );
```

The **ouch()** function uses the JavaBean property shorthand notation described previously to get the **projectile** property for the **event**, then the **owner** property for the **entity**. The entire function body is just a single JavaScript statement.

```
echo(event.projectile.owner,'ouch!')
```

I wrote it like this so I could create a short callback function at the in-game prompt. Functions at the in-game prompt are limited to just 100 characters on a single line. If I were writing the function in a module, I might be more verbose and write it like this instead:

```
function ouch( event ) {
  var projectile = event.projectile;
  var shooter = entity.owner;
  echo( shooter,'ouch!');
}
```

The one-line version of the code avoids the need to create new variables for the projectile and the owner but is probably less readable—especially for beginning programmers. Once again, whichever style you use is up to you. You should experiment with different styles as you become more comfortable writing JavaScript code.

Summary

In this chapter, you completed all of the code needed to add a teleporting ender bow to the game and learned more about inheritance and how to use it when browsing the CanaryMod API reference.

Chapter 18

Protecting Your Server Against Griefing

ONE OF THE GREAT THINGS about running a CanaryMod server instead of the standard Minecraft server is the ability to customize the game by adding plugins. On a public non-whitelisted server where anyone can connect and play, one of the first things a server administrator will want to do is protect against griefing or wanton destruction. In this chapter, I'll show you how to prevent players from destroying property and how to prevent them from placing destructive blocks such as TNT and lava.

Simple Protection

The easiest way to prevent griefing is to prevent all players from breaking any blocks at all. This isn't very practical since breaking blocks and placing blocks is part of the process of building in Minecraft. The following code shows how to prevent any blocks from being broken:

```
/js function cancel( event ){ event.setCanceled(); }
/js var dontBreak = events.blockDestroy( cancel );
```

Canceling Events

If you run the previous code, then any attempt to break a block in the game will fail. The block will reappear just as it was about to be broken. This is because of the following statement:

```
event.setCanceled();
```

This statement cancels the event, preventing the normal procedure for breaking blocks from occurring. It was as if the block was never broken. Not all types of events can be canceled, but most can. You can see a list of all of the types of events that can be canceled at *https://ci.visualillusionsent.net/job/CanaryLib/ javadoc/net/canarymod/hook/CancelableHook.html* under the heading "Direct Known Subclasses."

Another type of griefing is when players place blocks where they shouldn't— for example, filling up another player's house with brick or other materials. You can also prevent all blocks from being placed using the same **cancel()** function defined earlier:

```
/js var dontPlace = events.blockPlace( cancel );
```

If you run the previous code and then try to place any block, the block you try to place will disappear. This **cancel()** event handler isn't very practical, but it does illustrate an important property of many types of events—they can be canceled.

How to Stop Listening for Events

You'll notice that I stored the return value from **events.blockDestroy()** and **events.blockPlace()** in variables in the previous examples. When you call any of the **events** module functions, an object is returned. This object can be used to *unregister* the events listener. If you want to listen for events only for a short while and then stop, you can do so in one of two ways. You can call the **unregister()** method on the object returned by any of the **events** functions:

```
var dontBreak = events.blockDestroy( cancel );
...
dontBreak.unregister();
```

Or you can unregister from within the event handling function itself:

```
var protectBlocks = 5;
function cancel( event ) {
   if (protectBlocks > 0) {
      protectBlocks = protectBlocks - 1;
      event.setCanceled();
   } else {
      this.unregister();
   }
}
events.blockDestroy( cancel );
```

In the previous code, the **cancel()** function will cancel only five block-break events and then will unregister itself. By unregistering, the function is telling the server not to call it any more when a block-break event occurs.

Prohibiting TNT

Prohibiting the placement of all blocks in the game wouldn't make for a fun Minecraft experience. You can adapt the code used earlier to provide a simple plugin that prevents anyone except operators from placing TNT. In your programming editor, create a new subfolder in **scriptcraft/plugins** called **protection** and in that folder create a new file called **no-tnt.js**. Then type in the code shown in LISTING 18.1.

LISTING 18.1 Preventing Placement of TNT

```
var items = require('items');
function noTNT( event ){
  var material = event.blockPlaced.type;
  if ( isOp( event.player) ) {
    return;
  }
  if (items.tnt( material ) ) {
    event.setCanceled();
  }
}


events.blockPlace( noTNT );
```

You can test this code by reloading the plugins using the `/js refresh()` command. You'll also need to use the `/deop` command to temporarily remove your operator privileges so you can verify that trying to place TNT when you're not an operator is impossible. You can re-enable your operator privileges later by running the **op** command at the server console prompt. With TNT in hand, try to place a block of TNT anywhere, and the TNT will appear briefly before disappearing.

In Listing 18.1 you declare a new function called **noTNT** that will be called whenever a player tries to place a block in the game. The first thing the **noTNT()** function does is get the material that was placed. It gets this via the event's **blockPlaced** property. Remember from the previous chapter that properties of Java objects can be read using **get** methods—in this case the `.getBlockPlaced()` method—or using the property's name. As you learned in Chapter 17, you can infer by the JavaBean rules that if there's a `.getBlockPlaced()` method of the **net.canarymod.hook.player.BlockPlaceHook** class (see *https://ci.visualillusionsent.net/job/CanaryLib/javadoc/ net/canarymod/hook/player/BlockPlaceHook.html*), then there must be a property called `blockPlaced` that is of type `net.canarymod.api.world.blocks.Block` (see *https://ci.visualillusionsent.net/job/CanaryLib/javadoc/net/canarymod/api/world/blocks/Block.html*). You can follow the same rule for the `blockPlaced` object and infer that since there's a `.getType()` method, there must be a `type` property that is the material the block is made from. You could have written this:

```
var material = event.getBlockPlaced().getType();
```

However, JavaScript lets you use the JavaBean properties without calling the getter methods.

```
var material = event.blockPlaced.type;
```

Next you check to see whether the player who placed the block is an operator.

The `isOp()` function returns true if the player is an operator (a player with administrative privileges or the console operator).

If the player is an operator, then you don't want to interfere with the normal course of events for placing blocks; that is, you don't want to prohibit operators from placing blocks.

Finally, you use the `items.tnt()` function, passing the material as a parameter to test whether the material is TNT. If it is, then you cancel the event.

Prohibiting Lava

The procedure for preventing the placement of lava is slightly different, but the principle is the same. You cancel the event if the event involves emptying lava into the world. Lava is not a material that can be held in a player's hand; instead, it's carried and emptied from a bucket. The event you want to listen for is not *block placement*; it's the *item use* event. In your editor, create a new file called `no-lava.js` in the `scriptcraft/plugins/protection` folder; then type the code in **LISTING 18.2**.

The code is similar to the TNT-prohibiting code. You just listen for the `itemUse` event instead of the `blockPlace` event. You'll find a table of `events` functions and their corresponding event types in the appendixes of this book.

LISTING 18.2 Preventing Placement of Lava

```
var items = require('items');
function noLava( event ){
  if ( isOp( event.player) ) {
    return;
  }
  if (items.lavaBucket( event.item ) ) {
    event.setCanceled();
  }
}


events.itemUse( noLava );
```

Player Plots

Preventing the placement of TNT and lava goes some way toward creating a safe server for players to create and collaborate. As the earlier examples demonstrated, in creating a safe environment where no griefing is possible, you can easily go too far and prevent any player from placing or removing blocks. What you want instead is to make it possible to create *plots* where players can build and collaborate with other trusted players without fear of griefing.

In the following sections of this chapter, you'll develop a set of functions that will enable operators to construct a *safe zone* where no one—except operators—can place or break blocks. Within this safe zone there will be plots—small parcels of land—that can be claimed by a player and once claimed can be built on. You'll also need to provide some way for players to claim a plot of land, and you'll need to keep a registry of players and their plots. You'll make it so players can claim only one plot.

Safe Zones

The first step in creating a safe server is adding the ability to create safe zones. Outside of these safe zones it should be possible for any player to place and break blocks, but inside the safe zones, only operators should be able to do so. You'll define a safe zone as an area of width and length that—for the sake of simplicity—extends indefinitely up and down along the y-axis. So, a zone can be defined using just two points in 3D space—the bottom-left corner and the top-right corner (**FIGURE 18.1**):

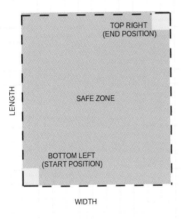

FIGURE 18.1 Safe zones

A safe zone starts at a location in the world and extends along the x-axis and z-axis, so a zone will have a start location and an *extent*, which is how far away it extends. You'll need to use this information when testing whether a broken or placed block is within the zone. You need three different components to manage safe zones:

- A module that will be responsible for creating zones, storing zones (persistence), and checking whether a given block or location is within a safe zone.
- A way to easily create safe zones. You'll add a new extension to the **Drone** object discussed in Chapter 12 to let you create zones without needing to work directly with locations.
- A few event listeners to prohibit block placement and breaking in safe zones.

The first step is to create a shared module. Open your editor and—if not already present—create a new folder called **protection** in the **scriptcraft/modules** folder. Create a new file called **zones.js** and enter the code in LISTING 18.3.

This module lets you add zones that will be loaded at startup (or when the module is first used) and saved automatically when the server is shut down.

LISTING 18.3 Safe Zone Management Module

```
var store = persist( 'zones', [] );

function addZone( a, b ){
  var result = {
    startX: 0,
    startZ: 0,
    extentX: 0,
    extentZ: 0
  };
  if (a.x < b.x){
    result.startX = a.x;
    result.extentX = (b.x - a.x);
  } else {
    result.startX = b.x;
    result.extentX = (a.x - b.x);
  }
  if (a.z < b.z){
    result.startZ = a.z;
    result.extentZ = (b.z - a.z);
  } else {
    result.startZ = b.z;
    result.extentZ = (a.z - b.z);
  }
  store.push(result);
  return result;
}
```

continued...

LISTING 18.3 *continued*

```javascript
function contains( zone, location){
  if ( ( location.x >= zone.startX &&
         location.x <= (zone.startX + zone.extentX)
       )
       &&
       ( location.z >= zone.startZ &&
         location.z <= (zone.startZ + zone.extentZ)
       )
     ) {
    return true;
  }
  return false;
}
function getBoundingZones( location ){
  var i = 0;
  var result = [];
  var zone = null;
  for (i = 0; i < store.length; i++ ){
    zone = store[i];
    if (contains( location, zone ) ){
      result.push(zone);
    }
  }
  return result;
}

exports.add = addZone;
exports.getBoundingZones = getBoundingZones;
```

Persistence is definitely something you want for safe zones—you want them to last. The module's **add()** function takes two parameters, both of them of type **net.canarymod.api.world.position.Location**, and stores their two-dimensional coordinates (the x and z properties). An additional function, **getBoundingZones()**, will return a list of encompassing zones for a given location. Zones can overlap, so it's possible that a location can be in more than one safe zone.

Next up let's create a new **Drone** extension called **zonemaker()**. In your editor, switch to the **scriptcraft/plugins** folder and create another subfolder called **protection**; then create a new file called **zonemaker.js** and enter the code in **LISTING 18.4**.

As you saw in Chapter 12, it's possible to extend the **Drone** object to build whatever you want. In this case, you want to be able to construct a bounding box in which no one except operators can place or break blocks. In addition to constructing a bounding box of whatever material you choose, the **zonemaker()** function gets the Drone's starting location and the farthest corner location and calls the **zones.add()** function to add a new safe zone. Once you've saved this file (and the **zones.js** file), you can test it by reloading your plugins (using the

LISTING 18.4 A Drone-Based Zone Creator

```
var Drone = require('../drone/drone').Drone;
var zones = require('protection/zones');
function zonemaker( material, width, length ) {
  var startLoc = this.getLocation();
  this.chkpt('zonemaker');
  if (material != null){
    this.box0( material ,width, 1, length);
  }
  var endLoc = this.fwd(length - 1).right(width - 1).getLocation();
  zones.add(startLoc,endLoc);
  this.move('zonemaker');
}
Drone.extend(zonemaker);
```

`/js refresh()`command) and then, at the in-game prompt, point at the ground and type the following command:

```
/js zonemaker( blocks.brick.chiseled, 20 , 20 )
```

A bounding box similar to that shown in FIGURE 18.2 should appear.

FIGURE 18.2 A safe zone (bordered)

Right now you can still break and place blocks within the area. The next step to "securing" the safe zone is to add event handlers that will prohibit placement and breaking of blocks. In your editor create a new file called **events.js** in the **scriptcraft/plugins/protection/** folder and enter the code in LISTING 18.5.

In Listing 18.5 you listen for two events and cancel the events if the block being placed or broken is within a safe zone. If the player is an operator, you return immediately because operators should be able to place and break blocks. Save these files and then reload your plugins using the `/js refresh()` command. Then temporarily use `/deop` for yourself and try to place or break blocks in the safe zone you created earlier. You should not be able to do so. Once you're satisfied you can't break blocks as a nonoperator player, re-enable your operator privileges by issuing the `/op` command at the server console prompt.

So far, you have a way to create safe zones where non-operators can't break or place blocks. What you need to do next is provide a way to create player plots within this safe zone where players—once they've claimed a plot—can build.

LISTING 18.5 Event Handling for Protection

```javascript
var zones = require('protection/zones');

function onPlace( event ) {
  if ( isOp(event.player) ) {
    return;
  }
  var block = event.blockPlaced;
  var boundingZones = zones.getBoundingZones(block.location);
  if (boundingZones.length == 0){
    return;
  }
  event.setCanceled();
}
function onBreak( event ){
  if ( isOp(event.player) ) {
    return;
  }
  var block = event.block;
  var boundingZones = zones.getBoundingZones(block.location);
  if (boundingZones.length == 0){
    return;
  }
  event.setCanceled();
}
events.blockPlace( onPlace );
events.blockDestroy( onBreak );
```

Refactoring

Before I get into the mechanics of creating, claiming, and sharing player plots, let's think about what a player plot is and how it's similar to something you've already created—safe zones. A zone and a plot are both *regions* within the world where certain rules apply. A region has a starting point and extends in two directions (along the x-axis and the z-axis). So, zones and plots are really just parcels (or regions) of land. For any block placed or broken, you'll want to test to see whether the block is within a given region. There's going to be much in common between zones and plots, so let's *refactor* the code you've already written. *Refactoring* is the process of changing code you've already written so that it can be made more reusable. The goal of refactoring is to improve the code so you don't write the same code over and over. What you're going to do is take some of the code from the **zones.js** module you created earlier and move it into a new more reusable module called **region.js**. In your editor, create a new file called **region.js** in the **scriptcraft/modules/protection/** folder and edit the file so it matches the code in **LISTING 18.6**.

   You'll notice the **create()** function is similar to the **addZone()** function from the **zones.js** module. That's because it is the same except the statement **store.push(result);** from the **addZones()** function is not present in the **create()** function. If you want to take a shortcut, I recommend copying and pasting the body of the **addZone()** function into the **copy()** function and then removing the **store.push(result);** line from the **create()** function. The **contains()** function can be copied directly from the **zones.js** file into the **region.js** file and requires no changes.

   Once you've saved changes to the **region.js** file, edit your **zones.js** file so it looks like **LISTING 18.7**.

LISTING 18.6 Region Management Module

```
function create( a, b ){

  var result = {
    startX: 0,
    startZ: 0,
    extentX: 0,
    extentZ: 0
  };
  if (a.x < b.x){
    result.startX = a.x;
    result.extentX = (b.x - a.x);
  } else {
    result.startX = b.x;
    result.extentX = (a.x - b.x);
  }
  if (a.z < b.z){
    result.startZ = a.z;
    result.extentZ = (b.z - a.z);
  } else {
    result.startZ = b.z;
    result.extentZ = (a.z - b.z);
  }

  return result;

}
```

continued...

LISTING 18.6 *continued*

```javascript
function contains(region, location){
  if ( ( location.x >= region.startX &&
         location.x <= (region.startX + region.extentX)
       )
       &&
       ( location.z >= region.startZ &&
         location.z <= (region.startZ + region.extentZ)
       )
     ) {
    return true;
  }
  return false;
}

function getBoundingRegions(regions, location ){
  var i = 0;
  var result = [];
  for (i = 0; i < regions.length; i++ ){
    if ( contains(regions[i], location) ){
      result.push(regions[i]);
    }
  }
  return result;
}

exports.create = create;
exports.contains = contains;
exports.getBoundingRegions = getBoundingRegions;
```

LISTING 18.7 Zones Using Regions

```
var region = require('./region');
var store = persist( 'zones', [] );

function addZone( a, b ){
  var result = region.create(a,b);
  store.push(result);
  return result;
}
function getBoundingZones( location ){
  return region.getBoundingRegions(store, location);
}

exports.add = addZone;
exports.getBoundingZones = getBoundingZones;
```

The **addZone()** function is greatly simplified, and the **getBoundingZones()** function now calls **region.getBoundingZones()**. Now that you've completed the refactoring, you're ready to begin working on player plots. There are a few things you'll want to be able to do with player plots.

- Operators will want to be able to create plots.
- Players will want to be able to claim plots.
- Players will want to be able to share plots with other trusted players.
- Players will want to be able to abandon their claim to a plot.

Before you look at creating plots, you'll need to create a **plots** module that will support each of these operations. In your programming editor, create a new file called **plots.js** in the **scriptcraft/modules/protection/** folder and enter the code in **LISTING 18.8**.

LISTING 18.8 Plot Management Module

```
var region = require('./region');
var store = persist('plots',{plotCounter: 1, plots: []});

function addPlot( a, b ) {
  var result = region.create(a,b);
  result.number = store.plotCounter++;
  result.claimedBy = null;
  result.sharedWith = [];
  store.plots.push(result);
  return result;
}

function getBoundingPlots( location ){
  return region.getBoundingRegions(store.plots, location);
}

function removeAllPlots(){
  store.plots.length = 0;
}

exports.add = addPlot;
exports.getBoundingPlots = getBoundingPlots;
exports.removeAllPlots = removeAllPlots;
```

So far, the **plots** module looks like the **zones** module. When you add a plot, there are three extra properties you want to store:

- The plot's number (the .**number** property). The plot number is incremented (increased by 1) every time a new plot is added. The .**plotCounter** property of the store is persisted so that even across server restarts, each plot is guaranteed to have a unique number.
- The name of the player who has claimed the plot (the .**claimedBy** property).

■ The list of players the plot is shared with (the `.sharedWith` property). You want players to be able to collaborate with other trusted players so they can build on the same plot.

Now let's flesh out the `plots` module some more by adding functions for claiming plots. Add the code in LISTING 18.9 to your `plots.js` file.

LISTING 18.9 Claiming Plots

```javascript
function claim( player, plotNumber) {
  var i ;
  var plot;
  var result = getClaim(player);
  if (result != null){
    // player already has claimed a plot
    return result;
  }
  for ( i = 0; i < store.plots.length; i++){
    plot = store.plots[i];
    if (plot.number == plotNumber){
      // is the plot already claimed by another?
      if (plot.claimedBy){
        echo( player, 'This plot is already claimed');
        return null;
      } else {
        plot.claimedBy = player.name;
        return plot;
      }
    }
  }
  return null;
}
```

continued...

LISTING 18.9 *continued*

```
function getClaim( player ){
  var i ;
  var plot;
  for ( i = 0; i < store.plots.length; i++){
    plot = store.plots[i];
    if (plot.claimedBy == player.name){
      return plot;
    }
  }
  return null;
}

exports.claim = claim;
exports.getClaim = getClaim;
```

Creating Plots

You're starting to put in place functions that will be used by operators and players to add and claim plots. The next step is to extend the **Drone** module yet again, this time adding a **plotmaker()** function that operators will use to create plots that players can later claim. In your editor, create a new file called **plotmaker.js** in the **scriptcraft/plugins/protection/** folder and add the code in LISTING 18.10.

Once you've saved this file and reloaded your plugins using the **/js refresh()** command, you can create a plot using the following command (target a block at ground level first):

```
/js plotmaker( blocks.brick.red, 10, 10)
```

A new plot outline will be created, and a sign will appear with instructions for players (see **FIGURE 18.3**).

LISTING 18.10 **Creating Plots**

```
var Drone = require('../drone/drone').Drone;
var plots = require('protection/plots');
function plotmaker( material, width, length ) {
  var startLoc = this.getLocation();
  this.chkpt('plotmaker');
  this.boxO( material ,width, 1, length);
  var endLoc = this.fwd(length - 1)
                   .right(width - 1)
                   .getLocation();
  var plot = plots.add(startLoc,endLoc);
  this.move('plotmaker');
  var claimMesg = [
    '#' + plot.number +
      ' (' + width + ' X ' + length + ')',
    'To claim:',
    '1. move inside',
    '2. /jsp claim '
  ];
  this.up().sign(claimMesg,63).down();
}
Drone.extend(plotmaker);
```

FIGURE 18.3 A player plot

Claiming Plots

Right now the instructions that appear on the sign (move inside the plot area and issue the `/jsp claim` command) don't work. The next step is to provide a `/jsp claim` command for players to claim plots in which they are standing. In your editor, create a new file called **claim.js** in the **scriptcraft/plugins/ protection/** folder and enter the code shown in **LISTING 18.11**.

Save this code and then reload your plugins using the `/js refresh()` command.

Preventing Griefing on Plots

When a player successfully claims a plot of land, they're sent a message of congratulations, and a firework launches at their location. You're nearly there. Now all you need to do is update the **events.js** file in the **scriptcraft/plugins/ protection/** folder so that it checks to see whether the player is in a plot and owns it. Change the **events.js** file so it matches the code in **LISTING 18.12**.

LISTING 18.11 The /jsp claim Command

```
var plots = require('protection/plots');
var fireworks = require('fireworks');
function claim( params, player ){
  var existingClaim = plots.getClaim( player );
  var boundingPlots = plots.getBoundingPlots( player.location );
  if ( existingClaim ) {
    echo( player, 'You already have plot number ' +
                      existingClaim.number);
    return;
  }
  if (boundingPlots.length == 0){
    echo(player, 'You are not in a plot!');
    return;
  }
  for (var i = 0;i < boundingPlots.length;i++){
    var plot = boundingPlots[i];
    if (!plot.claimedBy){
      // convert from Java to JavaScript string
      plot.claimedBy = '' + player.name;

      echo(player, 'Congratulations! You now own plot ' + plot.
          number);
      fireworks.firework( player.location );
      return;
    }
  }
  echo(player, 'No available plots!');
}
command(claim);
```

LISTING 18.12 Event Handling for Plots

```javascript
var zones = require('protection/zones');
var plots = require('protection/plots');
/*
 can a player build on a location?
*/
function playerCanBuild( player, location ) {
  // for now just check if player has a plot on this location
  return playerOwnsPlot( player, location );
}
/*
 does the player own a plot of land at location?
*/
function playerOwnsPlot( player, location ) {
  var boundingPlots = plots.getBoundingPlots( location );
  for (var i = 0;i < boundingPlots.length; i++){
    var plot = boundingPlots[i];
    if (plot.claimedBy == player.name){
      return true;
    }
  }
  return false;
}
function onPlace( event ) {
  if ( isOp( event.player) ){
    return;
  }
  var block = event.blockPlaced;
  if (playerCanBuild(event.player, block.location)){
    return;
  }
```

continued...

LISTING 18.12 *continued*

```
    var boundingPlots = plots.getBoundingPlots( block.location );
    var boundingZones = zones.getBoundingZones( block.location );
    if (boundingPlots.length == 0 && boundingZones.length == 0){
      return;
    }
    event.setCanceled();
  }
  function onBreak( event ) {
    if ( isOp(event.player) ){
      return;
    }
    var block = event.block;
    if (playerCanBuild( event.player, block.location ) ){
      return;
    }
    var boundingPlots = plots.getBoundingPlots( block.location );
    var boundingZones = zones.getBoundingZones( block.location );
    if (boundingPlots.length == 0 && boundingZones.length == 0){
      return;
    }
    event.setCanceled();
  }
  events.blockPlace( onPlace );
  events.blockDestroy( onBreak );
```

Now you check to see whether the block being placed or broken is in a player plot and whether the plot is owned by the player. If it is, then the event proceeds as normal. If the block is within a region and that region is not owned by the player, then the event is canceled.

So, now you have a basic working protected server where operators can create safe zones and within those zones (or even outside them) create plots of land for claiming by players. Players can build uninhibited in unsafe zones but must claim a plot of land if they want to build without worrying about griefing.

Abandoning Plots

The next step is to provide a way for players to abandon their plots so they can claim new ones. You'll do this by providing yet another new command, /jsp abandon, which will cause the player who issues the command to give up any claim they have on a plot so they are free to claim a new one. Open the scriptcraft/plugins/protection/claim.js file from earlier and add the code in LISTING 18.13.

Now reload your plugins using the /js refresh() command. Your players are now upwardly mobile and can move from plot to plot as different plots become available!

LISTING 18.13 The /jsp abandon Command

```
function abandon( params, player ) {
  var existingClaim = plots.getClaim( player );
  if (existingClaim){
    existingClaim.claimedBy = null;
    echo(player, 'You have given up your claim on plot ' +
                    existingClaim.number);
  } else {
    echo(player, 'You do not have any plots to abandon!');
  }
}
command(abandon);
```

Sharing Plots

You're almost there. You have one last feature to add to this protection plugin. You'd like players to be able to choose collaborators who are allowed to build on their plots. To do this, you need to do the following:

1. Add a new /jsp share command that will let players choose one or more trusted players.

2. Adjust the event-handling rules for block breaking and block placement to accommodate players who don't own a plot but who are trusted.

Let's start with the new /jsp share command. Open your claim.js file again and add the code shown in LISTING 18.14.

LISTING 18.14 The /jsp share Command

```javascript
var utils = require('utils');
function share( params, player ) {
  // convert from Java to JavaScript string
  var trustedPlayer = '' + params[0];

  var existingClaim = plots.getClaim( player );
  if (existingClaim){
    if (typeof existingClaim.sharedWith == 'undefined'){
      existingClaim.sharedWith = [];
    }
    existingClaim.sharedWith.push( trustedPlayer );
    echo( player, 'You have shared with ' + trustedPlayer);
  } else {
    echo( player, 'You do not have any plots to share!' );
  }
}
command(share, utils.playerNames);
```

Save the `claim.js` file and then reload your plugins, and you can now share your plot with others by issuing the following command:

`/jsp share [TAB]`

If you hit the Tab key after typing `/jsp share` with a space after it, you'll notice that a list of player names will show up as possible completions for the command.

Dynamic Command Options

I already covered the topic of the `command()` function, how it can be used to add new custom commands for players to use, and how it can be provided with a list of possible options for tab completion. The `command()` function either can take a static list of options (as you saw previously with the `icecream` and `chatcolor` examples in Chapter 15) or can take another function as a parameter. If the `options` parameter is a list, then that list will be used for tab completion. If the `options` parameter is a function, then the function will be executed and should return a list of strings to be used for tab completion. In Listing 18.14 you pass the `utils.playerNames` function as the second parameter to `command()`. This means the `utils.playerNames()` function will be invoked whenever a player issues the `/jsp share` command and presses the spacebar followed by Tab. If you can't know ahead of time the possible options for your custom command, then providing a function that returns a list of options when the player issues the command is the way to go. In the previous example, you won't know what players are online at the time the command is issued, so providing a static list of player names would not work. That's why you pass the `utils.playerNames` function as the second parameter.

Updating Event Handling to Accommodate Trusted Players

Next you must update the event-handling code related to protection. You want to allow players to place or break blocks if they are within a plot and are in the plot's `.sharedWith` list. Open the `scriptcraft/plugins/protection/events.js` file, add the new `playerIsTrusted()` function, and update the `playerCanBuild()` function as shown in **LISTING 18.15**.

LISTING 18.15 Event Handling for Trusted Players

```
/*
 can a player build on a location?
*/
function playerCanBuild( player, location ) {
  // check if player has a plot on this location
  // or is trusted
  var result = playerOwnsPlot( player, location ) ||
    playerIsTrusted( player, location );
  return result;
}


function playerIsTrusted( player, location) {
  var playerName = ''+ player.name;

  var boundingPlots = plots.getBoundingPlots( location );
  for (var i = 0;i < boundingPlots.length; i++){
    var plot = boundingPlots[i];
    var sharedWith = plot.sharedWith;
    if (!sharedWith ) {
      continue;
    }
    for (var j = 0; j < sharedWith.length; j++){
      if (sharedWith[j] == playerName){
        return true;
      }
    }
  }
  return false;
}
```

There's a new `playerIsTrusted()` function in this revision of the `events.js` file. This function returns **true** if the player is trusted to work on the plot. There are two interesting things to note in this function. The first is how you use the player's name to test whether the player is in the **sharedWith** list.

Java Strings and JavaScript Strings

The **String** type in JavaScript and the **String** type in Java—they both share the same name—are slightly different, so there are some things you can do with a JavaScript string that you can't do with a Java string, and vice versa. When comparing two strings—one of them a JavaScript **String** type and the other a Java **String** type—it's safest to convert the Java string to a JavaScript string. The easiest way to convert a Java string to a JavaScript string is to insert an empty JavaScript string at the front of the Java string like this:

```
var jsString = '' + javaString;
```

This is what you do in the first statement of the **playerIsTrusted()** function:

```
var playerName = '' + player.name;
```

This assigns the value of **player.name** to a new JavaScript variable called **playerName**. The **player** variable is a Java object, so it follows that all of its **String** properties are Java strings. Java does not behave consistently across all platforms and versions when comparing Java and JavaScript strings, so you should convert Java strings to JavaScript strings by prepending **''** (an empty JavaScript string) if you want to compare strings or use standard JavaScript string-based operations.

Loops Within Loops

The second thing to note about the **playerIsTrusted()** function is its use of nested loops. A *nested* loop is a loop within a loop. In this case, you loop through all the plots, and for each plot you loop through all of the plot's trusted players.

```
for (var i = 0;i < boundingPlots.length; i++){
  var plot = boundingPlots[i];
  var sharedWith = plot.sharedWith;
  if (!sharedWith ) {
    continue;
  }
```

```
for (var j = 0; j < sharedWith.length; j++){
  if (sharedWith[j] == playerName){
    return true;
  }
}
}
```

In the innermost loop you use a different looping variable to the outermost loop. The outermost loop uses the **i** variable as an index and counter, while the innermost loop uses the **j** variable. This is important. When you have nested loops, you must be careful not to reuse the outermost loop's index variable in the innermost loop. This is a common mistake—one that I myself made while writing this code.

It's possible to have any number of nested loops, but if you find yourself writing a function that has many nested loops, you should consider refactoring the function so it is easier to read and understand.

Summary

In this chapter, I walked you step-by-step through the process of adding protection to your server. You can see from the amount of code and number of files you used that protecting servers is no easy task! However, if you tackle the problem by breaking it down into smaller problems and solving each of these in turn, it becomes easier. Programming is an iterative process—you write some code, test it, make changes as you go, and gradually improve the code adding new features piece by piece until it does what you want. Throughout this chapter you revisited code you had written earlier, making gradual improvements and additions each time. This is how programming is typically done. Even the best programmers in the world don't arrive at a perfect solution first time!

While not a comprehensive protection plugin, the code you created in this chapter provides a good basis for a more fully functional protected server plugin. There are a couple of outstanding features you'd need to address to make this plugin better, like what should happen to plots once they're abandoned? Right now, there's no way for a player to tell whether a plot that has buildings has been abandoned. Ideally there should be a sign put in place that says "This plot is available" when plots have been abandoned. That's just one of many possible improvements; I'm sure you can think of more!

Chapter 19

Snowball Fight!

IN THIS CHAPTER you're going to create a player-versus-player mini-game called Snowball Fight (see **FIGURE 19.1**). The aim of the game is to hit your opponents with snowballs as many times as possible while avoiding being hit yourself or hitting players on your own team. In the game players can form opposing teams.

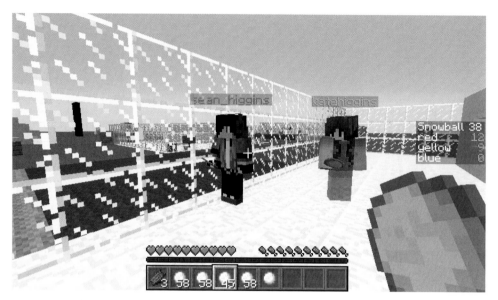

FIGURE 19.1 Snowball Fight

The game will be kept simple for the sake of providing example code, which you might want to adapt and extend to create your own mini-game.

The game will be started using a JavaScript function, and its duration and team structure will be passed as parameters. If no parameters are passed, then the default game duration will be 60 seconds, and each player will be allocated to one of three teams.

First I'll present the game in a single JavaScript module with a function that operators will use to start the game, and later in this chapter I'll cover how players can start the game using in-game mechanisms. I'll also cover how to create an arena for the game to be played in and a command for use by players to start the game.

Game Rules

Before you begin coding, let's lay down some of the rules of the Snowball Fight mini-game.

1. Players will each be allocated a number of snowballs when the game begins.
2. Each player will be a member of a team. There can be up to three teams: red, blue, and yellow. Each player's name appears in the color of their team.
3. Players gain a point if they hit an opponent.
4. Players lose a point if they hit a member of their own team.
5. A scoreboard of players and their scores will be displayed during the game.
6. At the end of the game, the scoreboard will remain onscreen for a few seconds so players can see the final score for each team. Fireworks will launch over the winning team.

Logistics

For the game to work, players should be in close proximity to one another. Later in the chapter you'll construct a special arena for the game to make it more fun. Much of the fun of Minecraft mini-games comes from the anticipation of the game and the ceremony surrounding it. For example, many player-versus-player mini-games have a holding area where players wait to jump into the mini-game or choose teams to participate in prior to the game starting. The mechanism for starting a game can vary from mini-game to mini-game. Initially you'll keep things simple—only the operator may start a Snowball Fight mini-game using the /js SnowballFight() command. Later you'll improve the game so any player can start.

Keeping Score

In Chapter 11 you used a JavaScript array to create a simple leaderboard that sorted players by how many times they had jumped. Minecraft has some built-in commands that let you easily create and display an in-game translucent sidebar with a leaderboard, or *scoreboard*, of players.

The /scoreboard Command

The /scoreboard command provides a neat way to specify what should be displayed in the in-game list view, in the sidebar view, and above players' heads. For example, revisiting the leaderboard code from the earlier chapter, you could display the same leaderboard using the following built-in commands in Minecraft:

```
/scoreboard objectives add Jumping stat.jump
/scoreboard objectives setdisplay sidebar Jumping
```

Notice that once you've run these commands, whenever you or any other player on the server jumps, the scoreboard is updated.

This is a really nice feature and one you'll definitely want to use in your Snowball game.

Executing Commands from JavaScript

It's possible to execute any built-in command from JavaScript using the **server.dispatchCommand()** method. To execute the scoreboard commands already mentioned, you'd use the following code:

```
server.executeVanillaCommand(server,
   'scoreboard objectives add Jumping stat.jump');
server.executeVanillaCommand(server,
   'scoreboard objectives setdisplay sidebar Jumping');
```

The **server.executeVanillaCommand()** method is really useful when you want to call built-in commands or commands provided by other plugins from JavaScript. The appendixes include more information on using other plugins via JavaScript.

ScriptCraft's Scoreboard Module

ScriptCraft provides a module for working with the scoreboard. We'll use this module to add teams at the start of the game and update scores during the game.

The Game Source Code

We have a lot of ground to cover, so let's dive right in and write the core game code. In your editor, create a new folder called **snowball** in the **scriptcraft/ plugins/** folder. Inside the **snowball** folder, create a new file called **game.js** and enter the code shown in LISTING 19.1.

LISTING 19.1 Snowball Fight Core Game Source

```
var items = require('items');
var utils = require('utils');
var scoreboard = require('minigames/scoreboard');
var cm = Packages.net.canarymod;
var cmSnowball = cm.api.entity.EntityType.SNOWBALL;
var cmCreative = cm.api.GameMode.CREATIVE;

function start( duration, teams, onGameOver ) {
  var players;
  var i;
  var game;
  var teamName;
  var ball;
  if ( typeof duration == 'undefined' ) {
    duration = 60;
  }
  if ( typeof teams == 'undefined' ) {
    teams = {};
    players = utils.players();
    var teamNames = ['red','blue','yellow'];
    var playerCount = players.length;
    for ( i = 0; i < playerCount; i++ ) {
      var playerName = players[i].name;
      teamName = teamNames[ i % playerCount ];
```
continued...

LISTING 19.1 *continued*

```
    if (teams[ teamName ] == undefined){
      teams[ teamName ] = [];
    }
    teams[ teamName ].push(playerName);
  }
}
game = {
  teams: teams,
  duration: duration,
  teamScores: {},
  eventListener: null,
  onGameOver: onGameOver
};

function loop(){
  if ( game.duration-- ){
    updateScoreboard( game );
    setTimeout( loop, 1000 );
  } else {
    end( game );
  }
}

function onSnowballHit( event ) {
  var snowball = event.projectile;
  if (snowball.entityType != cmSnowball ){
    return;
  }
  var thrower = snowball.thrower;
  //var thrower = snowball.handle.j().getCanaryEntity();

  var damaged = event.entityHit;
  if (damaged == null){
```

continued...

LISTING 19.1 *continued*

```
      // snowball did not hit another player
      return;
  }
  var throwerTeam = getPlayerTeam( thrower, game.teams );
  var damagedTeam = getPlayerTeam( damaged, game.teams );

  if ( !throwerTeam || !damagedTeam ) {
    return; // thrower/damagee wasn't in game
  }
  if ( throwerTeam != damagedTeam ) {
    game.teamScores[ throwerTeam ]++;
  } else {
    game.teamScores[ throwerTeam ]--;
  }
} // end onSnowballHit

scoreboard.create('snowball', 'Snowball Fight!');
ball = items.snowBall(1);

for ( teamName in game.teams ) {

  scoreboard.addTeam( teamName, teamName );

  game.teamScores[ teamName ] = 0;
  team = game.teams[ teamName ];

  for ( i = 0; i < team.length; i++ ) {
    scoreboard.addPlayerToTeam( 'snowball', teamName, team[i]);
    player = server.getPlayer( team[i] );
    player.mode = cmCreative;
    player.inventory.addItem( ball.type.id, ball.amount, 0 );
  }
}
```

continued...

LISTING 19.1 *continued*

```
    updateScoreboard(game);
    game.eventListener = events.projectileHit( onSnowballHit );
    setTimeout(loop, 1000);
}

function updateScoreboard( game ) {
  var teamName;
  var team;
  var teamScore;
  var i;

  for (teamName in game.teamScores) {
    teamScore = game.teamScores[ teamName ];
    team = game.teams[ teamName ];
    for (i = 0;i < team.length; i++){
      scoreboard.updateScore( 'snowball', team[i], teamScore);
    }
  }
}

function end( game ) {
  var teamName;
  scoreboard.remove('snowball');
  var winningTeam;
  var highestScore = 0;
  for ( teamName in game.teams ) {
    if (game.teamScores[teamName] > highestScore){
      highestScore = game.teamScores[teamName];
      winningTeam = teamName;
    }
    scoreboard.removeTeam( teamName );
  }
```

continued...

LISTING 19.1 *continued*

```javascript
    server.broadcastMessage('The ' + winningTeam + ' team won!');
    game.eventListener.unregister();
    game.onGameOver( game, winningTeam );
}

function getPlayerTeam( player, teams ) {
  var teamName;
  var team;
  var i;
  if ( !player ) {
    return null;
  }
  for ( teamName in teams ) {
    team = teams[ teamName ];
    for ( i = 0; i < team.length; i++ ) {
      if ( team[i] == player.name ) {
        return teamName;
      }
    }
  }
  return null;
}

exports.SnowballFight = start;
```

Running the Game

Once you've saved the file, reload your plugins using the `/js refresh()` command. Then with two or more players connected to the server, issue the following command:

```
/js SnowballFight()
```

The game should begin. Each player is allocated a number of snowballs, and as soon as any player strikes another with a snowball, the scoreboard is updated. Every participant in the mini-game can see the scoreboard. The game will continue for 60 seconds. At the end of the game, the scoreboard remains for a couple of seconds, so the victors can savor the moment.

Allocating Teams

The mini-game is created using the **start()** function, which takes three parameters: **duration**, **teams**, and **onGameOver**. If neither a **duration** nor a **teams** parameter is provided, then the default values are 60 seconds for the duration and a set of teams comprised of all the players on the server. The following section of code in the **start()** function creates a set of up to three teams, and each player is allocated to a team in turn:

```
if ( typeof teams == 'undefined' ) {
  teams =  {};
  players = utils.players();
  var teamNames = ['red','blue','yellow'];
  var playerCount = players.length;
  for ( i = 0; i < playerCount; i++ ) {
    var playerName = players[i].name;
    teamName = teamNames[ i % playerCount ];
    if (teams[ teamName ] == undefined){
      teams[ teamName ] = [];
    }
    teams[ teamName ].push(playerName);
  }
}
```

If you had eight players online when the game started, the **teams** object might look something like this:

```
{
    red: ['sean', 'moe', 'curly'],
    blue: ['walter', 'larry', 'oliver'],
    yellow: ['john', 'paul']
}
```

In this game there should ideally be only up to three teams where each team name is one of the following three colors: red, blue, yellow. Try to avoid having green and red teams because the colors can be difficult to tell apart for some players. Each player's name will appear in the color of their team to make it easier for players to tell who is an opponent and who is on the same team. Next you create a variable called **game** that will be used to store the state of the game and will be passed to other functions in the module.

The Game Loop

The **loop()** function is called once every second using the **setTimeout()** function and subtracts 1 from the game's duration counter, updates the scoreboard, and schedules another call to itself in 1 second. If the game's duration counter is 0, it means that time has run out and the game is over, in which case the **end()** function is called.

Scope and Functions

You might be wondering why the **loop()** function is declared inside the **start()** function. The **loop()** function must be declared inside the **start()** function because it needs to use the **game** variable. Because both the **game** variable and the **loop()** function are declared inside the **start()** function, the **loop()** function can see the **game** variable. If the **loop()** function was declared **outside** the **start()** function, it would not be able to see the **game** variable because variables are private to the function in which they're declared. Normally you'd declare the **loop()** function outside the **start()** function and pass the **game** variable as a parameter, except you schedule the call to **loop()** using a **setTimeout()** call.

There are actually a couple of ways to handle scope and functions in JavaScript, but I think declaring the **loop()** function inside the **start()** function so it can see and work with the **game** variable is the simplest.

Listening for Snowball Hits

Next you declare a new event-handling function called **onSnowballHit()** that will be called every time there's a *projectile hit* event. The **events.projectileHit()** function can be used to listen for projectile hits in the game. In your case, you're concerned only with snowballs thrown by mini-game participants. The **getPlayerTeam()** function will return the team a player belongs to. If the thrower and damaged player are on different teams, then the thrower's team score is increased; otherwise, it's decreased.

```
if ( throwerTeam != damagedTeam ) {
  game.teamScores[ throwerTeam ]++;
} else {
  game.teamScores[ throwerTeam ]--;
}
```

Starting the Game

The main part of the **start()** function is at the end of the module. The following three statements are responsible for starting the game, listening for events, and starting the game's loop:

```
game.eventListener = events.projectileHit( onSnowballHit );
  setTimeout(loop, 1000);
```

The **start()** function is responsible for initializing the game's scoreboard and team scores, and giving each player snowballs to throw.

Initializing and Updating the Scoreboard

The first group of statements in the **start()** function use the scoreboard module's **create()** function to initialize the mini-game's scoreboard, add teams and team members, and allocate snowballs to each player. Each player is placed in Creative Mode so they have an infinite number of snowballs to use during the game.

```
scoreboard.create('snowball', 'Snowball Fight!');
ball = items.snowBall(1);

for ( teamName in game.teams ) {

  scoreboard.addTeam( teamName, teamName );

  game.teamScores[ teamName ] = 0;
  team = game.teams[ teamName ];

  for ( i = 0; i < team.length; i++ ) {
    scoreboard.addPlayerToTeam( 'snowball', teamName,
                                team[i]);
    player = server.getPlayer( team[i] );
    player.mode = cmCreative;
    player.inventory.addItem( ball.type.id, ball.amount,
0 );
  }
}
```

The next step in starting the game is to loop over all of the teams in the game and, for each team, call the **scoreboard.addTeam()** function. The **scoreboard.addTeam()** function takes two parameters: a team name and the team's color. Since, in this game at least, the teams are named after colors, we use the team name for both the name and color:

```
scoreboard.addTeam( teamName, teamName );
```

Displaying the Score

The `updateScoreboard()` function is called once at the start of the game. It's also called from within the `loop()` function every second of the game.

Ending the Game

The `end()` function is responsible for ending the game. Any snowballs that were given to the player at game start are taken away. The event listener is unregistered, and the main scoreboard is restored for each player.

Creating an Arena

So far you've created a single JavaScript function for use by operators to start a new Snowball Fight game. The game works but could be made much more fun by constructing an arena to play in and making it fun and easy for players to join and start and game and choose a team. Let's use the **Drone** (again) to construct a simple 24 by 24 block arena of snow with some walls to make an interesting place to play the game. The arena will have a glass wall so spectators can watch and will have three large colored waiting areas outside the walled arena where players can choose their team simply by waiting in one of the three colored zones. The entire arena and waiting areas will be protected from griefing using the **zonemaker** and **region** modules you developed in Chapter 18, so if you haven't already added the protection modules from that chapter, I recommend doing so now.

Later you'll add the ability for any player waiting in a colored zone to start the game using the `/jsp snowball` command. First let's write the code to build an arena. Create a new `scriptcraft/plugins/snowball/arena.js` file and enter the code shown in **LISTING 19.2**.

LISTING 19.2 Constructing a Snowball Fight Arena

```javascript
var region = require('protection/region');
var Drone = require('../drone/drone').Drone;
var blocks = require('blocks');
var arenas = persist('snowball-arenas', []);
var instructions = [
  'Snowball Fight',
  'In color area:',
  '/jsp snowball'
];

function snowballArena() {
  var arena = {};

  this.chkpt('sbarena');
  // construct team waiting areas
  this.box( blocks.wool.red, 8, 1, 8);
  this.right(8).box( blocks.wool.blue, 8, 1, 8);
  this.right(8).box( blocks.wool.yellow, 8, 1, 8);
  this.move('sbarena');
  // construct arena
  this.fwd(8);
  this.box( blocks.snow, 24, 1, 24);
  // construct some walls to make it interesting
  this.fwd( 6 ).right(3).box(blocks.snow, 10, 4, 1);
  this.right(2).up(2).box(blocks.air, 6, 1, 1);
  this.down(2)
      .right(1)
      .fwd(6).box(blocks.snow, 10, 4, 1);
  this.right(2).up(2).box(blocks.air, 6, 1, 1);
  this.move('sbarena');
  // construct glass wall around arena
  this.up()
```

continued...

LISTING 19.2 *continued*

```
    .fwd(8)
    .box0(blocks.glass_pane,24, 3, 24);
this.move('sbarena');
this.up().sign(instructions,63).right(8);
this.sign(instructions,63)
    .right(8)
    .sign(instructions,63);
// make whole area protected
this.move('sbarena');
this.zonemaker( null, 24, 32 );
// store the coordinates of the blue, red and
// yellow waiting areas these will be used to
// determine who's on each team
var loc = this.getLocation();
var loc2 = this.fwd(8).right(8).getLocation();
arena.redZone = region.create(loc, loc2);

loc = this.back(8).getLocation();
loc2 = this.fwd(8).right(8).getLocation();
arena.blueZone = region.create(loc, loc2);

loc = this.back(8).getLocation();
loc2 = this.fwd(8).right(8).getLocation();
arena.yellowZone = region.create(loc, loc2);

// store the locations of the red, blue and
// yellow spawn points
this.move('sbarena');
loc = this.fwd(10).right(1).getLocation();
arena.redSpawn = { x: loc.x, z: loc.z, y: loc.y+1};
```

continued...

LISTING 19.2 *continued*

```
loc = this.right(8).getLocation();
arena.blueSpawn = { x: loc.x, z: loc.z, y: loc.y+1};

loc = this.right(8).getLocation();
arena.yellowSpawn = { x: loc.x, z: loc.z, y: loc.y+1};

this.move('sbarena');
arenas.push(arena);
}

Drone.extend( snowballArena );
```

The **snowballArena()** function is a new **Drone** extension and is meant for use by operators to create an arena for play. Operators can use this function as they would use any **Drone** function. In the game (with operator privileges), target a block at ground level and issue the following command:

```
/js snowballArena();
```

An arena should appear shortly. The arena looks like **FIGURE 19.2** from above (plan view).

Unlike other **Drone** functions you've created, you want to save some information about the newly created arena for later (so when you develop the **/jsp snowball** command, you can tell which players are on each team using the player's starting zone). You used the **persist()** function you first learned about in Chapter 15 to load and automatically save the arena data. I recommend issuing the **/js refresh()** statement after you create each snowball arena so that the arena data is saved immediately.

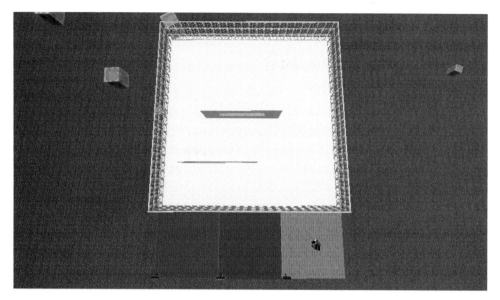

FIGURE 19.2 Snowball arena

In each of the colored zones is a sign with instructions for players who want to play. The instructions read as follows:

```
Snowball Fight
In color area:
/jsp snowball
```

These signs are created using the Drone's **sign()** function, which makes it easy to produce signposts or hanging signs with messages.

Protecting the Arena

The arena is protected using the **zonemaker()** function, which takes three parameters: a material, width, and length. If no material is provided, then the zone will be protected, but no border blocks are laid down. For this arena, you only want to protect it and don't need to lay down a border, so you call it like this:

```
this.zonemaker( null, 24, 32 );
```

When **null** is passed instead of a material, no border is built, but the area is protected from block-break and block-place events by non-operators.

Making It Easy for Players to Start the Game

Having created the core game code and an arena in which to play the game, the next step is to add some simple mechanics for starting and stopping the game and choosing teams. The **Drone**'s `snowballArena()` function creates not just the arena in which the game is played but a waiting zone outside the arena that is divided into three colored areas—one for each team. Players who want to play the game simply move into one of the three colored areas—the area they choose is important because this will be the team they belong to once the game begins.

Any one of the players in a waiting area can choose to start the game when other players are on at least one other color area by issuing the following command:

```
/jsp snowball
```

Let's complete the game by writing the code that will handle this command. In the **snowball** folder, create a new file called **command.js** and enter the code shown in **LISTING 19.3**.

This module also uses the **protection/region** module you developed in Chapter 18 as well as the **game** module you developed earlier in this chapter.

Where Is the Player?

The first thing the **snowball** command does is check the location of the player who invoked the command. If the player who issues the **/jsp snowball** command isn't on one of the three colored waiting areas, then the game won't begin (you don't want just anyone starting a game—only those who want to play the game should be able to start it). You use the **region.contains()** function from Chapter 18 to see whether the player is located in one of the three color waiting areas.

LISTING 19.3 A New Command, /jsp snowball

```
var region = require('protection/region');
var fireworks = require('fireworks');
var utils = require('utils');
var cm = Packages.net.canarymod;
var cmLocation = cm.api.world.position.Location;
var game = require('./game');
var arenas = persist('snowball-arenas', []);

function snowball( params, sender ){
  var duration = 60; // seconds
  var i;
  var arena = null;
  var gameOn = false;

  var allPlayers = utils.players();
  var player;
  var teams = {red: [], blue:[], yellow:[]};
  var spawns = [];
  var spawn = null;

  for ( i = 0; i < arenas.length; i++ ) {
    arena = arenas[i];
    if ( region.contains(arena.redZone,sender.location)
        || region.contains(arena.blueZone,sender.location)
        || region.contains(arena.yellowZone,sender.location)
      ) {
      // game on!
      gameOn = true;
      break;
    }
  }
  if (!gameOn){
    echo( sender,
```

continued...

LISTING 19.3 *continued*

```
        'You must issue this command while in a colored zone' );
    return;
  }

  for (i = 0;i < allPlayers.length; i++) {
    player = allPlayers[i];
    var playerLoc = player.location;
    inZone = false;
    if (region.contains( arena.redZone, playerLoc) ) {
      teams.red.push( player.name );
      inZone = arena.redSpawn;
    } else if ( region.contains( arena.blueZone, playerLoc) ) {
      teams.blue.push( player.name );
      inZone = arena.blueSpawn;
    } else if ( region.contains( arena.yellowZone, playerLoc) ) {
      teams.yellow.push( player.name );
      inZone = arena.yellowSpawn;
    }
    if ( inZone ) {
      var spawnLoc = new cmLocation( playerLoc.world,
                                     inZone.x,
                                     inZone.y,
                                     inZone.z,
                                     0,
                                     0);
      spawns.push( {
        participant: player,
        oldLocation: playerLoc,
        newLocation: spawnLoc
      } );
    }
  }
  if ( (teams.red.length == 0 && teams.blue.length == 0)
```

continued...

LISTING 19.3 *continued*

```
        || (teams.red.length == 0 && teams.yellow.length == 0)
        || (teams.blue.length == 0 && teams.yellow.length == 0)
      ) {
    echo( sender,
      'Need more than one team to play. ' +
      'Someone needs to choose a different color.');
    return;
  }
  function returnPlayers( gameData, winningTeam) {
    var spawn;
    for (var i = 0;i < spawns.length; i++) {
      spawn = spawns[i];
      var player = spawn.participant;
      player.teleportTo(spawn.oldLocation);
      if (gameData.teams[winningTeam].indexOf( '' + player.name) >
  -1) {
          fireworks.firework( spawn.oldLocation );
      }
    }
  }

  for (i = 0;i < spawns.length; i++) {
    spawn = spawns[i];
    spawn.participant.teleportTo(spawn.newLocation);
  }
  game.SnowballFight(duration, teams, returnPlayers);
}

command( snowball );
```

Who Wants to Play?

If the player is in one of the waiting areas, you keep a reference to the waiting area's arena. You then loop over all the players on the server, and if any players are in one of the arena's color zones, you add them to the appropriate team.

```
for (i = 0;i < allPlayers.length; i++) {
    player = allPlayers[i];
    var playerLoc = player.location;
    inZone = false;
    if (region.contains( arena.redZone, playerLoc) ) {
      teams.red.push( player.name );
      inZone = arena.redSpawn;
    } else if ( region.contains( arena.blueZone, playerLoc) ) {
      teams.blue.push( player.name );
      inZone = arena.blueSpawn;
    } else if ( region.contains( arena.yellowZone, playerLoc)
) {
      teams.yellow.push( player.name );
      inZone = arena.yellowSpawn;
    }
    if ( inZone ) {
      var spawnLoc = new cmLocation( playerLoc.world,
                                     inZone.x,
                                     inZone.y,
                                     inZone.z,
                                     0,
                                     0);

      spawns.push( {
        participant: player,
        oldLocation: playerLoc,
        newLocation: spawnLoc
      } );
    }
  }
```

The **spawns** array is a list of players and their locations just before the game begins. You need to keep a list of such locations because you'll teleport the players inside the arena (see **FIGURE 19.3**) when the game begins and would like to return each player to their original location when the game ends. Each arena also has three spawn points where players will be teleported when the game begins.

FIGURE 19.3 Snowball Fight waiting area

How Many Teams?

Next the **snowball** command function checks how many teams have players. If there's only one team, then the game won't begin.

```
if ( (teams.red.length == 0 && teams.blue.length == 0)
   || (teams.red.length == 0 && teams.yellow.length == 0)
   || (teams.blue.length == 0 && teams.yellow.length == 0))
{
   echo(player, 'Need more than one team to play. ' +
           'Someone needs to choose a different color.');
   return;
}
```

Starting and Stopping the Game

Finally—assuming the player who issued the command wants to play and there are enough teams/players to play—you teleport the players into the arena and begin the game using the `game.SnowballFight()` function, which is mapped to the `start()` defined earlier in this chapter. You also schedule a deferred function call using the `setTimeout()` function. The `returnPlayers()` function will be invoked when the game has ended and will return each player to the waiting area they were in before the game started. A firework will launch above each player of the winning team so everyone—players and spectators—will know which team won the game.

Summary

In this chapter, you built a player-versus-player mini-game from scratch. You reused many of the functions you wrote in earlier chapters and made good use of the **Drone** object to create an arena in which to play the game. This has been the most complex of the new features you've added to Minecraft over the course of this book, but it's also one that is fun to play with your friends.

Playing games is fun, but writing your own games can be hugely rewarding, especially when you get to see your friends play a game you created!

Conclusion

While this brings you to the end of the book, you have only just begun to explore the world of Minecraft plugin development. My aim with this book was to provide a solid foundation from which to begin developing your own Minecraft plugins. I've tried to cover all of the basics and some advanced topics and provide examples along the way. There's still much to learn about Minecraft plugin development, but I hope this book gives you the confidence to begin creating your own plugins.

It's been a lot of fun writing this book, and I hope you've enjoyed reading it and have learned something about programming along the way.

Index

Symbols

A

O

object literals, 184
object types, 239
objects
  `console`, 182
  creating with **new** keyword, 224
  defined, 64
  `exports`, 182
  in JavaScript, 182
  as lookup tables, 185–188
  making, 182–184
  `Math`, 77
  modules as, 74–75
  name and value pairs, 210
  nesting, 191–192
  as parameters, 190
  and references, 188–189
  types of, 184
  as variables, 64
`onChat()` function, 206
`onInput()` function, 188
`/op` command, 253
operator, creating oneself as, 21
operators, `instanceof`, 239
`ops.cfg` file, 18
`OR` (| |) operator, 115–116
`ouch()` function, 242

P

parameter passing, `varargs`, 226
parameter values, defaults, 84–85
parameters
  comparing to variables, 83
  converting case of, 126
  explained, 81
  objects as, 190
  passing arrays as, 226
  types in CanaryMod, 219
  using, 82–83
parentheses (()), using with **if** statement, 107
`parseInt()` function, 38–39
period (.), using with functions, 159
permissions for CanaryMod, 18–19
`persist()` function, 207–208, 210–211
player plots, 248
`playerCanBuild()` function, 269–271

`playerIsTrusted()` function, 269–271
players. *See also* greeting players
  finding for Snowball Fight, 295–296
  greeting, 101–102
  locating for Snowball Fight, 291–294
  returning to waiting area, 297
  sorting by experience, 136–138
  sorting by name, 135–136
  sorting by rules, 138–139
  statistics, 139–140
Plot Management Module, 259
plots
  abandoning, 267
  adding, 259–260
  claiming, 263
  creating, 261–263
  event handling for, 265–266
  preventing griefing on, 263–267
  sharing, 268–269
plugin, defined, ix, 59
plugin data
  loading, 207–209
  saving, 209–210
plugin methods and classes, using, B-2
private variables, 63–64, A-2
privileges, checking, 21
programming, event-driven, 92–93
projectile
  API hierarchy, 234
  inheritance diagram, 234
prompt, bringing up, 71
`prompt()` function, 105–106
properties
  defined, 65
  `length`, 94
public variables, 63–64
`push()` method, 96
pyramids, creating, 162–164

Q

questions, asking, 105–106
`quit` command, 110
quotes
  double (" "), 32
  escaping, 32
  single (' '), 32